New Visions of
Collaborative Writing

New Visions of Collaborative Writing

Edited by Janis Forman

Boynton/Cook Publishers
HEINEMANN
Portsmouth, New Hampshire

Boynton/Cook Publishers, Inc.
A Subsidiary of
Heinemann Educational Books, Inc.
361 Hanover Street   Portsmouth, NH 03801
Offices and agents throughout the world

Library of Congress Cataloging-in-Publication Data

New visions of collaborative writing/edited by Janis Forman.
      p.   cm.
   Includes bibliographical references.
   ISBN 0-86709-295-5
   1. Authorship—Collaboration.   I. Forman, Janis.
PN145.N447 1992   91-29274
808'.02—dc20   CIP

Cover design by Jenny Jensen Greenleaf
Printed in the United States of America
92 93 94 95 96 10 9 8 7 6 5 4 3 2 1

To Honor the Memory of Sandra Schor

Contents

Acknowledgments

This collection took shape at the 1989 *Conference on College Composition and Communication* in discussions with Bob Boynton, my editor, and with most of the authors. To them I am deeply grateful. Bob's enthusiasm for the project and considerable knowledge of composition studies has significantly added to the pleasure of working on the project. The authors were ideal collaborators. I am indebted to them for their wisdom, collegiality, and cheerful persistence in working through to the final form of their essays.

My special thanks also go to the readers who offered insightful comments on drafts of individual essays. For this important assistance, I acknowledge Nancy Roundy Blyler, Iowa State University, English; Margaret Ecker, Michigan Technological University, student in the Rhetoric and Technology Communication Program; Michele Forman, National Institute of Health (Cancer Institute), Lisa Gerrard, UCLA Writing Programs; Gail Hawisher, University of Illinois at Champaign, English; Thomas Kent, Iowa State University, English; Cynthia Koch, University of Michigan School of Business Administration, MBA Writing Program; Michael McCormick, The Center for Machine Intelligence; Beverly J. Moss, The Ohio State University, English; Carol Mohr, University of Michigan School of Business Administration, MBA Writing Program; Marsha Reichman, National Institute of Health (Cancer Institute); Jone Rymer, Wayne State University School of Business Administration; Barbara Shwom, Northwestern University's Writing Programs; Betsy Stevens, University of Michigan School of Business Administration, MBA Writing Program.

Acknowledgment is due the Ella Sharp Museum of Jackson, Michigan; The University of Michigan's Rackham Research Partnership Program; The Schlesinger Library at Radcliffe College, and those who assisted with the production of the book: Don Gibson of the Anderson Graduate School of Management at UCLA and Cheryl Kimball at Heinemann-Boynton/Cook.

I also want to thank my husband, Don Brabston, and our son, Benjamin, for their emotional support throughout the project and, especially, for the pleasures of collaboration that they offer.

Introduction

"I cannot keep my subject still. It goes along befuddled and staggering, with a natural drunkenness. I take it in this condition, just as it is at the moment I give my attention to it. I do not portray being; I portray passing."

Michel de Montaigne,
"Of Repentance" (660−661)

"I do not portray being; I portray passing" is an apt summary statement for *New Visions of Collaborative Writing*, for the essays capture the movement in our profession's thinking about collaborative writing, the sometimes confusing — even dizzying — shifts in awareness about the subject viewed from one perspective and then from another. And in the spirit of Montaigne, the essays are "tests" or "attempts" that, taken as a whole, play with and against one another. Although individual essays do not exhibit the internal reversals and contradictions characteristic of some of Montaigne's, the juxtaposition of one essay to another or to a group of others often yields apparent or real contradictions about fundamentals — the definition of collaboration, the characteristics of collaborative practices, the application of theory to research and to pedagogy. How, for instance, does one essayist's view that all writing is collaborative match up against any of the other essayists' more narrowly circumscribed definitions? How can one team of authors' claims about the benefits of face-to-face collaboration make sense in light of another author's argument for electronic conferencing as a way to diminish the negative effects of face-to-face collaboration? This volume poses such questions rather than provides answers, and suggests that some kinds of resolutions may depend, in Kenneth Burke's words, upon "perspectives by incongruity," that is, upon juxtaposing one essay to another, and in this process illuminating the complex discussions about collaboration. The definitions and practices offered here also suggest that future new visions of collaborative writing will be necessary if consensus is to be reached.

The purpose of this introduction is to provide entry into the essays: first through a brief discussion of the motivation for the volume and of early scholarship on collaboration, second through a short summary of the essays, and third through a longer discussion of the "new visions," the common patterns in the essays that present points of stability within the ongoing dynamic exploration of the subject.

Motivation for the Volume: A Personal Note

To the extent that beginnings are traceable, the idea for this collection arose in the midseventies when I was thinking about a dissertation on European first-person narratives for a Ph.D. in comparative literature while I began teaching remedial composition as a Graduate Fellow in Writing at Queens College, the City University of New York (CUNY). This was an exciting period in CUNY's history. The system was for the first time opening its doors to an underprepared student population; consequently, the writing faculty on the Queens campus began to collaborate on ways to work with these students effectively. Like other Graduate Fellows at Queens, I was better prepared to teach an undergraduate course on Montaigne than to be of any use to these students. My underpreparedness as a writing instructor bred informal collaboration out of necessity, a process foreign to almost all of the Graduate Fellows since most of us spent our nonteaching days working alone in study carrels and ingesting "high culture" literary values, including the fixed belief that invention and composition are the province of the individual talent alone. On one level, then, collaboration about teaching writing meant lots of discussions with other Graduate Fellows about what to do on Monday morning, and what links might exist between Monday morning's basic writing class and Tuesday's reading of Montaigne. For these discussions, I am particularly grateful to John Clifford, Sharon Friedman, and Jonna Semeiks.

Fortunately, the "Queens Experience" also included formal collaboration led by the then Directors of the Queens Writing program, Bob Lyons, Don McQuade, and Sandra Schor, each of whom brought a special kind of open-mindedness and imaginative leadership to the work. Among other things, they encouraged novices and experienced teachers alike to write our way into understanding our new teaching situations by collaborating on syllabi for freshman writing that were then discussed and used by other instructors. In the midst of this activity, Kenneth Bruffee's early work on collaborative learning began to surface on the campus, and then Graduate Fellow John Clifford invited two of us to participate as research subjects for his dissertation; that is, as teachers of basic writing in collaboratively organized classes.

These mutually reinforcing experiences with collaboration in the midseventies convinced me of the power of collaborative learning as an educational innovation and of collaborative writing as a classroom practice. Working as a director of a management communication program in the eighties and nineties has confirmed and expanded my sense of the contribution of group work to developing an understanding of self (as problematic as this notion is) in relation to others and to organizational structures.

Early Scholarship on Collaboration

Within composition circles, Bruffee is deservedly credited with introducing a collaborative pedagogy, motivated at its inception in the early seventies by the exigency of finding ways to teach nontraditional students previously excluded from colleges, and supported by social changes that favored collaborative groups (such as women's support groups, "free university" classes, and antiwar groups). From the seventies to the eighties, Bruffee's work evolved from a focus upon teaching practices to a broader concern with a philosophy of education based upon the notion that knowledge is socially constructed. (See "Collaborative Learning" as an example of his early thinking; and "The Structure of Knowledge," "Liberal Education," "Writing and Reading," and "Social Construction" for his later views.) For this expanded notion, Bruffee has drawn upon thinkers from various fields such as anthropology, developmental psychology, literary theory, and philosophy.

Before the mideighties, collaborative pedagogy was embattled philosophically and politically, especially as many of its advocates taught and administered writing programs housed in and subordinate to English departments, which found the ideas and practices of collaboration to be, at best, foreign, and, at worst, anathema to literary theories and practices that were fashionable until the advent of postmodernism.[1] So new a concept and practice in writing programs and so vulnerable to attack from the outside, collaboration was, then, less subject to scrutiny within composition circles.

But collaboration has received growing acceptance — even ascendancy — in the late eighties and early nineties. As one index of success, witness the substantial historical and theoretical work on collaboration by Gregory Clark, Anne Ruggles Gere, and Karen Burke LeFevre. As further support, a substantial body of research has developed on collaborative writing as practiced by professionals, beginning with Lee Odell and Dixie Goswami's *Writing in Nonacademic Settings* on the social dimensions of business and technical writing, and continuing with studies by Nancy Allen, Dianne Atkinson, Meg Morgan, Teresa

Moore, and Craig Snow; Barbara Couture and Jone Rymer; Stephen Doheny-Farina; Lisa Ede and Andrea Lunsford; and Janis Forman and M. Lynne Markus. Indeed the very terms associated with collaborative writing, such as "community of knowledgeable peers" and "social construction of knowledge" — are verging on cliché in the literature.

With acceptance, however, has come examination of previously unquestioned claims about the benefits of the pedagogy. Does collaboration privilege compromise at the expense of debate about substantive issues (Karis)? Does Bruffee's notion of group consensus fail to account for the importance of individual differences within a group, the relative authority of these differences, and the underlying power structures upon which such authority is based (Trimbur)? Do the advocates of collaboration fail to acknowledge positive, alternative pedagogies (Stewart)? Are the benefits of a collaborative pedagogy superior to traditional classroom techniques for teaching cooperative problem solving, the social dimensions of language, and writing proficiency (Smit)?

Summary of the Essays

Considered sequentially, the focus of these essays shifts from history to diverse sites for collaboration, then on to conceptual frameworks for understanding collaboration, and to the interplay between collaboration and technology, a pairing that will increasingly dominate future collaborative studies.

Lest we think that collaborative practices arrived full-blown in the late sixties and early seventies, Anne Ruggles Gere and Laura Roop uncover a previously hidden strand in the history of collaboration and literacy — the use of collaborative practices by women's literary clubs in the nineteenth and twentieth centuries.[2] Their essay draws upon a century's worth of textual writing and reading by two such groups, including members' composition and commentary on club minutes, essays, plays, diaries, and histories, and uses archives that are generally unknown to the public.

John Trimbur and Lundy A. Braun then explore one relatively unknown site for collaboration — an internationally recognized cancer research laboratory and the broader scientific communities to which the lab belongs. They raise questions about how authorship is negotiated, on the basis of which individual careers as well as the prestige and power of laboratories are determined. Another site — a state agency — is the center of attention for Kitty Locker's essay, which looks at factors that contributed to the successful and unsuccessful collaborative efforts undertaken by teams of social service workers and lawyers who put together a legal complaint in support of eight thousand mentally disabled people in Ohio.

The next essays by Charlotte Thralls, Mary Lay, John Schilb, and Priscilla Rogers and Marjorie Horton emphasize how theoretical constructs, often adapted from other disciplines, may inform our understanding of collaboration. Thralls argues that, from a Bakhtinian perspective, all writing is inherently collaborative, serving as a response to preceding utterances and to subsequent ones that writers anticipate to their work. To establish the Bakhtinian perspective, she analyzes the fortunes of a manuscript as it moves from the author to editors and reviewers and back again to the author for revision. Lay builds a case for the importance of interpersonal dynamics for collaborative writing by drawing upon gender studies scholarship. Schilb works with C. Wright Mills's *The Sociological Imagination* and with cultural and literary studies to advocate a pedagogy of collaboration that emphasizes group exploration and debate about broad political and ethical issues inherent in acts of collaboration. Rogers and Horton adapt and extend Bruffee's work to argue for the benefits of *face-to-face* collaboration throughout the entire writing process.

Cynthia Selfe then uses the case of computer conference exchanges between writing instructors to show how the conference may serve as an alternative collaborative forum to the classroom, one that allows participants to break from traditionally unequal distributions of power that dominate the larger culture and are often replicated in face-to-face collaborative situations.

New Visions

What, then, are the *new* visions of collaborative writing claimed here? Viewed as a temporary stopping place in the ongoing exploration of the subject, the essays shed new light on the subject in four ways: through reassessment of earlier ideas, through a deepening of discussions about collaboration raised in the earlier research and scholarship, through expansion of the collaborative situations investigated and of the methods and concepts used for these studies, and through reaffirmation of the importance of research and scholarship to teaching.

Reassessment: Challenging Definitions and Early Assumptions

Several essays either challenge earlier definitions of collaboration or put in question assumptions about collaborative writing central to earlier work. Two of the essays undermine earlier definitions that seem commonsensical; for instance, that collaboration involves writing done by more than one person. For Thralls, the Bakhtinian concept of utterance substantiates the idea that all writing is collaborative.

According to Trimbur and Braun, at least in the world of scientific research, coauthorship may be assigned to those who have contributed nothing to the research or writing of a publication. The term "collaboration," then, is not even, in Wittgenstein's words, a "concept with blurred edges" — one for which there is shared agreement about some elements despite disagreement about others. There is no one definition of collaboration that can be pinned down across the essays.

In addition to challenging the definition of the term "collaboration," some of the essays continue the healthy skepticism and reevaluation of collaborative concepts begun in the eighties. For Schilb, the very term "collaboration" in its secondary meaning of "collusion with the enemy" opens up a host of ethical issues skirted or unseen by early theorists yet requiring attention in any collaborative act. For Selfe, Bruffee's notion of consensus can encourage student groups to accept as axiomatic to the group's dynamics the currently inequitable distribution of power in the larger culture.

Deepening of Discussions about Collaboration: Politics, and Ethics

The political and ethical dimensions of collaboration, which pervade the research from Bruffee's early studies to Ede and Lunsford's recent book on collaboration in the workplace, are of central concern to the essayists in *New Visions* as well. For Trimbur and Braun, the research lab is essentially a political animal, with much of the authority concentrated in the hands of the laboratory director; hence, those in authority can bestow credit and ultimately determine individual reputations. In addition, the broader scientific communities within which labs are themselves enmeshed are networks of authority that influence the relative prestige and financial health of individual labs. Locker partially attributes the success or failure of the two collaborative teams she studied to the nature of leadership and the distribution of power within each team. The failed effort was directed by an autocratic leader who claimed total ownership of the document and was impervious to the opinions of others and to the organization's expectations about how writing was to be handled. By contrast, the successful group handled leadership flexibly, divided work equitably, and was receptive to organizational expectations and to various stakeholders' concerns. For Rogers and Horton, *face-to-face* collaborative composing may compel group members to debate the ethics of their actions as embodied in the texts they are creating. For Schilb, ethical and political dimensions of collaboration are central as he advocates a broadened vision of collaborative pedagogy that engages students in questioning current distributions of power, and ultimately assists in their moral development.

As in Schilb's call for a critique of the distribution of power in the larger culture through collaborative activities, several other essayists argue that such activities provide opportunities to enfranchise marginalized populations and to privilege the attitudes and interactions of these silenced populations over those that dominate the culture. For instance, Geer and Roop find that the reading and writing practices of the women's literary clubs they studied provide an alternative to patriarchal forms of text production and use, particularly to the emphasis upon sole authorship and ownership through copyright. Further, the broad freedom with which women incorporated the texts of others in their collaborative compositions fostered a group environment of playful creativity rarely experienced by other kinds of groups, and worthy of emulation. Lay argues for the contributions that a female perspective on group maintenance and conflict management can offer collaborative teams. Selfe demonstrates how on-line conferences can help groups bypass class, race, and gender barriers to communication, and facilitate equitable involvement and power among team members.

Expansion: New Collaborative Sites and New Conceptual Frameworks

Several essays explore previously uninvestigated or inadequately investigated sites for collaborative writing — women's clubs, a research lab, a government agency composed of lawyers and social service workers, and on-line computer conferences. Rather than a mere descriptive backdrop to collaborative activity, each site emerges as an essential component of the activity, a Burkean scene, if you will, in which "the nature of [collaborative] acts and agents" is "consistent with the nature of scene[s]" (*A Grammar of Motives* 3). The meeting places for women's clubs that Gere and Roop describe provide the literal space for club members to create a gender-based sense of identity sheltered from the intrusions of male authority. The technological and financial requirements of the modern scientific lab described by Trimbur and Braun necessitate collaborative research. The state agency studied by Locker establishes organizational expectations about how collaborative writing projects are to be conducted, and allocates rewards and punishments on the basis of employees' measuring up to these expectations. The computer-based conference that Selfe describes can attenuate the negative effects of class, gender, and race that can come into play in the common alternative collaborative scene, the traditional classroom in which student groups work face-to-face. For these essayists, local conditions, not universal principles, dominate their inquiry about collaboration.

Essayists not only press the boundaries of the writing situations studied as collaborative scenes, but also extend the conceptual frameworks and bodies of knowledge used to study collaboration. Considered from this perspective, the essays bear witness to the need for diverse approaches to the subject, any single approach alone functioning, again in Burke's terms, as a "terministic screen" directing attention to some aspects of the subject while cutting off access to others. Essayists draw upon conceptual frameworks from a variety of fields — business communication, cognitive psychology, communication theory, composition theory, computer-supported cooperative work, cultural anthropology, cultural studies, ethics, feminist studies, law, linguistics, literary theory, social psychology, sociology of science, technical communication, and theories of organizational culture. In total, these represent theoretical richness that confirms the interdisciplinary status of research and scholarship on collaboration and condemns as reductive any single disciplinary approach.

Renewed Affirmation of the Centrality of Teaching to Research and Scholarship on Collaboration

Early interest in collaboration arose from the need to find effective ways to teach newly represented populations in our large universities; the essayists in *New Visions* confirm the importance of pedagogy by reflecting upon the implications of their research and scholarship for the classroom. Gere and Roop's historical study leads them to consider whether today's collaborative groups in the classroom might serve as a vehicle to strengthen gender identity, or, at a minimum, as a forum for discussing gender issues. They also encourage instructors to recognize the value of extra-institutional group learning that contributes to student's literacy. Trimbur and Braun argue for a necessary distinction between the aims of collaboration as a research activity and its aims as a pedagogy, pointing out how the egalitarian and participative processes aspired to in the classroom — the "dialogic" collaboration described recently by Lunsford and Ede (133) — often departs from the hierarchical organization of collaboration that researchers are likely to find in the field. Pedagogy, they argue, should selectively incorporate, not merely replicate, collaborative models derived from research.

From her study of collaboration at a state agency, Locker infers that instructors should help students to reflect on group and individual writing processes, to manage conflict, and to understand the particular demands of different rhetorical situations. Thralls explores how a writing pedagogy that looks on all writing as collaborative can reconcile two opposing pedagogical camps — the advocates of writing as self-expression and those of writing as the product of social forces. At the same time, her collaborative approach to all writing encourages an expanded notion of writing context that goes beyond a document's immediate writers and readers. Lay recommends the use of self-reflective exercises like journal and log keeping to improve collaborative processes. Such techniques, she argues, can help the individuals and the team as a whole to consider members' attitudes, behaviors, and motivations, and to react thoughtfully to conflict rather than revert to predetermined, often gender-stereotyped responses.

At the heart of Schilb's essay is an argument for a new kind of collaborative pedagogy that regards the classroom as a microcosm of the larger society in which ethical and political issues are played out, and collaborative groups in such a classroom as forums for critiquing the inequities of the larger society. Rogers and Horton show how drafting documents face-to-face is conducive to discussion of the rhetorical situation of a document and to group identification of and debate about morally difficult issues. Selfe offers on-line conferences as an alternative classroom that can attenuate the effects of inequities in power and foster intellectual divergence because conferences are a new, radical channel of communication unencumbered by set rules and conventions.

Review Essay and "Correspondence Between Writers on Collaboration"

Of the last two pieces in this book, the first represents a critical retrospective look at the earlier essays and the second considers possible directions for future research and scholarship on collaboration. John Clifford's response essay emphasizes a common theme across the essays, the ethical dimensions of collaboration. Clifford explains how collaborative sites, as depicted by the essayists, necessarily link ethics with the rhetoric and politics of the larger structures in which writing groups function. These sites can merely replicate the power structures of the larger culture or, ideally, can provide a space in which marginalized populations have a voice, dissensus is valued, and differences are negotiated.

The final selection, "Correspondence Between Writers on Collaboration," ends the collection with, in a sense, a new beginning—an opening up of issues and a cross-fertilization of ideas between authors. In this section, each author or team of authors has written an open letter to the writer(s) of another essay, suggesting ways to develop ideas presented in the current essay in further research and scholarship, and discussing ways that the essay has influenced the respondent's own thinking about collaboration. The suggestions for further study of collaboration that writers offer each other confirm a conclusion that the essays as a whole would have us draw: that it is *still* very premature to stake out a clearly defined territory known as collaboration and to establish its boundaries. If anything, *New Visions* suggests that collaborative territory more accurately resembles those medieval maps of the New World, which were more unknown frontier than defined places and place names. Yet, conversely, authors' explicit acknowledgment of affinities, or correspondence, between their work on collaboration — despite differences — reveals that certain core issues sustain our current discussions about collaboration: issues of power, conflict, and decision making; and influences of macro-organizational structures and norms, such as organizational expectations about writing, cultural norms, and socioeconomic and political structures. This commonality has emerged despite the lack of clear boundaries to the term itself, to frameworks for analysis of collaboration, to sites for investigation, and to relationships between theorizing about collaboration and teaching collaborative writing.

Finally, the letters themselves demonstrate further affinities between Montaigne's work and current thinking about collaboration. Montaigne believed, as we infer from versions of his *Essays*, that revision was often a matter of adding to earlier versions of his work rather than modifying it directly through substitution or deletion. Thus, some of his "revisions" amount to additional essays and leave earlier essays intact.[3] By analogy, the essayists in *New Visions* are invited to see their work again with new eyes, those informed by the perspective of another contributor(s) who comments on — and so adds to — the essay by suggesting additional avenues for thought and ultimately for additional essays, but does not modify the current vision. The final section, then, suggests that the present state of research and scholarship on collaboration requires us to take stock of a subject in motion, to review our ideas, to debate varying perspectives, to "portray passing," and then to move on.

Notes

1. For discussion of postmodernist theory in relation to collaborative writing, see Andrea Lunsford and Lisa Ede, *Singular Texts/Plural Authors* (Cardondale: Southern Illinois UP, 1990), 87–95.

2. See chapters 1 and 2 of Anne Ruggles Gere's *Writing Groups: History, Theory and Implications* (Carbondale: Southern Illinois UP, 1987) for further discussion of the historical dimensions of collaborative groups in the United States.

3. In *Montaigne's* Essais: *A Study* (Englewood Cliffs: Prentice-Hall, 1969), Donald M. Frame gives a brief synopsis of changes in those essays through the various versions.

Works Cited

Allen, Nancy, et al. "What Experienced Collaborators Say About Collaborative Writing." *Journal of Business and Technical Communication* 1.2 (1987): 70–90.

Bruffee, Kenneth A. "Collaborative Learning: Some Practical Models." *College English* 34 (1973): 634–43.

———. "Liberal Education and the Social Justification of Belief." *Liberal Education* 68 (1982): 95–114.

———. "On Not Listening in Order to Hear: Collaborative Learning and the Rewards of Classroom Research." *Journal of Basic Writing* 7 (1988): 3–12.

———. "Social Construction, Language, and the Authority of Knowledge: A Bibliographical Essay." *College English* 48 (1986): 773–90.

———. "The Structure of Knowledge and the Future of Liberal Education." *Liberal Education* 67 (1981): 177–85.

———. "Writing and Reading as Collaborative or Social Acts." *The Writer's Mind: Writing as a Mode of Thinking*. Ed. Janice N. Hays, et al. Urbana: NCTE, 1983. 159–69.

Burke, Kenneth. *A Grammar of Motives*. Berkeley. U California P, 1969.

———. *Language as Symbolic Action: Essays on Life, Literature, and Method*. Berkeley: U California P, 1966.

Clark, Gregory. *Dialogue, Dialectic, and Conversation: A Social Perspective on the Function of Writing*. Carbondale: Southern Illinois UP, 1990.

Clifford, John. "Composing in Stages: The Efforts of a Collaborative Pedagogy." *Research in the Teaching of English* 15 (1981): 37–53.

Couture, Barbara, and Jone Rymer. "Interactive Writing on the Job: Definitions and Implications of 'Collaboration.'" *Writing in the Professions*. Ed. Myra Kogen. Urbana: NCTE, ABC, 1989. 73–93.

Doheny-Farina, Stephen. "Writing in an Emerging Organization: An Ethnographic Study." *Written Communication* 3 (1986): 158–85.

Forman, Janis. "Novices Work on Group Reports: Problems in Group Writing and in Computer-Supported Group Writing." *Journal of Business and Technical Communication* 5.1 (1991): 48–75.

Frame, Donald M. *Montaigne's Essais: A Study*. Englewood Cliffs: Prentice-Hall, 1969.

Gere, Anne Ruggles. *Writing Groups: History, Theory, and Implications*. Carbondale: Southern Illinois UP, 1987.

Karis, Bill. "Conflict in Collaboration: A Burkean Perspective." *Rhetoric Review* 8 (1989): 113–26.

LeFevre, Karen Burke. *Invention as a Social Act*. Carbondale: Southern Illinois UP, 1987.

Lunsford, Andrea, and Lisa Ede. *Singular Texts/Plural Authors Perspectives on Collaborative Writing*. Carbondale: Southern Illinois UP, 1990.

Montaigne, Michel de. *The Complete Essays of Montaigne*. Trans. Donald M. Frame. Stanford: Stanford UP, 1958.

Odell, Lee, and Dixie Goswami, eds. *Writing in Nonacademic Settings*. New York: Guilford, 1985.

Smit, David W. "Some Difficulties with Collaborative Learning." *Journal of Advanced Composition* 9 (1989): 45−58.

Stewart, Donald C. "Collaborative Learning and Composition: Boon or Bane." *Rhetoric Review* 7 (1988): 58−83.

Trimbur, John. "Consensus and Difference in Collaborative Learning." *College English* 51 (1989): 602−16.

1

For Profit and Pleasure: Collaboration in Nineteenth Century Women's Literary Clubs

Anne Ruggles Gere
Laura Jane Roop

By examining the reading and writing practices of nineteenth-century women's clubs, this essay explores forms of collaboration that appear in these clubs. It describes the intertextual, intergenerational collaboration that blurred boundaries between reading and writing and strengthened gender identity. Contemporary writing classes, it argues, manifest continuity with these clubs in themes such as the role of gender, the pleasure of friendship, and the empowerment of textual ownership in writing groups.

During the latter half of the nineteenth century, once the chaos of the Civil War had subsided, Americans continued their practices of collaborative self-education. As Daniel Boorstin has noted, from Colonial times forward, residents of this country differed from their European counterparts in two significant ways: they took an egalitarian view of knowledge; and they tended to join with others to initiate change. Unlike Europeans who "depended on the monumental accomplishments of the few" (150), Americans saw knowledge and its development as the province of all. As Boorstin puts it: "Out of all the limitations and opportunities of colonial America grew an American ideal, which sprang from the conviction that knowledge, like the New World itself, was still only half-discovered" (188). This view of knowledge, combined with an impulse to join with others in effecting change, created a climate in which mutual education or collaborative learning groups flourished. One of the earliest, the Junto, was formed by Ben

1

Franklin and a group of his friends in 1728 (Gere 32). Such collaboration grew as the United States developed. The Lyceum, a mutual education system created in 1826, had established 3,000 member groups in 15 states by 1834, and in the 1840s "every state had Lyceums which not only sponsored lectures but maintained libraries and museums, organized classes and published teaching materials" (Nye 360).

Although the collaborative learning groups formed after the Civil War represented a continuation of the Lyceum concept, it was a continuation with a difference: women became active participants in collaborative learning. To be sure, women had often accompanied their husbands or fathers to Lyceum meetings, there had been women's Bible study groups affiliated with churches, and a few women had paid subscriptions to attend Margaret Fuller's "Conversations for Women" between 1839 and 1844, conversations designed to help women address the questions "What were we born to do? and How shall we do it?" (Dall 5). After the Civil War, when significant numbers of women's groups convened for mutual education, they transformed the club tradition, weaving women's clubs into the fabric of nearly every American city, town, and village.

Two clubs, the New England Women's Club and New York's Sorosis, both founded in 1868, claim to be the first women's club in this country. Actually several short-lived clubs predated both of these contenders, but the real force of the women's club movement gathered in the early 1870s, and the years between 1870 and 1920 saw tremendous growth in club membership. The General Federation of Women's Clubs, formed in 1890, claimed over 800,000 members by 1908 and 1,600,000 in 1914 (Blair 142). An even greater number of clubs remained outside the Federation. The number of nonfederated women's clubs is difficult to calculate because they had no central recording agency, and many members, adhering to the principle that a woman's name should appear in the newspaper only at the time of her marriage and her death, avoided publicity. Federated and nonfederated clubs differed in size, specific purpose, racial and social class of members, range of activities, degree of formality, and many other ways, but they all fostered learning through collaboration, a collaboration that gave prominence to both the pleasures and profits of reading and writing.

These days, collaboration appears frequently in discussions of learning. Strategies for implementation, evaluation of effectiveness, and epistemological underpinnings of collaboration have been elaborated by contemporary theorists. In the late nineteenth century, discussions about collaboration were much less common, but groups such as women's clubs practiced collaboration much as rhetoricians practiced their art long before Aristotle described rhetoric systematically.

In this essay, we will examine closely the collaborative learning that occurs in two very different clubs, the Saturday Morning Club of Boston and the Friday Club of Jackson, Michigan. The two clubs differ in many respects, and their differences illustrate the tremendous variety included under the general term "collaborative learning." Among the issues we will consider are preservation and use of club texts, the relationship between reading and writing, the relationship of texts to one another, and the strengthening of gender identity that characterized each of these clubs.

The Saturday Morning Club was started by Julia Ward Howe, president of the New England Women's Club, for her daughter Maud and several of her young friends in 1871. As might be expected of the daughter of Julia Ward Howe, Maud's friends included members of Boston's most prestigious families. Club size varied across the years from twelve to fifty members, but twenty-five was the most consistent number. Although the club occasionally met in members' homes, most meetings were held in rented public spaces such as hotels. Many of the resources of the city were available to the Saturday Morning Club, and lecturers included Ralph Waldo Emerson, Bronson Alcott, and many other intellectual leaders of the period. Originally these lectures by nonmembers alternated with members-only discussions, but discussions soon gave way to papers written by members. These papers were highly valued by the club. A 1946 letter from Maud to the Saturday Morning Club illustrates the club's emphasis on preservation of its own texts at the same time that it provides some insight into the club's origins:

> When I was seventeen, I was a saucy brat of a spoiled child living with my parents.... My mother had recently become an ardent suffragist, one of the editors of the *Women's Journal* and the leader of a women's peace crusade. There was much talk and many meetings concerning the founding of a women's club. The ladies interested had meetings at our house. One day after such a meeting I said something like the following to my mother: "Why do you bother so about these terrible old frumps?" (The bonnets of some of those early suffragists were fierce!) "It might be worth while to have a girls' club." The seed sown by a reckless hand took root, flourished, and grew into your worshipful body. (Series VIII Box 1)

Maud, then ninety-two years old, wrote this letter because she was unable to attend the seventy-fifth anniversary celebration of the club in person. Her letter was read aloud to the assembled group and the members voted to send her a telegram, "which was dispatched before dessert" (11/2/46). This letter was put in the club archives and served as a resource for future club members.

The Friday Club of Jackson, Michigan, was intentionally small: the membership goal was twenty-four, a number that could be entertained in spacious parlors or living rooms (Figure 1.1). Founded in 1887 by a core group of experienced club members, Jackson's Friday Club took for its object "the gaining of Emersonian ideas" (Minutes, August 9, 1889, taken by F. E. Porter). The Friday Club's collaboratively written statement of purpose reflects the spirit of playful community that characterized this club:

> We the undersigned, feeling the need of some intellectual stimulus, and painfully realizing that there is one day in the week in which mental pablum (sic) is not offered to us in chunks; do hereby resolve: To close that gap in the calendar; and to apply ourselves with unwearied devotion to the consumption of knowledge — not to speak of such slight refreshments as may be offered by the hostess — enhancing the feast of reason with that flow of soul which can only characterize Two Dozen mutual admirers. (1887)

The Friday Club's resolution to "apply ourselves with unwearied devotion to the consumption of knowledge" is purposely undercut by the notion "not to speak of such slight refreshments as may be offered by the hostess." The women of the Friday Club, though serious in their pursuit of intellectual matters — as evidenced by the consistent record of text-based, sometimes passionate discussion — refused to take themselves too seriously.

Club members were the wives and daughters of the town's prominent citizens — elected officials, lawyers, and businessmen — although these women were not of the same social class as the Saturday Morning Club members. Women of the Friday Club seem to have been fairly well schooled; some apparently attended college or seminary. Responsibility for hosting meetings was shared equally among members; since each woman hosted no more than two meetings a year, painstaking preparation went into every occasion. The hostess made sure that her house was spotless, her flowers arranged, her refreshments lavish, and her children neatly attired. Members clearly loved the chance to visit one another's homes; descriptions of refreshments, flower arrangements, children, husbands, and pets were sometimes included in records of the meetings. The Friday Club chose to forgo a public meeting place or clubhouse. "These weekly bits of travel from one house to another — each a reflection of the tastes and personality of the homemakers — are a delightful feature of the Friday Club, that no Clubhouse meeting place could improve upon," wrote Zelie Emerson, after describing the setting of one meeting (Minutes, April 16, 1897). The intimate social dimension of the club was at least as important to these women as was the scholarly aspect. "I confess to having been more interested in the sight of the dear, familiar, new-old faces, than at first in the reading,

Figure 1.1

Women of The Friday Club of Jackson, Michigan, at the turn of the century. (Photo courtesy of the Ella Sharp Museum, Jackson, Michigan.)

and to have paid very little attention to its own selection from Lubbock, read by Mrs. Root," wrote Mrs. Loomis, scribe for the September 20, 1889, meeting.

The Friday Club collaborated to lead and maintain the community, choosing not to create a hierarchy of leadership roles. Members rotated responsibility for hosting meetings and keeping records. The meeting facilitator, termed the "Bell ringer," was initially elected on a yearly basis, but after several years, even that responsibility rotated from meeting to meeting. One member, Lydia Robb, an active club woman who had founded several clubs, served as the club's mentor, encouraging the other women to pursue learning with the same passion that she did. While other members regarded Mrs. Robb as their "Lady Teacher," she shared responsibilities for hosting, minute taking, and facilitating meetings with them. Mrs. Robb may have chosen this arrangement in order to give others the chance to acquire leadership skills and to gain confidence in their own intellects.

"Intergenerational" Collaboration

Both the Saturday Morning Club and the Friday Club honored the texts that their members produced by preserving them; records spanning at least a century for each club were placed in local archives. These letters, papers, minutes, and momentos served as a resource for future club members. For example, Frances Darling's 1968 paper about Maud Ward Elliot includes a long excerpt from Maud's letter to the Saturday Morning Club, referred to as Maud's "As It Was in the Beginning" letter (Series VIII, Box 1). Subsequent histories of the club, including the club book published for the hundredth anniversary celebration in 1971, likewise quoted excerpts from Maud's letter. From its earliest days the Saturday Morning Club carefully preserved its important texts in the "green trunk," whose history is recounted at an April 26, 1958, meeting of the club:

> At the Annual Meeting held at the apartment of Mrs. Rugg, the members of SMC were invited to examine the contents of the famous "Green Trunk," a very small affair indeed, that contained the earliest records of the Club. As the records multiplied, another larger trunk was procured to hold the "Green Trunk" itself, plus the overflow, and later a third still larger one to hold these two. And still our records accumulate.

The "green trunk" has important symbolic value for members of the Saturday Morning Club. The fiftieth birthday celebration in 1921 featured a masque written by club member Abbie Farwell Brown titled "The Green Trunk." In addition to recounting some of the club's history, the masque underscores the importance of preserving club texts by making the club archive—the green trunk itself—the star of the drama. (Of course, the masque was added to the club's collection of texts.)

The value the Saturday Morning Club assigned to its own texts is illustrated by the fact that one of the highest compliments club members could pay one another was to suggest that one's paper be put in the "green trunk." The manilla envelope containing the papers given at the club's seventieth anniversary has written on the outside: "for green trunk." The pleasure members take in one another's texts appears to be the primary motive for preservation. For example, the October 19, 1870, minutes include this: "It was agreed that Miss Tetlow could read an old paper rather than write a new one. This gives the club a particular treat because her papers are ageless in their interest and stimulating." Collaboration often played a role in the texts preserved by the Saturday Morning Club. Records of the May 2, 1891, meeting mention that a club album had been commissioned and "the handsome book whose cover Miss Hallowell decorated, whose essay Miss Morrison wrote and whose report Miss Ellen Dennie made was added to the archives" (Series I, Box I).

Clearly, sharing club texts with the larger world was not a motive for preserving them. Access to the "green trunk" and its contents was carefully controlled. A 1921 letter from one club member to another discusses who may have access to the trunks and specifies that a letter of permission is required. As a general rule, the Saturday Morning Club avoided (and avoids) publicity. A skit written in 1946 imagining the Saturday Morning Club in 1971 concludes with this comment from a reporter: "Your club sure is the berries, avoiding publicity and yet living for a hundred years. Can you beat it?" (11/2/46). Preservation of SMC texts, then, fostered an intertextual collaboration. Members separated by time and space could (and can) borrow one another's language, appropriate one another's texts, and literally speak in one another's voices because the collected texts of the club were available to become part of new texts.

Although the Friday Club preserved fewer texts than the Saturday Morning Club, the handwritten autobiographical records, termed "little books" by members, served as an informal literary publication, a valued permanent record, in much the same way as the SMC's Green Trunk. Some entries in the little books show an awareness that record keepers were writing a "history":

> If the history of the Friday Club is ever written for the benefit of future generations, our "little books" of autobiography will serve to furnish materials for such an important work. We may smile at such an idea but more improbable things have happened and may again. Whatever may appear of strength, or weakness, or wisdom, or folly, the good comradeship will be apparent. (Minutes, November 27, 1896, taken by Mary Kellogg)

By choosing to write "autobiographical literature" collaboratively, the Friday Club created a permanent record of personalities and friendships. The entries in the little books were read out loud at the start of each meeting; judging from intertextual references, the observer sees that the weekly record keepers reread many entries privately as they would a magazine or journal before adding to the book.

In preserving their texts, both the Saturday Morning Club and Friday Club created an alternative canon that allowed for "inter-generational" collaboration. The texts contained in the "green trunk" and its successors and the texts of the "little books" took on a special quality for club members. These are the texts from which the "truth" about the club can be extracted because club members created histories of themselves. These histories served as sources of guidance for decisions about the future. When members of the Saturday Morning Club were, for example, undecided about how to respond to World War I relief efforts, they reread Julia Ward Howe's poem "Our Orders" and on the basis of that reading decided to "follow individually, rather than as a Club, the standard set by our Founder" (Series VIII, Box i). More importantly, though, club texts reinforced members' sense of group identity. Though this benefit of collaboration is sometimes dismissed as trivial, it was significant for club women at the turn of the century, in a world that denied them access to educational institutions, and even denied them the right to vote.

Blurring the Boundaries Between Reading and Writing

According to its constitution, the Saturday Morning Club was to "promote culture and social intercourse" and from its beginning to the present the Saturday Morning Club has employed combinations of reading and writing to achieve this goal. During the early years of the club, lectures by nonmembers alternated with members-only discussion meetings, and no writing was required of members. After a series of underattended discussions, President Marion P. Gray read an address to the club on November 28, 1874, in which she remonstrated members for the small attendance on discussion days, for a failure to address all talk to the chair, and for inadequate preparation. The seriousness attached to this address is evident in the fact that it was written by President Gray in advance and by the fact that it was copied in its entirety by the recording secretary (usually the secretary recorded only summaries of speeches). The written text was read aloud and then recorded again in writing, thus merging the acts of reading and writing.

Members of the Saturday Morning Club evidently took President Gray's admonition to heart because somewhat later in the minutes for the day this appears: "It was suggested that some might like to put their thoughts in writing on the subject under discussion which idea was favorably received and the president expressed her willingness to read any short paper which might be sent to her anonymously if the writer so chose" (Series I, Box l). The SMC paper requirement thus emerged, and it soon became a requirement for membership that endures to the present: "Women who are proposed for membership have to remain 'substitute' members for two seasons until they have presented two papers that meet the group's standard" (GLOBE 7/30 1973). Initially, four papers were given at each meeting, but this did not allow enough time for discussion so the number was reduced to three. Implicit in this requirement is the assumption that all members should contribute something to the intellectual life of the club. This collaborative spirit is further emphasized by another requirement, one that continues to appear in today's SMC program book: "Papers shall be read to the president (or to someone designated by her) at least a week before the discussion date" (1986–87 Program Book). The SMC president's role as previewer of papers not only demonstrates the collaborative dimension of writing club papers but also shows how the lines between production and consumption of texts were blurred. The president read and responded to a written text, which would be revised in writing and then read aloud, summarized in the written record of the club meeting, and preserved in written form in the club records.

Club records themselves represented an interesting combination of reading and writing. The recording secretary typically took written notes during the meeting and then revised them before copying them in the club record book and reading them aloud at the next meeting. The effort represented in these records is suggested by a secretary's marginalia on the record for the meeting of March 8, 1947: "This was written at the President's special request, after borrowing and reading all three of the papers and getting the Treasurer's which was on the business of the day." Another marginal comment written during the same period suggests the sense of performance attached to the reading of the minutes. A penciled addendum notes: "They applauded it; wasn't I pleased?" (11/2/46). And another, added after the word "accepted" states "by hand-clapping. I *was* gratified" (2/1/47). The oral transactions recorded in writing appear in oral form again when the records are read aloud, and at every stage the writer works closely with and receives support from the audience.

Reading and writing activities were expressly collaborative for Friday Club members. Like the Saturday Morning Club, the Friday Club read the written records of the previous meeting out loud. Since the minutes were written to entertain, the reading of them became a dramatic performance to which the "audience" often responded. Subsequently, during a typical meeting, women took turns reading passages aloud—Emerson first, usually, then contemporary articles, poems or stories—while the rest listened, doing handwork, minding any small children present, and following along in their own copies of texts, when possible. Readers were sometimes interrupted by listeners, who would comment on passages and ask for clarification from other group members. Discussion followed each passage, and sometimes grew quite heated, as evidenced by the following:

> Mrs. Robb began the afternoon by reading in a half-hearted way from that most unsatisfactory essay of Emerson's—as *she* thinks— "Love"—interrupting herself every three sentences by protests against the truth of the statements.... But the battle of the afternoon was fought over the story "Where Ignorance is Bliss" by Margaret Deland,

which Mrs. Root placidly called into our midst — the variety of ethical opinions in the Friday Club is only limited by its number of members, and the joyous part of it all is that we are all so satisfied that we are right, secretly excusing our sisters' lack of accord with us — with the charitable thought "that though a dear woman she is a little narrow-minded," in a word, that we have reached a higher moral plane of development — this makes us all happy and hurts nobody. We decided once or over again, singly, doubly, in groups, *all together* by turn in season and out of season (especially sister Ruth) that the hero was a fool & so was she, that the hero was indeed a moral hero, but the girl a fool, that the hero was a fool and the girl wise. (Minutes, March 26, 1897, taken by Zelie Emerson)

Mrs. Emerson conveyed the energetic twists and turns this conversation apparently took, while poking fun at the way the women's seeming civility and tolerance masked their own stubborn interpretations of texts. Such conversations served more than one function: club members practiced articulating their own interpretations of texts and learned to negotiate differences of opinion. When written accounts like Zelie Emerson's were read aloud at meetings, the women had the opportunity to reflect upon and critique their own processes of making meaning.

Boundaries between activities such as reading, writing, and speaking were blurred and softened in women's clubs, where collaboration was the rule. Because written texts were so often read aloud in club meetings, the authority of the written text was diminished. Read out loud, the texts, regardless of their authors' status, became new voices in a conversation among equals.

Intertextual Collaboration

With the institution of copyright laws in the eighteenth century, the concept of authorship became inextricably bound to economic interests. Authors claimed ownership of their texts and of the monetary profits generated by them. As texts became identified as intellectual property, authorship evolved into an ideology that privileged solitary production of writing and that viewed texts as commodities to be bought and sold. Within the space created by clubs, women subverted the ideology of authorship and appropriated texts with a spirit of playfulness.

This appropriation included but extended beyond texts written by club members. Members of the Saturday Morning Club borrowed from a wide range of texts. In lighthearted fashion, Mrs. Milet issued invitations to a Mother Goose party (3/27/11) in verse, and her guests responded in verses parodying various nursery rhymes. The Century Party held on January 1, 1901, featured a new club song using the air of Michael Roy. Over the years the Saturday Morning Club staged a number of dramatic productions. Several of these were based on texts written by club members (as in the case of the "Masque of the Green Trunk"), but many were based on the texts of others. The Saturday Morning Club produced "A Winter's Tale" in 1895 and its version of *Pride and Prejudice* in 1904. Although they retained much of Austen's language, club members shaped her text to suit their own purposes.

Club records indicate that the most prized of its productions was the 1891 version of *Antigone* (Figures 1.2 and 1.3). In addition to cutting Sophocles' text, SMC members appropriated the text in several ways. The cast was composed entirely of women and both public productions were open to women only. Because the women's voices were lighter and did not carry as well as men's, SMC members decided to augment the Chorus of Theban Elders with a Chorus of Maidens. A few days after the final production, SMC members gathered for a celebratory breakfast, and the toasts and speeches delivered on this occasion appropriated, as we shall see below, language from several other texts. The record of the breakfast meeting includes this:

> The first toast, "The Managers," was drunk standing. The next, "the originator of the idea of giving the Antigone," was answered by Miss Dennie, who took advantage of the opportunity to express publicly the thanks of the Managers to all present and absent for the valuable aid rendered in the previous months. Miss Tower was next toasted and gave some amusing anecdotes, incidents and comments heard about the play. The "Founder of the Club" brought Mrs. Howe to her feet with complimentary remarks upon the play and a poem written for the occasion. Miss Butler also read a poem written by her for the occasion. Miss Quincy responded for the "Elders" with some very amusing verses in the style of "Hiawatha." (VII-lv)

Ellen Dennie responded to the toast in her honor with a poem that began:

> Theban Elders! Theban Elders
> Are there, in the English Language,
> Fitting words for just this moment
> To express the joy and rapture
> Which I owe to your great kindness
> For a gift so rare and perfect,
> Full of gen'rous thought and feeling;
> Thing of beauty, joy forever,
> Keeping fresh in mem'ry's vision
> Beauty evanescent, fleeting?
> If so, I have failed to find them.

Most of the toasts and responses took the form of verse, and as this one indicates (with its "thing of beauty, joy forever"), borrowed freely from other texts. Collaboration among club members thus extended to

Figure 1.2
The Saturday Morning Club's 1891 production of *Antigone*. (Photo
courtesy of The Schlesinger Library, Radcliffe College.)

a wider form of intertextuality, one that did not concern itself with the
"authority" of texts so much as with the pleasure they could create.

The Friday Club's decision to accentuate subjectivity and individuality in its record-keeping practices allowed for a kind of collaboration
that was rare. Scribes tried to make their entries stylistically distinctive

Figure 1.3

The Saturday Morning Club's 1891 production of *Antigone*. (Photo courtesy of The Schlesinger Library, Radcliffe College.)

and amusing, writing verse, biblical parodies, and mock-heroic descriptions. Club members viewed club record-keeping duties as aesthetic transactions with other members. Unlike the Saturday Morning Club and most other clubs, the Friday Club rejected uniformity in its records—the date, the hostess's name, and the works studied were the only consistent pieces of information included in each entry. Because the central purpose of making a record of club meetings was to entertain, the record keeper was free to include descriptions of the weather, the hostess's home, the refreshments, and the nuances of discussions. Often, the record keeper stated her own views on texts, even on the process of writing itself. Minutes were used to tease and encourage other members, and to mock oneself. Zelie Emerson referred to the stylistic choices of other recorders in this passage:

> Shall I allow myself to be carried away by the poetic fancies and melodious measure of a Carlton, or imitate the quaint humorous style of a Robb, steal the deep wisdom & philosophy of a Gibson, or making *their* best my own, fuse the whole into one gigantic and glorious production, or thus cast a suspicion on the originality of their matter and style, since mine must necessarily be the *Epitome* of what is best in all? (Minutes, November 8, 1889)

Zelie hinted at the way club members used other entries: they imitated them. Once a writer tried an entry in verse, other rhyming entries would follow, sometimes using the same rhythmic pattern.

The appropriation of models, ranging from "Twas the Night Before Christmas" to Emerson to the Bible, gave the women of the Friday Club a sense of power over the texts they read and wrote. When Lydia Robb wrote "And it came to pass that the words of the wise man, even Emerson, became as goads to the Club, yea verily like the arrow that findeth the joint in the harness," she was gaining control over a sacred text, establishing a new stylistic possibility for minutes, and encouraging members to search out their own models (Minutes, October 16, 1889). Such playful imitation and commentary was not only amusing for the club members; it also generated a level of irreverence toward published texts that carried over into their discussions:

> The meeting was called to order and reading commenced by Mrs. Robb; after reading a few pages she pantingly resigned the book to Mrs. Mathison who heroically began her struggle to keep in breath to the end of one of Dr. Edward's sentences. The excitement of the club was intense as idea after idea were tacked together and no sign of a period, the club dropped their work and leaned forward straining every nerve to catch every new thought, on, on, she went, could she, would she hold out, the club were wild with agitation, but at last she conquered, flushed with the effort so nobly accomplished she resigned the book and the club tremblingly resumed their work. (Minutes, August 9, 1889, taken by Mrs. F. E. Porter)

In this account of a meeting, Mrs. Porter captured the humorous struggle the readers had with the text by creating similarly cumbersome sentences in the minutes. By being able to laugh together at published texts, club members could gain a certain power over them.

By appropriating texts freely both the Friday Club and the Saturday Morning Club developed an alternative aesthetic, one that created and enacted its own standards. Club members were not writing for a public that valorized originality and individual authorship; they were more concerned with the pleasure they could create than with the "authority" of texts.

Strengthening Gender Identity through Collaboration

Historians such as Karen Blair and Penny Martin describe women's clubs as way stations between private and public life, arguing that the safety of clubs gave women opportunities to develop skills and confidence that enabled them to move into the public sphere. While we acknowledge that this interpretation has validity, we believe there is more to the story. Clubs such as the Saturday Morning Club strengthened the gender identity of women, allowing them to take pleasure in themselves without reference to the patriarchal world. Indeed SMC members avoided the kind of competitiveness and honing of oratorical skill that would have enabled them to enter the public arena, preferring to concentrate on language designed to strengthen their relationship to one another. The playful verses for the Mother Goose party and those celebrating the production of *Antigone* are but two illustrations of SMC members' continuing interest in using language to delight one another. Even in more serious moments, such as the death of a member, club language differed from public language. The account of a woman's life published in the newspaper obituary was very different from the memorial read at the club meeting. The club memorial emphasized the deceased's relationship to the Saturday Morning Club. Mary Gray Morrison, for example, was memorialized on December 4, 1937, by Helen Cheever. The six typewritten pages included statements such as these: "...in 1888 Mary Morrison joined the SMC.... How many papers she has given the club in those years, papers clever as well as witty, always awaited with eagerness and received with gratification! A few of her Club friends go back to her girlhood days, some members who welcomed her to the Club are with us today..." (VIII-l). In addition to including information about the deceased's relationship to the club, club memorials offered a more sentimental and intimate view of its former member. Comments such as "I have never heard her say an unkind word of anyone" and "she had been an inspiration to him" punctuate Cheever's account of Morrison's life.

In the Friday Club as well, women chose to privilege friendship and good feeling over conventional notions of educational activity. Writing and reading to enhance friendships and to interpret experiences, *not* for a public audience, permitted them to create a space outside the academic world where learning could be safe and joyful. The women in the Friday Club chose to keep their meetings small, private, and noncompetitive. When a dinner was held where each member was to come dressed as a character from literature, a group of ten wrote a petition protesting the policy of giving three-minute speeches:

> ...whereas, the undersigned do favor the custom of three-minute speeches in all members save those whose names are affixed to this document; but
> Whereas, the undersigned do as earnestly deprecate the habit of speech making in such as are not accustomed to extemporaneous remarks, spontaneous wit and the like; be it therefore
> Resolved, in the name of independence of woman, the courage of Emerson and the memory of Dickens we do assert in hard words and good set terms that the undersigned contingent flatly refuse to comply with said edict....(February 27, 1897)

These women, who signed the names of their chosen literary characters instead of their own, asserted that they had the right as independent women to alter the social "rules" so they would feel comfortable. If "forced" to speak, they threatened to walk out. One of the highlights of the party was the reading of this petition. Their refusal to be put in a public, possibly competitive situation was applauded by other members.

Such assertion of themselves as women marked many of the discussions and record entries. In fact, several entries mention the Friday Club's "unwritten" motto: "Men may come, and men may go, but we go on forever." One rather subversive conversation was recorded in a biblical imitation:

> (The book) told a true tale, how that one called Addison was overcome by a woman, yea verily, by Sarah his wife; and behold the four and twenty (members of the Friday Club) did clap their hands and laugh aloud and they spoke to one another, saying, we too will rebel and he to whom we are espoused shall take a back seat, and the houses and lands which are his shall become ours, and we will rule over the houses and lands as seemeth good. (March 26, 1897)

Though this version of discussion was obviously recorded for comic effect, empowering, subversive talk apparently took place at club meetings on a regular basis.

Another rather intriguing way that both women's clubs strengthened gender identity was through cross-dressing. In addition to assuming the clothing and roles of men in their dramatic productions, SMC members had "favorite author" parties where they came dressed as male and female writers. While the Friday Club did not produce plays, club members occasionally dressed as favorite literary characters — male or female. While cross-dressing may be seen as women's attempt to borrow some of the power assigned to men by borrowing their clothing, it also made them feel self-sufficient. They did not need men's help to produce plays or to fill a role at a party.

Pedagogical Implications

Women's clubs such as the Friday Club and the Saturday Morning Club may seem distant from, or even irrelevant to contemporary classrooms. Unlike the women of those nineteenth-century clubs, students and teachers alike take for granted women's right to vote, to pursue an education, to embark upon a career. Women's clubs may now seem a throwback to a distant era, even though many such clubs still thrive in various communities. However, we'd like to claim that the self-initiated, extra-institutional collaborations between nineteenth-century women have a great deal to teach us about literacy practices in our own classrooms. At the very least, thematic continuity between nineteenth-century club experiences and current discussions of collaboration may inform future conversations and questions.

Grouped by gender, the members of the Friday Club and the Saturday Morning Club were able to speak to one another in ways that may not have been possible in mixed gender groups. When the Saturday Morning Club chose not to permit men to attend their discussions or even their play performances, and when the Friday Club adjourned abruptly each time the head of the household arrived, members were refusing to subject themselves to male judgment. The supportive, noncompetitive social environments they had created could have been considered frivolous or subversive by men. While striking changes have occurred in gender roles and relationships during the past hundred years, psychologists, sociologists, and linguists have documented marked differences in the ways men and women interact. (Belenky et al., Gilligan; Weiler). Thus, classrooms and collaborative relationships should not necessarily be regarded as gender-neutral sites. The experiences of nineteenth-century club women suggest that collaborative groups can be formed to strengthen gender identity or consciously to examine gender issues.

Most striking to us was the sheer pleasure nineteenth-century club women expressed about attending club meetings. They reveled in one another's company; the friendships were intertwined with, and sometimes more important than, reading and writing activities. While some club members were friends before joining clubs, friendships were often enhanced as a result of participation. The club experience clearly points to the power of friendship and community as motivation to pursue reading and writing. If teachers understand the importance of community as a motivation to learn, they must do what they can to foster such interaction, not ignore it or relegate it to the fringes. The role of good company, of friendship, is often critical to effective collaborative relationships, though seldom mentioned by researchers.

The extra-institutional nature of women's clubs such as the Friday Club and the Saturday Morning Club also seemed to contribute to their success. The multiple forms of empowerment evidenced in these two clubs suggest that ownership plays a central part in individuals' literacy development. By determining the nature of their interactions with one another, setting their own guidelines, and negotiating changes, club women were able to create places where they could "think aloud with less timidity and more directness" (Friday Club minutes, September 20, 1889). By implication, classrooms that attempt to foster such empowerment would permit students' ownership of texts, conversations, and even classroom rules for interaction.

The extra-institutional aspect of these clubs may remind us that our students have literate lives outside the confines of the classroom. In fact, some literacy activities outside of schools may be marked by greater degrees of flexibility and collaborative energy than those inside; they may be more potent forces in a learner's life than any school experience. Teachers would do well to tap into their students' potentially rich backgrounds and to encourage reflection upon extra-institutional literacy experiences.

The experiences of these nineteenth-century club women highlight the artificiality of many boundaries and divisions in educational institutions — between students' academic and home lives, between reading and writing. When we see their easy transitions between roles — from being readers to being writers, from being mothers, wives, and friends to being teachers and critics, then back again, it reminds us how flexible and adaptive humans can be. Collaboration — four students teaming up on a research project, twenty-four nineteenth-century women setting up a study club for themselves, two colleagues working on an article together — may spark a kind of connection making or boundary blurring that makes learning exciting, memorable, and above all pleasurable.

Works Cited

Blair, Karen. *The Clubwoman as Feminist: True Womanhood Redefined, 1868–1914*. New York: Holmes and Meier, 1980.

Boorstin, Daniel. *The Americans: The Colonial Experience*. New York, Random House, 1956.

Gilligan, Carol. *In a Different Voice: Psychological Theory and Women's Development*. Cambridge, MA: Harvard UP, 1982.

Dall, Caroline Wells Healey. *Margaret and Her Friends or Ten Conversations with Margaret Fuller upon the Mythology of the Greeks and Its Expression in Art*. Boston: Roberts Bros., 1895.

Friday Club of Jackson, Michigan. Papers. Bentley Historical Archive, University of Michigan.

Gere, Anne Ruggles. *Writing Groups: History, Theory and Implications*. Carbondale: Southern Illinois UP, 1987.

Martin, Theodora Penny. *The Sound of Our Own Voices: Women's Study Clubs 1860–1910*. Boston: Beacon, 1987.

Nye, Russell. *Society and Culture in America 1830–1860*. New York: Harper, 1974.

Saturday Morning Club. Papers. Schlesinger Library, Radcliffe College.

Weiler, Kathleen. *Women Teaching For Change: Gender, Class and Power*. South Hadley: Bergin and Garvey, 1988.

2

Laboratory Life and the Determination of Authorship

John Trimbur
Lundy A. Braun

This essay argues that the collaborative organization of scientific work has produced structural and epistemological ambiguities about the nature of individuals' contributions to common projects and the credit to which they are entitled. By analyzing the determination of authorship on a number of scientific papers from a leading molecular biology laboratory, the essay explores the social processes of negotiation and networking that allocate credit to individual scientists. It closes with a cautionary note about the relationship between research on collaborative writing and pedagogy.

Let's begin with a scene from laboratory life at a research university. A junior faculty member struggling to develop an independent research program in a highly competitive field of biomedical research has produced a significant finding. The finding, our researcher believes, may be enough to establish a niche and a heightened visibility in his field. This is precisely the kind of recognition his institution requires for tenure and what he needs to secure continued grant funding to support his research. He is justifiably excited by the results of his hard work and the professional credit his finding appears to promise.

As it turns out, however, publishing a paper presenting the finding is more complicated than we might expect. It entails considerably more than simply writing up the results and sending a manuscript to a journal. Our researcher's work has involved collaboration with a laboratory in Europe. The European lab, the biggest and most prestigious in the field, has supplied our researcher with a cell line necessary for his experiments. Our researcher and his European colleagues have agreed that their collaboration will deal with the influence of a particular molecule on the cells. Because of this, our researcher prepares a manuscript and sends it immediately to the head of the lab in Europe. He follows up the transmission of the paper a few days later with a phone call. The head of the lab in Europe likes the paper and suggests a further experiment to strengthen it. They agree that our researcher will perform that experiment and incorporate the results in a new draft of the paper.

Our researcher is relieved. For one thing, his European collaborators have not performed the experiments his finding is based upon; no one, as far as he can tell, has scooped him; his finding is news. Second, our researcher knows that the head of the European lab could have insisted on doing the second experiment in his own lab, thereby taking control of the project and diminishing the credit our researcher would receive. Our story about laboratory life has a happy ending. Our researcher did indeed publish the paper as its first author, with his collaborators listed in proper order as coauthors. But we want to sidestep the discursive pleasures of narrative closure in this exemplary tale to examine more closely the social dynamics involved in what seems to an outsider to be the simple transmission of a scientific finding to a co-worker. There is more being communicated here than just scientific information.

On one hand, sending a manuscript to European collaborators is indeed an episode in an ongoing collaboration between two laboratories, a matter of conferring with co-workers in order to present scientific information. From an outsider's perspective, sending the manuscript seems to represent the dissemination of knowledge necessary to ensure the progress of science through the free and open exchange of information. From another perspective, however, sending the manuscript also represents what S. Michael Halloran calls a "proprietary claim," an assertion of ownership of the finding and a bid for the status of first authorship. What we may begin to discern in our researcher's apparently simple act of sending a manuscript is that the kind of collaboration that has become the standard operating procedure in most scientific fields produces not only scientific knowledge. It also produces careers in science.

There can be no question in this case that collaboration between the two laboratories played a generative role in the extension of scientific learning. But the point we want to emphasize is that the sheer fact of collaboration simultaneously makes it difficult to assess the relative contributions of individual co-workers and to distribute credit among them. As we will see, the technical and intellectual division of labor that characterizes contemporary science creates a number of ambiguities when it comes to deciding who should be included as an author on a particular paper and in what order the authors' names should appear.

For this reason, the authorship of a scientific paper is rarely a simple matter of writing up experimental results. Each of the authors listed on a multiauthor paper, after all, is not necessarily involved in its actual composition. Authorship, that is, may have less to do with the act of writing than with processes of negotiation by which recognition is allocated. It is a fluid and potentially contested social status that is determined concretely at particular conjunctures of laboratory life in science. The purpose of this essay is to explore some of the complexities that surround the determination of authorship on scientific papers.

The Problem of Collaboration in Studies of Writing

One reason to explore the social dynamics of multiple authorship in scientific writing is that collaboration has become one of the central preoccupations in studies of writing. The notion of collaboration has not only generated an important body of research and pedagogical innovation, but the term "collaborative" has now entered into the discourse of studies of writing as a part of the conventional wisdom. The value of collaborative learning and collaborative writing has taken on a kind of self-evident and self-valorizing status. As Joseph Harris suggests of its associated term "community," the term "collaboration" has acquired a kind of "warmly persuasive" rhetorical force. Collaboration has come to refer to a set of practices in the teaching of writing — collective work, mutual aid, nonauthoritarian styles of classroom life — that no one would think to dissent from.

There are certainly some good reasons to valorize collaboration. As many writing instructors have discovered, the social practices of working and writing together represent important and useful correctives to the unquestioned primacy of the solo performance and the intertwined ideologies of authorship and possessive individualism that have dominated the humanities. Recent research by Ede and Lunsford, Odell, Goswami et al., and Forman reveals that the traditional literary view of the single author has obscured the fact that coauthorship is the norm in many academic and professional fields, and their investigations have started to chart the ways writing in business, industry, government, the professions, and in technical and scientific research actually gets produced through the multiple contributions of individuals in complex divisions of labor.

The results of this research, however, and the accompanying sense that we now know how people actually write out in the world, can produce certain blind spots, especially when we use such research as a measure of our pedagogical practices. Writing teachers and theorists increasingly have justified the use of collaborative learning and collaborative writing on the grounds that students are likely to be involved in team projects and group writing in their jobs and careers. Collaboration, as one of us has suggested elsewhere, has been invested with a kind of "real world" authority because it appears to model the forms of social organization that produce written texts, documents, and reports in contemporary America (Trimbur). But it is precisely because of the authority that has been invested in collaborative practices that there is the danger of idealizing collaboration out in the "real world" without considering substantial differences between what professionals do in the world of work and what we want our students to do in our classrooms.

Lunsford and Ede point to a crucial difference when they distinguish between "hierarchical" and "dialogic" forms of collaboration. Collaboration among students, as it has been organized by writing teachers such as Kenneth A. Bruffee and Peter Elbow, operates in a "dialogic" mode that regards students as peers and status-equals involved in the shared activity of learning to write. One of the central purposes of collaboration, therefore, is to make sure everyone gets the opportunity to speak and to be heard. The point of collaboration is to stage a dialogue, to orchestrate a multiplicity of voices so that students can become the coauthors of the curriculum and of their own learning. Collaboration in scientific research, on the other hand, relies upon a stratified division of technical and intellectual labor that is organized and administered along "hierarchical" lines. In scientific publication, the status of coauthorship is not only an acknowledgment of participation in a common project. Coauthorship is also a device to allocate credit differentially by distinguishing the relative importance of individual contributions to a joint enterprise. For this reason, as we will see, the determination of authorship in scientific work can create troubling ambiguities, which in turn may lead to conflicts among co-workers and may inhibit instead of facilitate communication within a collaborative group.

The Problem of Multiple Authorship

Science is often thought to be one of the purest forms of meritocracy, because its universalistic norms prescribe that recognition be accorded solely on the basis of a scientist's work. Since Francis Bacon, one of the central projects of modern science has been to divorce personality and individuality from scientific investigation. For Bacon, the scientific method exerts a kind of leveling effect that makes the particularities of a scientist's social situation — status, gender, professional connections — extraneous to the activity of science. Science, that is, appears to reward its practitioners for what they have achieved rather than for what has been ascribed to them.

Accordingly, scientists have been concerned historically with the issue of priority — of determining who was the first to make a particular discovery or to present a significant finding. Histories of science often tell the story of the race to get there first, as in the case of James Watson's account of the discovery of the structure of DNA in *Double Helix*, or of the complications that arise from parallel discoveries such as that of Darwin and Wallace, who independently formulated the law of natural selection. The story of science as the race for priority has produced the popular image of the scientist as a lonely and perhaps misunderstood individual battling competitors to be the first to solve a problem or make an important discovery.

Nowadays, of course, we need to refigure the scientist. As *Double Helix* indicates, for all of Watson's self-promotion, the heroic figure is no longer the individual scientist but the laboratory and the research group. As Derek Price argues in *Big Science, Little Science*, the days of the individual scientist puttering late at night in the lab are over. For Price, it is the trend toward increasing collaboration that most clearly distinguishes premodern from modern science. Until late in the nineteenth century, scientific work was still organized largely as craft labor and the individual scientist performed the manual work required to execute experiments. By the mid — twentieth century, however, scientific laboratories had been transformed along industrial lines to harness the cooperative labor of a collective work force.

There are a number of reasons for this shift from a craft to an industrial model of scientific work. The expense of scientific equipment, the technical complexities of research, the patterns of grant funding (which favor large groups), the extended apprenticeship systems of training graduate students and postdoctoral fellows, and the growing specialization within scientific fields have increasingly necessitated both a division of labor within laboratories and the entrepreneurial activity of laboratory heads to raise and manage capital, organize production, and circulate results. The typical contemporary well-funded lab contains a senior scientist who directs the lab and a range of subordinate figures — research faculty and associates, postdoctoral fellows, graduate students, and technicians. The senior scientist who conceptualizes a program of research is rarely the person who performs the actual experiments. Instead, the division of labor that operates in most laboratories separates mental from manual labor, senior scientists and laboratory heads from technicians and research assistants. By assigning work to subordinates, principal investigators can manage their laboratory's work more efficiently and pursue their own research interests and professional careers more vigorously.

One of the by-products of this shift to an industrial model has been an increase in the number of multiauthor papers. According to

Zuckerman and Merton, single-author papers accounted for 75 percent of publication in the biological and physical sciences in 1900—1909, but by 1950—1959 the number had dropped to 19 percent (547). Meadows reports the following figures on the incidence in 1950—59 of multiple authorship: 83 percent in chemistry, 70 percent in biology, and 67 percent in physics, as compared to 15 percent in mathematics and 4 percent in history (128). Not only has the number of scientific papers with multiple authors increased, but the size of the author set has increased as well. The two articles cited most frequently in the physical sciences in 1976 and 1977, for example, had 41 and 40 authors respectively, from the SLAC-Lawrence Berkeley Laboratory (Over 996), and scientists in such specialties as high-energy physics "frequently publish papers with 70 or 80 authors; a recent example had 139" (Piternick 22). As Price notes, "three-author papers are accelerating more rapidly than two-author, four-author more rapidly than three-author, and so on. . . if the trend holds, . . . we shall move steadily toward an infinity of authors per paper. It is one of the most violent transitions that can be measured in recent trends of scientific manpower and literature" (79).

What makes this transition so "violent" is a problematic tension between the collaborative structure of scientific work and the matter of assigning credit to individual scientists. As scientific work increasingly relies upon a complex division of labor, it becomes increasingly difficult to assess the relative contributions of individual members of a research group working on a common project. As Robert K. Merton notes, "The continuing change in the social structure of research, as registered by publication, seems to make for greater concern among scientists with the question 'How will my contribution be identified?' in collaborative work than with the historically dominant pattern of wanting to ensure their priority over others in the field" (409). The rise of collaborative work, Harriet Zuckerman says, has produced a "malintegration" of the reward system and individual scientists' interest in recognition and visibility, on the one hand, and the actual social organization of laboratory life, on the other. This "malintegration" has created considerable and troubling ambiguity about how to identify the individual "role performances" of scientists working within a research group. According to Zuckerman, the various patterns of name ordering used by scientists on publications represent symbolic attempts to cope with this ambiguity. Name ordering, that is, appears as what Louis Althusser might call an "imaginary relation to the real conditions of existence," a fictional effort to harmonize the potentially conflicting interests of individual scientists' concern for their careers and the prevailing collaborative organization of work.

According to Stokes and Hartley, the conventional pattern of name ordering on papers with multiple authors can be stated fairly straightforwardly: the position of first author is reserved for the scientist who designed and performed the experimental work; the last author is the senior scientist or laboratory head who superintended the work; and those who provided assistance are listed in relative order of importance left to right. This convention, however, is often manipulated deliberately. In some institutions, the position of last author is an honorific one: the head of a laboratory is listed on all papers the lab produces, whether he or she genuinely contributed or not. In other cases, as Zuckerman found, Nobel laureates decided at times not to attach their names to papers to which they had contributed in order to highlight the work of junior colleagues. A common pattern of name ordering attempts to equalize the contribution of all individuals by listing names in alphabetical order (or, alternatively, in reverse alphabetical order) or by cycling individuals through from first to last author on successive papers. Still another variation is to single out the contribution of one member of the group by putting either the first or last author out of sequence, thereby isolating a figure against a ground, whether the pattern is ZABC or XYZA. Others have suggested that papers be identified by the name of the research group instead of a list of individual authors.

Patterns of name ordering, Zuckerman says, are "devices to reduce the stress of collaboration" (290) and to minimize ambiguity about the nature of individuals' contributions and the credit to which they are entitled. Ambiguity, however, seems guaranteed not only by the difficulties of assessing the contributions of individuals but also by the ways scientists read and remember the order of names on papers with multiple authors. As one Nobel laureate in physics suggests, reputation seems to be a bigger factor than name order: the "man who's best known gets more credit, an inordinate amount of credit" (Merton 443). A laureate in physiology and medicine describes the way he responds to papers with multiple authors:

> You usually notice the name you're familiar with. Even if it's last, it will be the one that sticks. In some cases, all the names are unfamiliar to you, and they're virtually anonymous. But what you notice is the acknowledgments at the end of the paper to the senior person for his "advice and encouragement." So you will say: "This came out of Greene's lab or so-and-so's lab." You remember that rather than a long list of authors. (Merton 444)

Moreover, abstracts, literature reviews, and review essays also tend to operate selectively, reducing a large number of coauthors to a central figure or a short list of important authors. A passage from Carlo M. Croce and George Klein's recent article in *Scientific American*, "Chromosome Translocations and Human Cancer," shows how this selective reduction works: "Other experiments. . . [showed] that a similar rearrangement occurs in translocations underlying mouse plasma-cytomas. These studies were first carried out by Michael D. Cole *and his associates* at the St. Louis University Medical Center" (quoted in Stokes and Hartley 118, emphasis ours). The paper Croce and Klein refer to lists four coauthors, of which Cole is the last-named.

The ambiguities involved in the way coauthor order is constructed and decoded suggest that Zuckerman is right when she says that "in the long run, functional requirements of the evaluation system and of collaborative groups are incompatible and so call for different and sometimes conflicting procedures for making role performance visible" (290). Such "conflicting procedures," furthermore, raise serious ethical issues about the allocation of credit. Heffner, for example, indicates that "publication credit is not always accorded on the basis of univer-salistic criteria" (377). Authorship status may be withheld from those who occupy subordinate positions in a scientific laboratory — technicians, research assistants, and graduate students. As one laboratory technician reported to Heffner, "I performed all of the data collection work, prepared data over 75 percent of the time, and worked out most of the 'bugs' in the experimental design. For this I received an acknowledgment for technical assistance only" (379). Because the person assigning publication credit is normally the head of a lab or a senior scientist, the potential for the exploitation of subordinates is an ever-present one in laboratory life.

Authorship of scientific papers is highly charged, in part because of the ambiguities involved in allocating credit and in part because author-ship mediates in a very real sense between the production of scientific knowledge and the formation of individual careers. As Stokes and Hartley note, the "question of who will be a coauthor, and in what order, is a matter of great interest; it is therefore the cause of much friction and bad feeling within research groups" (105). There may be significant tensions between the collaborative production of knowledge and individual scientists' interest in visibility and mobility within the socially stratified world of academic science. To say that scientific knowledge is collaborative or socially constructed, while certainly true, hardly suggests the complexity of the processes of negotiation and the dispositions of power that determine authorship in concrete instances. To see in more detail what these negotiations and plays of power look like in laboratory life, we turn now to a particular laboratory.

The Weinberg Laboratory as a Site for Collaborative Work

Robert Weinberg's laboratory at the Whitehead Institute for Biomedical Research, associated with Massachusetts Institute of Technology, is one of the leading molecular biology labs in the world. Weinberg's lab is at the forefront of oncogene research and a prestigious site for graduate students and postdoctoral fellows to make their way into academic science. While one of the most distinguished in its field, Weinberg's lab, of course, is only one example of what "big science" looks like today and of how authorship on scientific papers is determined concretely. Nonetheless, Weinberg's lab, as described in *Natural Obsessions*, Natalie Angier's account of current research on the role of oncogenes in human cancer, can serve as a kind of case study, not to develop a comprehensive account of the social dynamics of laboratory life but to raise questions about the problematic nature of collaboration in contemporary science.

At any given time, fifteen to eighteen junior faculty, postdocs, and graduate students—some with their own fellowships and others supported through Weinberg's grants—and a cadre of technicians populate Weinberg's lab. The size of the workforce in his lab presents Weinberg with what he describes as a "managerially difficult problem"—namely, that of assigning projects so that the overall division of labor within the lab can proceed smoothly and yet simultaneously offer young scientists significant research opportunities. For Weinberg, collaboration is not just a technical necessity but also a positive intellectual force in laboratory life. As Weinberg puts it, "If one wants to move somewhere on a project, one doesn't want to have a person working on it alone. One needs cross-fertilization and synergy" (Angier 266). At the same time, however, Weinberg recognizes that scientific collaboration is fraught with potential difficulties. Weinberg's "great horror," he says, "has been the fear of having people in my lab compete with one another." His goal, therefore, "has always been to have people working on complementary aspects of a project" (Angier 267).

The Potential for Conflict in Scientific Authorship

What Weinberg seems to perceive is that the potential for conflict between the collaborative organization of work and the interests of individual scientists is structurally given and can surface at any time. A small and extreme example will illustrate how this can happen. In the early eighties, the Weinberg lab was involved in a race with other molecular biology labs to be the first to isolate and clone a human oncogene. Weinberg assigned the cloning project to a graduate student and two postdocs. "The trouble started," Angier writes, "when [one of the postdocs] suggested that they keep open the authorship of any future papers on the cloning of the oncogene, deferring decisions on the order of the three authors until they saw who had done what" (103). The graduate student had been the first to transfer tumorigenicity by introducing DNA from human cancers into normal cells and felt proprietary about the gene he had isolated. He was determined to clone the gene — and to do it on his own. This led to a rather sorry sequence of intellectual hoarding, secretiveness, and misinformation on the graduate student's part. Ultimately, the collaboration dissolved into separate and parallel research, precisely the kind of intralaboratory competition Weinberg feared, with the graduate student working alone to clone an oncogene from bladder cancer cells and the postdocs working to clone an oncogene from colon tumors.

The outcome — the graduate student succeeded in isolating an oncogene but was scooped by a rival lab while the postdocs ran into technical difficulties — is less important to our purposes here than the fact that the issue of authorship in this instance was instrumental in disrupting collaboration and inhibiting communication of scientific information. The case admittedly is an extreme (and no doubt exceptional) instance of social dysfunction. Nonetheless, the extremity of this example would seem to result in large part from a heightened consciousness of the potential conflict between the social organization of scientific work and an individual's interest in recognition and credit. As the graduate student put it, speaking of Weinberg, "What does it matter to him who the first author of the paper is? The important thing for him is that the work gets done. The important thing is that his lab gets the paper. That's true of every lab in the world — in Taiwan, everywhere" (Angier 104). The technical and intellectual division of labor Weinberg devised to push ahead on the work to clone an oncogene produced the kind of situational ambiguity about credit that Zuckerman describes and the graduate student found unendurable. Once the position of first authorship was put up for grabs, the graduate student attempted to resolve the ambiguity by closing himself and his work off from his erstwhile collaborators.

Each instance of multiple authorship, we might say, contains such potential for conflict — between the head of a lab's interest in managing a complex technical and intellectual division of labor and the interests of individual scientists. It is unusual, of course, for these potential conflicts to take the counterproductive direction we have just described. Most often, the tensions that can arise from the ambiguity of collaboration are deflected or evaded by a number of strategies, both formal and informal.

In some laboratories, co-workers agree in advance on who will be listed as an author on scientific papers and sometimes codify such agreements in writing. In other laboratories, first authors have the prerogative to decide which co-workers to list on papers. Perhaps the most common situation, however, is the one that obtains in Weinberg's lab, where the prerogative to determine authorship belongs to the head of the lab. In these instances, informal processes of intercession and negotiation often take place at the level of lab talk about who will be listed among the authors of a paper and in what order. Angier notes two cases when first authors interceded with Weinberg to include in the list of authors co-workers he had left off. In one case, Weinberg agreed and in the other he refused.

Difficulties in Managing the Ambiguities of Collaboration

Weinberg's explanations of his decisions illustrate some of the ambiguities involved in distributing credit among collaborators and distinguishing major from minor contributors. The ambiguity of determining who should be included as a secondary author derives in part from the absence of clear-cut criteria to assess contributions to a collaboratively produced piece of research. The line that divides "technical assistance," which is usually recognized in a "gratefully acknowledged" footnote, from a substantive intellectual contribution, which entitles one to authorship status, is a slippery and fluid one, subject to local and contradictory interpretation. In the first case, for example, Weinberg initially resisted including on an important paper presenting the cloning of the retinoblastoma gene the name of a graduate student who had built the cDNA library, containing all the messages in retinal cells, which was necessary to clone the gene. As one of the postdocs in his lab remarked, Weinberg "thought that making a cDNA library wasn't a huge intellectual contribution, and he thought that too many authors would take away from the importance of Steve and Ted [the two first-listed authors]" (Angier 351). Ultimately, Weinberg relented to pressure from one of these authors and did include the maker of the cDNA library as the third author. In this case, Weinberg's desire to strengthen the rhetorical effect of the paper by limiting the number of authors was overridden by the persistent expression of solidarity with a co-worker.

In the second instance, however, Weinberg turned down a first author's request to list a co-worker, but this time for apparently contradictory reasons. In this case, a graduate student had been involved in the early conceptual stages of a project to identify for the first time a specific gene mutation linked to human cancer. Subsequently, however, the graduate student had taken a personal leave of absence from Weinberg's lab. When he returned, the project was reaching its culmination and the results were being prepared for publication. The first author of the paper interceded with Weinberg to include the graduate student on the list of authors, and, Angier reports, the following conversation took place:

> Did he contribute any data to the paper? Weinberg asked.
> No, he didn't, Cliff [the first author] admitted. But he did contribute ideas to the mix-and-matches.

> Ideas are cheap, said Weinberg. If you didn't use any of his data, I
> don't think it would be appropriate to list him. (Angier 130)

What appears to be an inconsistency on Weinberg's part — excluding
one person on the basis that she had not made an "intellectual
contribution" but another on the grounds that "ideas are cheap" — is
not, however, just a matter of individual capriciousness. Weinberg's
explanations reveal the difficulty of applying the distinction between
"technical assistance" and "intellectual contribution" as a criterion for
determining authorship.

There is, to be sure, a relatively clear-cut line between mental and
manual labor in scientific work — a division of labor in which intellectual
workers design experiments and manual workers carry them out. This
division between mental and manual labor is so engrained in laboratory
life that it produces an aversion toward "benchwork" on the part of
many scientists. As one of Weinberg's graduate students put it, "I
find benchwork incredibly boring. . . . Here you've had all this expensive
education, and you're spending most of your time either looking for
equipment or labeling tubes" (Angier 30). But if mental and manual
labor are clearly marked along class lines (and rewarded accordingly),
the routine nature of benchwork disguises the difficulty of distinguishing
ideas from data and data from material and supplies.

As Latour and Woolgar argue, scientific ideas are perpetually
materializing themselves not only in the form of data but also in the
form of laboratory materials and technical equipment. A piece of
scientific equipment, according to Latour and Woolgar, is itself a form
of reified knowledge, an object that has acquired a kind of facticity by
effacing the intellectual labor that conceived and designed it in the first
place. By the same token, what appears today simply as material or
supplies may in fact be yesterday's data, the results of scientific experiments that have been absorbed into the domain of science and taken
for granted.

These epistemological difficulties, rooted in the technical division
of labor in science, not only create ambiguity in assessing the contributions of individual collaborators, and especially of secondary figures.
They also make the determination of authorship more of an interpretive
act than an application of universalistic criteria. To put it another way,
authorship is negotiated, not discovered. The determination of authorship is indeed subject to certain conventional understandings, but, as
Stokes and Hartley put it, these are "conventions on interpretation"
(106).

Authorship and Social Networks: Collaboration Beyond the Lab

If we look at the determination of authorship on a particular paper, we see what may well appear to be inconsistent and contradictory efforts to deal with the structural and epistemological ambiguities of collaborative work in science. If, however, we look at patterns of authorship *across* a number of papers within a scientific specialty, the picture changes dramatically. The determination of authorship, from this wider perspective, suggests that something beyond formalized prior agreements or local and informal processes of intercession and negotiation are involved in assigning credit. For one thing, the status of the journals in which a particular laboratory or individual scientist publishes must be taken into account. It is important to note that scientific articles are not reviewed "blind," as is generally the case in the humanities. Submitted manuscripts in science include the names of the authors. For this reason, once a paper from a particular laboratory appears in a prestigious journal such as *Science* or *Nature*, others from that lab are likely to be published more easily. There is a kind of cumulative weight assigned by reviewers to the names of scientists and laboratories they recognize — what one of the readers of an early version of this essay calls a "splurge effect." In this sense, the determination of authorship across a number of scientific papers reflects and amplifies the established reputations of leading scientists.

Such determinations of authorship, moreover, are involved not only in enhancing reputations but also in elaborating social networks that extend beyond a particular lab and across a number of papers. As Stokes and Hartley have suggested, citation and co-citation counts have been useful in social studies of science to identify influential papers within a field and to fashion a cognitive map of the intellectual influences within a specialty. Such counts, however, will not necessarily account for social influences or produce reliable information about the social structure of the specialty in question. This is so, Stokes and Hartley argue, confirming the ambiguities of multiple authorship, because "coauthor order is not a dependable guide to the relative contribution of individual coauthors" (107). For a "specialty to have a *social* dimension," Stokes and Hartley write, "it needs more than a certain number of members. The members need to *interact*" (108). Citation counts simply cannot provide information about the interactions that take place within a specialty or serve as a way to distinguish major from minor figures. However, by examining patterns of coauthorship to determine "with whom a scientist is associated as a coauthor, and who not," Stokes and Hartley continue, "the social cohesiveness and differentiation of the specialty as a whole can be determined from its published work" (109–10).

By examining patterns of coauthorship across a number of papers in two specialties — DNA polymerases and the c-*myc* oncogene — Stokes and Hartley reveal coauthorship linkages among scientists that define important and influential social networks within these fields. What emerges from their analysis is the picture of a number of collaborative groups of various sizes — some whose efforts are interconnected and others whose work is isolated from all the other groups. Bibliometric maps of patterns of coauthorship disclose that scientists working within these particular specialties do not, in fact, form a socially cohesive whole. Rather, the social structures of these specialties are internally differentiated in ways that make some scientists more influential than others. Stokes and Hartley identify both "key" figures who coauthor all or most of the papers produced by a group and "bridging" figures whose involvement as coauthors connects groups together in loose collaborative networks. As Stokes and Hartley conclude, the "collaborative groups in which these figures work, and the collaborative connections between groups which bridging figures establish, demarcate socially mediated influence" (122).

The "bridging" function of collaboration may be seen in the case of an important paper from the Weinberg lab that linked DNA mutation to human cancer. Weinberg had acquired *ras* antibodies from Edward Scolnick's lab at the National Cancer Institute and a normal *ras* gene from Esther Chang, who had taken the gene with her when she moved from Scolnick's lab to Douglas Lowy's. In return, Weinberg promised to list Chang in the prestigious position of last author. What resulted, as Cliff Tabin, the first author of the paper, describes it, is not simply a list of authors but the articulation of a complex web of social influence:

> Then I got the second draft of the paper back from Bob [Weinberg], and it had the list of authors. Scott was second. Cori was third. Esther Chang was the last author, just as Weinberg had promised, but that wasn't going to fool anybody out there. Bob played all these political games with NIH. Alex Papageorge was listed because he took some *ras* out of Scolnick's freezer and sent it to us. Scolnick was listed because he was Scolnick. Doug Lowy was listed because...Esther [Chang was] in his lab. (Angier 130)

Authorship, as this small example suggests, is not only achieved by the intellectual merits of a scientist's work. It is also negotiated socially to form social, professional, and financial linkages among laboratories. The tendency toward collaboration that Price and others have recognized as the hallmark of modern science may, in fact, serve largely, as Stokes and Hartley argue, to promote the internal stratification within a specialty and the concentration of influence within a few large and interconnected labs.

In this sense, collaboration in scientific research offers a pointed example of what Merton calls the "Matthew effect." According to Merton, the "Matthew effect" — named after the biblical injunction "For everyone that hath shall be given" — describes the ways in which credit, visibility, and influence in science will tend to accrue to the already-famous. One of the complications of collaboration in contemporary science that teachers and theorists of written communications have largely overlooked is its tendency to consolidate the reputations of leading figures and to reproduce a scientific elite. The actual workings of scientific laboratories do, of course, rely upon the cooperative efforts of many hands and minds. And, as our opening scenario indicates, collaboration among laboratories has become a necessity in many scientific fields. Nonetheless, collaboration, as John Ziman argues, also appears to put "direct power into the hands of the seniors, and opens the way to careerism, personal autocracy, and other evils" (quoted in Merton 553). Formalized prior agreements about authorship, expressions of solidarity among co-workers, and informal processes of intercession and negotiation may in particular instances, as we have suggested, work as a counterbalance to such a monopoly of power and authority. Still, the determination of authorship remains inevitably caught up in structural, political, and epistemological ambiguities that result from the very complexity of the technical and intellectual division of labor in science.

Pedagogical Implications: A Cautionary Note

Research on collaborative writing in professional settings — whether in science, industry, law, government, or business — poses a particular problem for the study and teaching of writing, namely the problematic relationship between research and pedagogy. While the study of writing has conceived of itself for the most part as an applied field, we want to suggest that research on collaborative writing does not necessarily or automatically present writing instructors with any particular consequences, one way or another, that *ought* to inform their pedagogy. As we indicate above, we worry about the tendency among some writing instructors to model classroom practices on "real world" writing as researchers have described it. We view this tendency as unfortunate in part, because it takes as its starting point the current organization of writing "out in the world" and, if enacted literally, would run the risk of reproducing stratified divisions of labor and asymmetrical relations of power and authority. Now, at the same time, we do not want to suggest that writing instructors should ignore the growing body of research on collaborative writing in the workplace and in the professions. Our point is that pedagogy constitutes its own starting point, and its interests may differ in important respects from the interests of researchers. Pedagogy means what it says etymologically: it refers to applied theories that aspire quite literally to instruct the young, not to replicate another social practice, such as the present state of "real world" writing. The goals of writing instruction may diverge in significant ways from the goals of writers in professional settings. While the term collaboration seems to call up "warmly persuasive" images of participation and the empowering of multiple voices in the classroom, collaboration in the workplace and in the professions may in fact be embedded in hierarchical social structures and produce monopolies of expertise and differential access to prestige and credit.

In many respects, we are faced here with a terminological problem because the term collaboration seems to mean different things depending on its use. It is, on the one hand, a descriptive term researchers use to identify how people work together in complex technical and intellectual divisions of labor. On the other hand, writing instructors tend to use the term collaboration normatively to refer to pedagogical techniques to transform the social relationships in the classroom, between teachers and students and among the students themselves. The impetus for this normative use of the term has less to do with the collaborative organization of work in the "real world" than with a critique of traditional methods of teaching and an effort to reform the social dynamics of classroom life. For this reason, it may be useful to distinguish more sharply than we often do between the various uses of the term collaboration, between the way researchers use it and the way teachers use it.

To draw this distinction between the descriptive and normative uses of the term collaboration, moreover, may help to clarify the relationship between research on collaborative writing and pedagogies that employ collaborative writing assignments in the classroom. The point is not to sever the connection between research and pedagogy but to recast it, so that we think of pedagogy not so much as practices *based upon* the latest research findings but instead as practices that, for their own purposes, *draw upon* research.

This distinction may sound slight, but it is, we believe, a telling one. What it suggests, to us at least, is that the rationale for collaborative writing projects should not be limited to imitating "real world" writing situations but should include the study of collaborative writing, as it is organized and enacted in various social settings. Students need not only to practice collaborative writing but also to understand the problematic nature of collaboration in complex technical and intellectual divisions of labor. Rather than justify collaborative writing assignments by reference to current research that demonstrates how frequently coauthorship takes place, we might ask students to do their own research on how collaborative writing is practiced by groups of scientists or engineers at their university or in professional firms outside the academy. What they might learn is how authorship is negotiated and credit allocated. They might learn, that is, how the professions they may eventually enter are organized and how, in at least one important respect, these professions function. This, it seems to us, is a kind of "real world" knowledge worth having.

Our account of the determination of authorship on scientific papers amounts finally to a kind of cautionary tale. It is cautionary in part because of its limited authority. Clearly, we need further studies of collaborative writing to pursue the questions we have tried to raise here in a preliminary way. What we think such research might yield is not a general model of collaboration but, as Lunsford and Ede's work suggests, a wide range of possible collaborative practices adapted to local conditions. But our account is also intended to sound a cautionary note about the present tendency to idealize collaboration and multi-authorship outside the humanities. One undercurrent in professional talk about the study and teaching of writing is the idea that the organization of work in business, government, science, and industry is more collaborative than work in the humanities. The apparent truth of this idea—the very fact that more people are involved in common projects—misses, it seems to us, precisely what the work, whether collaborative or individual, shares: namely, that it is involved in the production not only of knowledge but also of individual careers. To remedy this oversight, and the illusions about the nature of collaborative work it can foster, we suggest that both teachers and researchers pay attention not only to the collaborative production of written communications but also to the social processes that have articulated complex divisions of labor and that allocate credit and prestige differentially.

Works Cited

Angier, Natalie. *Natural Obsessions: The Search for the Oncogene*. Boston: Houghton Mifflin, 1988.

Forman, Janis. "The Discourse Communities and Group Writing Practices of Management Students." *Worlds of Writing: Teaching and Learning in Discourse Communities of Work*. Ed. Carolyn Matalene. New York: Random House, 1989. 247–54.

Halloran, S. Michael. "The Birth of Molecular Biology: An Essay on the Rhetorical Criticism of Scientific Discourse." *Rhetoric Review* 3 (1984): 70–83.

Harris, Joseph. "The Idea of Community in the Teaching of Writing." *College Composition and Communication* 40 (1989): 11–22.

Heffner, Alan G. "Authorship Recognition of Subordinates in Collaborative Research." *Social Studies of Science* 9 (1979): 377–84.

Latour, Bruno, and Steve Woolgar. *Laboratory Life*. Beverly Hills: Sage, 1979.

Lunsford, Andrea, and Lisa Ede. *Singular Texts/Plural Authors: Perspectives on Collaborative Writing*. Carbondale: Southern Illinois UP, 1990.

Meadows, A. J. *Communication in Science*. London: Butterworths, 1974.

Merton, Robert K. *The Sociology of Science*. Ed. Norman W. Storer, Chicago: U. of Chicago P, 1973.

Odell, Lee, and Dixie Goswami, eds. *Writing in Nonacademic Settings*. New York: Guilford, 1985.

Over, Ray. "Collaborative Research and Publication in Psychology." *American Psychologist* 37 (1982): 996−1001.

Piternick, Anne Brearly. "Traditional Interpretations of 'Authorship' and 'Responsibility' in the Description of Technical and Scientific Documents." *Cataloguing and Classification Quarterly* 5 (1985): 17−33.

Price, Derek J. de Solla. *Big Science, Little Science*. New York: Columbia UP, 1963.

Stokes, T. D., and J. A. Hartley. "Coauthorship, Social Structure, and Influence Within Specialties." *Social Studies of Science* 19 (1989): 101−25.

Trimbur, John. "Consensus and Difference in Collaborative Learning." *College English* 51 (1989): 602−16.

Zuckerman, Harriet A. "Patterns of Name Ordering among Authors of Scientific Papers: A Study of Social Symbolism and Its Ambiguity." *American Journal of Sociology* 74 (1968): 276−91.

Zuckerman, Harriet, and Robert K. Merton. "Age, Aging, and Age Structure in Science." Robert K. Merton. *The Sociology of Science*. Ed., Norman W. Storer. Chicago: U. of Chicago P, 1973: 497−559.

3

What Makes a Collaborative Writing Team Successful? A Case Study of Lawyers and Social Workers In a State Agency

Kitty O. Locker

In April 1989, The Ohio Legal Rights Service filed a complaint initiating a class-action suit on behalf of eight thousand people with mental retardation in Ohio. The fifty-five page complaint was a collaborative document; a second group wrote it after another group at the same agency was unsuccessful. An examination of the two groups' processes and products suggest that four constellations of factors interacted to make the second collaborative writing team successful. First, the two groups' processes — both group processes and writing processes — differed markedly. Second, the central author of the first group's drafts never seemed to understand the standards of the agency's discourse community. Third, the first group's failure can be partially explained by the incomplete socialization of three of its members into the agency's organizational culture. Finally, the organizational environment had changed in subtle but important ways by the time the second group began work, removing some of the forces that exacerbated the first group's problems.

Not all collaborative efforts succeed. Of the seven hundred professionals in various disciplines who responded to Andrea Lunsford and Lisa Ede's survey, 42 percent found writing as part of a team or group "not too productive" or "not at all productive" (50). Geoffrey A. Cross has documented the startlingly inefficient process that led eight participants to spend seventy-seven working days on the two-page executive letter for an annual report, only to produce a flawed document that ignored its major audience and contained redundant and poorly explained information (196). Contrasting the process Cross observed with the more numerous accounts of productive collaboration given by Lunsford and Ede allows us to draw inferences about the factors that lead to successful collaborative writing. However, such inferences force us to compare groups in different organizations working on different tasks; we rarely have a chance to study two different on-the-job teams that have attempted the same task with markedly different results. Serendipitously, I have had the chance to study just this situation: two teams in the same organization working on the same task.

In April 1989, The Ohio Legal Rights Service filed a complaint initiating a class-action suit on behalf of eight-thousand people in Ohio with mental retardation or other developmental disabilities. The fifty-five page complaint was a collaborative document; the four-person team produced nine drafts in about eight months. By draft 6, the supervisors described the document as "better than [the supervisors] thought it could ever be." (The team revised the document three more times while the agency's director completed the political groundwork necessary before the complaint could be filed.) Yet this successful project had previously been undertaken by another group at the same agency, a group whose thirteen drafts, according to supervisors, "never got any better."

An examination of the two groups' processes and products suggests that four constellations of factors interacted to make the second collaborative writing team successful. First, the two groups' processes — both group processes and writing processes — differed markedly. Second, the central author of the first group's drafts never seemed to understand the standards of the agency's discourse community. Third, the first group's failure can be partially explained by the incomplete socialization of three of its members into the agency's organizational culture. Finally, the organizational environment had changed in subtle but important ways by the time the second group began work, removing some of the forces that exacerbated the first group's problems.

Access to the Organization and Sources of Data

This qualitative case study was unusually accidental and serendipitous. I gained access to this organization because my husband worked there; I knew many of these people socially. Before I decided to study these groups, I heard about their progress at office parties. Of the four people in the second group, two are friends whom I see socially outside of office functions; a third, whom I would call the team leader, is my husband.

I asked for and received permission from the agency to study the process after the complaint had been filed. My data include the extant drafts (drafts 1, 2, 7, and 8 from the first group and drafts 1−6 of the second), a videotape made by the agency of one staff meeting during the first group's work, and, primarily, retrospective interviews with each of the participants (including those who no longer work for the agency). One interviewee consulted notes to refresh his memory as we talked; the others did not. These interviews, which took place long after the events people were recalling, have the advantages of hindsight but the disadvantages of fallible memories. The third portion of my data consists of my own memories (only rarely substantiated by contemporary notes) of conversations with participants at parties or over the dinner table and my evaluation of these people from our interactions over the years.

The various sources of data and the stories from different participants provide triangulation. However, this account is still a story based on my interpretation of the data available to me. The participants still at the agency have read this article and accept my descriptions of events and of the organization's culture. But other stories from other perspectives might also seem plausible and might offer other truths.

The Setting: The Organization, the Exigency, and the Participants

The Ohio Legal Rights Service is a state agency that advocates on behalf of people labeled mentally ill, mentally retarded, or developmentally disabled. As a "protection and advocacy" agency, it is empowered "to receive and act upon complaints" about "institutions for the mentally retarded and hospitals for the mentally ill," even when these institutions are licensed or operated by the state. Ohio law further specifies that the agency "be completely independent of the department of mental health and the department of mental retardation and developmental disabilities and...independent of the office of the attorney general," and empowers the agency to bring lawsuits when negotiation fails (Ohio Revised Code §5123.60 (A), (E), and (G), respectively). As a result, the agency is unusual: it is a state agency, which sometimes sues other state agencies. The agency receives funds both from the state and from the federal government. Every state has such an agency, but enabling legislation and agency philosophies vary. Some agencies publish newsletters, dispense grants, and serve as watchdog agencies but do little litigation. Some focus on individual cases, whereas others also seek system wide change.

The Ohio Legal Rights Service prides itself on being one of the largest and most active such agencies in the country. The agency is conscious of advocating the "cutting edge" of treatment and policy; it actively works to change laws through lobbying and to challenge existing practices through lawsuits. The agency's 800 number gets scores of calls every day from people in institutions, parents, and providers complaining about the care (or lack of it) that clients are receiving or charging that clients' rights have been violated. Much of the agency's work involves investigating these complaints, attempting to negotiate agreements with providers of care, and bringing lawsuits when negotiation fails.

Members of the agency are convinced that people with mental retardation should live in the least restrictive environment possible. That means that most should live not in big institutions but in "group homes"—homes for four to sixteen people with mental retardation, living together with another adult who provides guidance and re-sources—or in "supported living" situations where a case manager looks in once a day or several times a week. For some time, the agency had wanted to file a class-action suit to challenge Ohio's failure to create more small group homes and supported living services for, the nearly eight thousand people in Ohio who could benefit from such environments.

The need for more "residential" beds comes from at least four sources. First, large institutions often are unable to give clients— especially those with multiple disabilities—as much individual attention as they need. Second, several large facilities in Ohio (and across the nation) have been decertified in the last ten years because they fail to meet federal Medicaid standards. Without Medicaid reimbursements, many of the facilities close, shrinking the number of beds available for people with mental retardation. Third, many people with mental re-tardation are housed in nursing homes that provide only custodial, not developmental, care. Finally, many parents whose adult children with mental retardation live at home are aging. Placements are needed for these adults when their parents are no longer able to be care-givers.

The agency is comprised of lawyers and social service staff; the latter work as ombudsmen or as investigators. Lawyers as a group enjoy more status in our society than do social service workers, but investigators in this agency are lawyers' peers, not their subordinates. This status derives partly from the agency's history and partly from the fact that investigators in this agency know more about mental health and mental retardation than do lawyers who are new to the agency. Most lawyers join the agency straight out of law school, and few of them have taken courses in this specialized area of the law. In contrast, most of the investigators have several years of experience in the field before they join the agency. They know more about the complex government regulations, about treatments and their side effects, and about the "system." Lawyers in the agency file suits and negotiate settlements, just as do lawyers in other organizations. Investigators' duties, in contrast, do not parallel those of social service workers in other organizations. Investigators are not case workers or case managers providing direct services to clients; instead, their work is more systemic, more investigative, and more evaluative.

Eight months before this case began, a social service worker had been named director of the agency—the first nonlawyer to head the agency in its fifteen-year history. She brought in a new legal director, a lawyer who had at one time worked at the agency but who had been doing poverty law for the past four years. They agreed that the agency's legal record was inadequate; even when agency staff agreed that a case was necessary, "nothing ever happened." As a result, "consumer" groups—associations of people with mental retardation and their parents—perceived the agency as ineffective and lacking zeal. Doing more litigation, especially more class-action lawsuits, was therefore a priority. The director had been interested in bringing a suit on residential housing for people with mental retardation for "years," even before she was named director in November 1986. Consumer groups across the state were clamoring for more and better placements; the agency was receiving calls from clients desperate for housing that did not exist. So the supervisors decided to "put a group together" to work on the issue.

In summer 1987, the agency assigned a group consisting of two 2-person teams, each comprised of a lawyer and an investigator, to pursue suits in state and federal court, respectively. Although the group (group 1) had two subgroups and was expected to produce two documents, the agency saw it as a single group working toward a common purpose. The two lawyers left before any document had been approved, so in August 1988 the agency created a second group (group 2), consisting of another two lawyers and the two investigators from the first team. This group was assigned to write a complaint for federal court. Their document was approved; the complaint was filed in April 1989. At this writing, the class has been certified and discovery has begun. (Discovery is the legal process of assembling support for a case through written questions and sworn depositions.) Defendants' motions to dismiss the case are pending.

Participants in Group 1

The case was an important one for the agency, and supervisors chose people who they hoped would be effective (see Figure 3.1). Jim, the attorney assigned to focus on the state suit, was seen as a "rising star" and a "favorite son" even though he had worked at the agency only

Figure 3.1
Group 1 (Summer 1987–June 1988)

Jim	Brian	(State Suit)
Attorney	Investigator	
Lisa	Dody	(Federal Suit)
Attorney	Investigator	

about two months. (Pseudonyms are used for all agency personnel except Bob, my husband.) He had previously worked as an aide to a state senator for two and a half years and then in another state agency before completing law school; in both jobs he had written extensively. After law school, Jim returned to the state Senate for four months and joined the agency in April 1987. Brian, an investigator, was a brand-new employee; he had six years' experience working in and supervising group homes for people with mental retardation. His supervisor hoped that he could "bring [Jim] along" by providing information about the system. Lisa, the attorney assigned to the federal suit, had worked for the agency for a year and a half. During that time, she had already worked on several cases with Dody, who had also been at the agency a year and a half. Before Dody came to the agency, she had worked as a caseworker and as a placement officer in a large institution under court order to close. In her previous positions, Dody says, she had become known for her writing; at this agency she had emerged as an expert on the Medicaid regulations that govern reimbursements to institutions. Supervisors felt that Lisa and Dody worked well together and that they would continue to work together "whether we assigned them to a case or not." Lisa left the agency in March 1988 to go to a protection and advocacy agency in another state; Jim left in June 1988 to join another state agency.

Participants in Group 2

In August 1988, two other attorneys, Bob and Nancy, were assigned to join Brian and Dody to work on a federal suit (see Figure 3.2). When Bob was assigned to this case, he had worked at the agency for sixteen months but had just recently transferred from a unit that handled individual cases to the systemic unit that controlled this class-action suit. Nancy had clerked at the agency while she was in law school, then worked as a lawyer at the Public Defender's office, and had joined the agency the previous January. Brian and Dody were retained to provide continuity with their experience on the topic. Supervisors saw Bob as

Figure 3.2
Group 2 (August 1988–April 1989)

Bob   Brian
Attorney   Investigator

(Federal Suit)

Nancy   Dody
Attorney   Investigator

"a good writer" and "a good worker bee" who would see that a product was produced; they saw Nancy as "a younger, less experienced lawyer who could bring some energy" to the project and do some of the legwork. Supervisors saw all four as being among "the brighter people in the office,...people that we knew would take the project and run with it." They were also, as supervisors knew, already friends.

Supervisors

Four supervisors read and responded to the drafts (see Figure 3.3): the agency director, Valerie; the advocacy director, Cheryl, who supervised the investigators and reported to Valerie; the attorney supervising the systems unit, Karen, who reported to Rick; and Rick, the legal director, who reported to Valerie. In spite of their different levels in the formal organizational structure, the four supervisors functioned as a single group meeting with the writers to give feedback; the document did not "cycle" separately to each supervisory level.

Valerie had come to the agency about a year after its inception, resigning a position as director of another state-level office to do so. She had twice been acting director and was named director when an amendment of a state law permitted nonlawyers to head the agency. Both Cheryl and Karen had worked at the agency for several years. Rick had returned to the agency in February 1987 as its legal director, responsible for helping the lawyers on staff to file more cases and litigate more effectively and for overseeing the development of the many new lawyers the agency had hired.

A Tale of Two Groups

Group 1 was created in summer 1987. In the next year, those writers produced thirteen "unacceptable" drafts of a state complaint and several handwritten pages of a federal complaint in longhand. In August 1988,

Figure 3.3
Supervisors

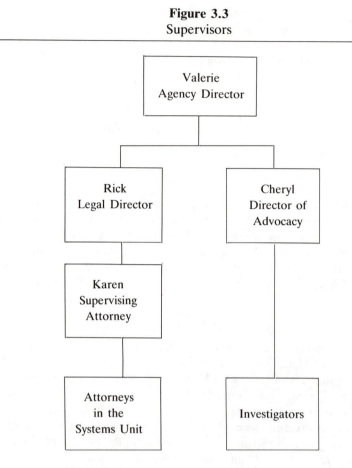

group 2 was assigned to write a complaint for federal court. Even their early drafts were viewed positively; their ninth draft was filed in April 1989.

Group 1: Summer 1987–June 1988

On October 2, 1987, thirteen people met to discuss the problem of residential housing for Ohioans with mental retardation so that "people who had been around the system a long time" could share their knowledge with Jim, who had worked for the agency for only a little more than five months. Jim asked some general questions and took notes. Valerie, Rick, Cheryl, and Dody contributed to the discussion, as did three people who were not assigned to the case. Lisa missed the first two-thirds of the meeting but contributed to the last third; Brian was not present.

Over the next several months, Lisa and Dody did considerable research; by March 1988 when Lisa left the agency, they had produced several pages of a longhand draft, which however, was never typed or distributed to supervisors. Dody's memory is that the agency saw the state suit as having a better chance and did not push for completion of the federal suit; Cheryl speculates that Lisa didn't get her own work done "because she was so busy working with [Jim]"; Rick believes that work on the federal suit was put "on hold" because the agency wanted to file the suits concurrently.

Jim circulated a first draft of a state suit on November 2, 1987, and a second draft on January 7. Thereafter drafts appeared much more quickly; draft 7 is dated April 13, 1988. Jim produced a total of thirteen drafts before leaving the agency in June 1988. According to the legal director, all of Jim's drafts were "totally inadequate"; "we could never get him to do a complaint that was going to be legally sufficient to survive a motion to dismiss." However, Rick remembers, "Part of the frustration was [that Jim would] sit in a meeting and he'd articulate exactly, orally, what it was that we wanted." In attempts to help him, supervisors "sat him down with the dictaphone, [and] said 'Just say that.'" Lisa helped him reorganize one draft, cutting up the parts and moving them around on the floor to show how the facts fit into the argument. Dody gave him suggestions. However, Jim's drafts never improved.

Group 2: August 1988–April 1989

When the second group was assigned, Rick gave Bob the last draft that Jim had submitted. Bob reports that Rick pulled the last page or two out of the stapled document, saying, "This is the only thing you'll be able to use," and threw the rest of it in a wastebasket. With this clear message, group 2 never looked at the surviving pages of Jim's last draft. The writers and supervisors met every two weeks in September and October 1988, brainstorming their strategy for the case, the causes of action, and the organization of the document. Dody dug out Lisa's notes. The group circulated an outline October 24, 1988, and presented its first draft on November 4. Supervisors felt that the draft "was certainly acceptable and probably better than that. It was very good. For a first draft." Supervisors' comments focused on "small technical pieces" and style, rather than on overall strategy. The next draft appeared three weeks later, on November 29. The longest period between drafts was seven weeks, when group members were on the road interviewing clients who might become named plaintiffs in the suit. Draft 4 (February 15) was good enough that discussion at the meeting with supervisors focused on preparing a press release and an article in the agency's newsletter to be ready when the case was filed. Draft 6 in early March was judged ready to file.

Although group 2 had started slowly in the supervisors' eyes, it gained momentum; a fileable draft was ready earlier than the director had expected. Before the suit could be filed, she needed to finish laying the political groundwork for the case with the defendants, consumer groups, legislators, and the agency's oversight commission. While she was talking with all these groups, the writers further revised the complaint, producing three more drafts. Draft 9 was filed in April 1989.

Group 2's first draft was judged to be far better than Jim's thirteenth draft. In ten months group 1 produced thirteen typed "unacceptable" drafts and several pages of a handwritten draft, which had not been distributed; in eight months group 2 went from brainstorming ideas to a complaint, which was filed in federal court. What enabled one group to succeed while the other had failed?

Differences in Group Processes and in Writing Processes

Seven differences in the two groups' processes partially explain the differences in their products. In terms of group process, the successful group distributed power in an egalitarian way, worked to soothe hurt feelings, and was careful to involve all group members. In terms of writing process, the successful group understood the task as a response to a rhetorical situation, planned revisions as a group, saw supervisors' comments as legitimate, and had a positive attitude toward revision.

Power and Leadership

In group 1, Jim assumed power and would not share it. Jim believed that attorneys should have "autonomy." He wanted to receive help only when he asked for it. His comments to me suggest that he expected to ask for only clerical assistance — in spite of the fact that Lisa, Karen, and Rick had all been at the agency longer than he: "And you need a co-counsel. Sometimes. And the co-counsel literally finds that paper that you're groping for and hands it to you and that's all they do." Jim also devalued the investigators, referring to them in his interview as "support staff," the same term he used in the interview to describe the typists at his current agency. Although Jim and Brian were friends, Jim basically ignored Brian. Brian never confronted Jim; he was new in the agency and "wasn't sure what [he] was supposed to do anyhow."

Jim's perception is that his ability to listen is one of the strengths of his "management style." But the other members assigned to the case felt shut out. Brian says, "I didn't feel very much a part of the group whatsoever." Dody feels that Jim "didn't kinda let you in on the ground floor." She remembers making many suggestions, which Jim almost never used. All the other group members and supervisors I interviewed claimed that Jim was sexist. However, he seems to have rejected Rick's criticisms just as much as Karen's or Dody's; an alternate explanation is that Jim was unable to accept criticism.

Although the supervisors saw Jim's shutting out the investigators as one cause of the group's failure, Bob perceived that the legal director and the supervising attorney wanted him to "take charge" of group 2. Bob consciously resisted this mandate, though his initial efforts were incomplete. Dody remembers an initial division of labor by job titles: "This is attorney stuff, this is investigator stuff." She told Bob and Nancy that she thought the investigators should be part of all the discussions. They were "very open" to her comments, and the process changed.

Brian believes that leadership in group 2 was flexible: "Throughout this whole process, there has usually been someone who's taken a lead. And it's never been the same person." Throughout the process of writing the complaint and for many months afterwards, Bob identified Dody as the leader of the group, and she seems to have contributed the most ideas to the final product. Bob "managed" the group's process, running group meetings, assigning work, and checking to see that it was done. He was egalitarian in having each member of the group draft part of the project and in encouraging other people's ideas. Some of Bob's actions seem deliberately designed to counter Jim's mistakes. Dody had argued that the complaint should include a section on "the crisis," which Jim was never willing to include. Bob not only included that topic in group 2's outline but asked Dody to write the section.

Dealing with Feelings

Jim was increasingly angry and unhappy as his drafts met with more and more criticism. Nancy—who was not assigned to the project until after Jim had resigned—remembers that he "was in my office constantly.... Complaining. He was miserable." These conversations may have been an unconscious effort to deal with his own hurt and anger, emotions that still surface when he recalls the case. He made no apparent effort to deal with anyone else's feelings; indeed, he seemed oblivious to the anger that Dody and Lisa felt toward him.

Group 2 rarely dealt with feelings about criticism and conflict in full-group meetings. Instead, members dealt with them in dyads after the meetings or on the next day: "How did you feel about that? Are you doing OK?" Members did not talk about feelings simply out of a theoretical desire to improve group dynamics but because they genuinely cared about each other. Members saw the group as a safe place and the group as a single unit standing together against the supervisors. Nancy reports, "We were able to bounce ideas off of each other without any fear of criticism.... It wasn't a personal attack.... It was all friendly,... It was meant to protect you from making a mistake as far as the supervisors were concerned." Much of the research on gender suggests that women are more likely to be concerned with maintaining relationships than are men, but both Nancy and Bob describe their efforts to maintain the relationships in group 2; Brian calls them "listeners" who "are concerned about other people's thoughts and feelings." The four liked each other at the beginning of the project and became close friends as the team progressed. Brian believes that the team "worked as well together as any four people could.... The process brought us closer together as professionals and as people."

The supervisors found the group's concern with process excessive: "They just processed and processed and processed to death." But while the talk may have slowed the group's progress, it made the group more cohesive.

Involvement of Group Members

Although he spent a lot of time talking to other people in the agency, Jim planned, wrote, and revised in isolation. Brian, Dody, and Lisa joined him in the meetings to discuss the drafts with supervisors, but everyone saw the draft as his product, not the group's. Group 2, in contrast, worked carefully to involve all members of the group. Dody had wanted to work in the first group and was eager to be a full-fledged team member. Both Brian and Nancy, however, disliked writing and would have been happy not to share in the drafting. Bob thought it was important that everyone write something. He made assignments in a low-key style ("Nancy, would you be willing to try writing that section?"). In their discussions of drafts, team members tried to be very supportive and to give specific suggestions.

Nancy presented an additional challenge. On December 24, the baby she and her husband had been trying to adopt from India finally arrived. She was required by the adoption agency to take three months' maternity leave, so she wasn't in the office during the crucial period when drafts 3−6 were completed. Bob mailed her the drafts, and group members phoned her to tell her how things were going; the team consciously tried to keep her as part of the group. When she returned she was able to step back in because she knew what had been happening.

Understanding the Rhetorical Situation

Jim tried to define the task in purely legal terms: establishing the law, the legal precedents, and the ways they had been violated. His cover memos on drafts 1 and 2 ask staff members to identify additional statutes he may not have included. Jim's model parallels the kind of writing that students often do in law school; it fits neatly with the bills that he had drafted while working for the legislature. Rick judges Jim's drafts as inadequate even for the narrow purpose of proving that statutes had been violated. However, Rick believes successful public interest law requires a much broader understanding of purpose and a consideration of audience. "If you just stayed within the confines of the existing law, you were going to lose. If you could manipulate the procedure or the substantive law in any way at all, the facts were so compelling, that you probably could win. But you needed a hook.... We talk a lot about 'hooks' here." To everyone but Jim, the best "hook" was obvious: "the current crisis" in residential housing, the need for eight thousand people with mental retardation to be placed in small group homes, homes that did not exist, and that the state was doing nothing to create.

A good class action complaint also serves nonlegal purposes. Valerie "knew that this was a document that EVERYBODY in the world would have their hands on." Workers and consumers in mental retardation and legislators would read the document. A good document demonstrated the agency's zeal and laid the groundwork for future legislative action if it became necessary.

Even in its first draft, group 2's complaint was designed to fulfill multiple purposes. The complaint establishes a legal case, but it also informs. As Dody explains, a class-action complaint must "educate a judge." The complaint does not assume that the judge will know that experts in the field favor helping people with mental retardation to live as normally as possible; instead, it explains the current philosophy. By draft 5, footnotes define technical and regulatory terms: "moderate" and "severe retardation," "habilitation plan," "Intermediate Care Facility," to name only a few. And—important for the case's political power as well as its legal success—the complaint seeks to move the reader. Seven and one-half of the fifty-five pages of the final document— just over fourteen percent—describe the history of the problem and the current crisis. This section uses emotional as well as logical appeals, listing the various subgroups represented within the class and showing how members of each group are prevented from reaching their full potential in large institutions that merely warehouse people.

Collaboration on Revisions

In both groups, team members and supervisors brainstormed strategy; in both groups, drafting and revision were done by individuals. However, members of group 2 discussed the necessary revisions in detail as a group before individuals made them. Jim, in contrast, rarely seems to have talked with other people about how he might implement the changes supervisors asked for.

I have been told of only one instance when Jim discussed the necessary revisions with someone else. Jim's first draft was criticized as being illogical: there was no "sense" to the order of paragraphs; the facts were not marshaled to support the causes of action. Lisa helped Jim reorganize the draft. Karen describes the scene: "[Lisa was] in her office with [Jim] and they had all these pieces of paper on the floor... cutting up the complaint, and putting the facts under each cause of action to see where they fit.... OK, this paragraph doesn't have a cause of action. Why do we need it? OK, throw that out. OK, this paragraph [is] related to this cause of action; therefore these paragraphs should be together."

Although group 2's early drafts were "on the right track," supervisors still had many suggestions for improving them. After hearing the supervisors' comments and critiques, group 2 met alone to go over all comments, figuring out how to make the necessary changes for the next draft. These meetings lasted several hours or even more than a day. If a passage had been termed "unclear" or "wordy," if the document "needed a section on x" or needed to be broken up, the whole group talked about how to achieve the change (even though one writer would later actually implement it). This discussion helped group members understand the reasons behind comments and gave them concrete strategies for making the necessary changes. After each member revised his or her sections, Bob checked the new version against the previous draft to make sure that the group had responded to all of the supervisors' comments. Group 2 revised so effectively that some of the supervisors decided they did not need to read all the later drafts.

Attitude Toward Supervisors' Comments

Jim saw supervisors' comments as arbitrary, inconsistent, and motivated by their desire for "control" rather than by objective problems in the draft. Most of the participants think that Jim simply did not understand the criticisms he received. In his interview with me, Jim described "cut and paste" changes as trivia, a sign that the supervisors could not find anything substantive to say about his draft. Lisa's attempt to show him how reorganizing a document could improve its logic had not left a lasting impression.

In a few cases, group 2 also rejected a supervisor's comment. Since they came to these decisions through conversation, they could articulate their rationales for deciding not to make the revision called for. But such cases were the exception. Often the team not only agreed with the comment but had anticipated it: "Yes, we knew that was a problem and we're going to do that; we just didn't have time to do that for this draft." The successful team had internalized the supervisors' standards.

Attitude Toward Revision

Jim clearly resented having to revise. He saw the cycling process as failure, as evidence of the supervisors' unfairness toward and bias against him, as an example of bureaucratic madness. At the beginning he had paid at least lip service to the likelihood of revision. His first draft was accompanied by a cover memo whose first and last sentences read (in full caps) "ATTACHED IS THE FIRST OF MANY DRAFTS OF THE RESIDENTIAL SUIT" and "SPEAK UP!!!" However, he uses the heading "Remaining Issues" after the first sentence, suggesting that he really expected comments only on three points the draft does not fully address. Jim's previous employers had put a premium on handling many assignments quickly. He had "never had time to do a lot of redrafting," and he did not see extensive drafting as valuable: "If an attorney can't get something right on the second or third draft, he ought to be removed. IF that's what the real issue is!"

Brian recalls that Jim "complained that he wasn't getting much direction as to what they wanted." Jim's memory is that "maybe on one of those drafts there might be one or two cryptic comments scribbled." However, I have seen a copy of draft 7, which Karen, Jim's supervisor, annotated extensively. Some words and sentences are crossed out; others are added. Marginal notes on almost every page call for stylistic changes, for reorganization ("Put this later"), for tightening ("Redundant"), and for more elaboration ("How has the Dept. failed to act?" "What is an IHP? Why important? *Relate* to residential beds." "Expand — 1. How many do they operate? 2. All are full. 3. By law can't exceed capacity. 4. Waiting lists.").

Draft 7, Brian recalls, "was called more or less a piece of trash. Not even close to what we're looking for." However, by this time Jim had stopped trying to revise. Draft 8 makes a very few stylistic changes (minuscule in relation to the number of stylistic suggestions in the margins of draft 7) and adds twenty-eight paragraphs describing named plaintiffs, a section that has no text in draft 7. The rest of draft 8 is identical to the maligned draft 7. Supervisors were accurate in their complaint that feedback "wasn't being reflected in the next draft," though they may not have realized just how little change occurred. Jim says, "They weren't even smart enough to catch that. . . . I played their game, and I'd say, 'Oh, OK.' And I'd make little letters and paragraphs and move some lines. And then I'd disappear for a week. . . . And do a twenty-minute cut-and-paste and [come back] and say, 'Here it is.' Because I knew that wouldn't be good enough." Jim stopped trying to make substantive revisions because he was convinced that supervisors would criticize anything he did. But because he did so little, their criticisms became even harsher.

No one in group 2 made any negative comments to me about the revision process as a whole. Instead, they saw the task as a difficult one that would take a lot of work, a lot of trial and error. They knew nobody in the country had done a suit exactly like this one before. They had seen Jim's multiple drafts; they wanted to succeed where he had failed, but they did not expect success to come easily. Perhaps most striking, revisions became a way to improve a product in which their egos were invested: they did the last three drafts voluntarily, not because of pressure from superiors.

Differences in Assimilation into the Discourse Community

In the past ten years, it has become a commonplace in composition circles that no document can be judged in a vacuum; instead, documents succeed or fail in terms of the standards of the discourse community for which they are written. As James E. Porter explains, "A 'discourse community' is a group of individuals bound by a common interest who communicate through approved channels and whose discourse is regulated. . .[by] rules governing appropriateness. . . .A discourse community shares assumptions about what objects are appropriate for examination and discussion, what operating functions are performed on those objects, what constitutes 'evidence' and 'validity', and what formal conventions are followed" (38−39). A large part of Jim's inability to produce an acceptable draft may be attributed to his failure to understand the purposes and the kinds of evidence demanded by this agency's discourse community.

George Gopen (who holds a law degree as well as a Ph.D. in English and who is a consultant about legal writing as well as the director of Duke University's writing programs) argues that legal writing is difficult, in part, because lawyers must focus not on "interesting, human specifics...[but] instead on the relatively nonhuman (some would say inhuman) legal concepts" (152). This "purely legal" approach is privileged in the writing required of students in law schools; to judge from textbooks about legal writing and published accounts of the writing of lawyers, it is common in the writing of practicing attorneys. But it was not the kind of argument valued by this agency. The agency wanted a "compelling" document. Rick believes that judges are basically conservative; if public interest lawyers are to prevail, they "have to be better" than their opponents, using attention-getting "hooks" as well as sound legal arguments. Valerie, as we have seen, notes that documents enhance or weaken the organization's image in the eyes of its various publics. In this agency's discourse community, documents in important suits always have political and public relations as well as legal purposes.

According to Rick, "Our writing values, the value we put on writing here was something that [Jim] never shared." Jim may have carried the Perry Mason model of a trial attorney winning a case by brilliant oral arguments. However, Rick notes, "Civil litigation is not trial work now· it ïs writing." In response to rule changes in the 1960s and to crowded dockets, much legal work is done with written documents rather than with oral hearings. Good writing helps to establish the case, to withstand (written) motions to dismiss, to facilitate "discovery" of (written) facts that can substantiate the allegations of the complaint, and, perhaps, to persuade the other side to settle out of court. If the case should come to trial, the complaint or trial brief must raise all the issues that may be germane if the agency decides to appeal an adverse ruling. Jim, in contrast, saw the complaint as a formality. "You could amend the filing at any time.... Even if it's malpracticeable going in, you can probably fix that."

Further, Jim either did not understand or did not accept the organization's standards for quality. He had been praised for his writing in college and in his work for the legislature and another state agency. When supervisors at the agency discussed here criticized his writing, it never occurred to him that this community might legitimately have different standards for good writing than had the communities of which he had previously been a part. Instead, he assumed that his supervisors were acting out of personal bias.

Differences in Understanding the Organization's Culture

The discourse community's "rules governing appropriateness" and "shared assumptions" suggest that it is closely related to the concept of organizational culture popularized by organizational theorists Terrence Deal and Allan Kennedy. Organizational theorist Edgar H. Schein defines organizational culture as "a pattern of basic assumptions — invented, discovered, or developed by a given group as it learns to cope with its problems of external adaptation and internal integration — that has worked well enough to be considered valid and, therefore, to be taught to new members as the correct way to perceive, think, and feel in relation to those problems" (9). An organization's culture is revealed verbally in an organization's myths, stories, and heroes and nonverbally in the allocation of space, money, and power.

Three of the four members of group 1 were inadequately socialized into the organization's culture. They encountered difficulties with the organization's values in three areas: the value the organization accords collaboration, the roles and relative status of lawyers and investigators, and the importance of commitment to the organization's mission. Jim flouted the agency's norms in all three areas; Brian at the time of the first group's work inadequately understood the first two; and Lisa had problems with at least the first.

The Privileging of Collaboration

This agency privileges collaborative learning and collaborative writing. New employees are matched up with more experienced colleagues to learn what they need to know by doing it. Groups are viewed as the appropriate vehicle to deal with any important case. Indeed, the assigning of a case to an individual, I would argue, is evidence that the case is seen as routine or of minor importance. The decision that a case is ready to be filed is based on consensus. One member of group 2 perceived that Rick's and Cheryl's opinions carried the day and that it would have been more efficient to meet just with them rather than with all four supervisors. But Rick endorses the model of shared decision making. An "acceptable product," he says, is one "that the group finds acceptable. Not just me. . . . Not just [Valerie]. That the group finds acceptable."

Jim, Brian, and Lisa were all uncomfortable with collaboration in different ways. Jim rejected both supervisors and peers as possible collaborators. He argues that a supervisor should require changes in a draft only if it is "malpracticeable." In a college honors tutorial program and in his previous jobs, Jim had enjoyed a high degree of autonomy and had been praised for his independent work. Nothing in his experience before coming to this agency seems to have prepared him to collaborate or to have suggested to him that it could be profitable. Even when he discusses rugby, he describes success as an individual function — the ability to run — rather than a team effort. Jim functions independently in his current position and is highly successful. Brian's willingness to remain in the background was overcome in the second group, whose members deliberately involved him and created a supportive, risk-free atmosphere for him to stretch his abilities and gain confidence in his skills. Lisa enjoyed working with Dody but resented helping Jim: "I was put off by the fact that it was not my job to supervise him." In the large videotaped meeting to discuss the issue of residential housing, many people who were not formally assigned to the group offered suggestions; Lisa, perhaps because she entered thirty-six minutes after the meeting began, said little. Lisa sat in the doorway, outside the room, even though there was an empty chair near the door, which she could have taken without crossing in front of anyone. Her distance in that meeting and in this case may have been symptomatic of a larger distancing from the agency. She recalls her last year in the agency as sufficiently uncomfortable that she was "out of the office as much as humanly possible."

The Roles and Relative Status of Lawyers and Investigators

Lawyers in this agency do not enjoy automatic respect. In the words of the agency's advocacy director, lawyers straight out of law school don't yet know "how to handle an individual case, let alone how to handle a class action." To succeed in this agency, however, lawyers must not only master the pragmatic skills of filing and managing cases (skills rarely stressed in law school) and the body of law relating to mental retardation, developmental disabilities, and mental health, but they must be able to enter the intellectual and political conversations dealing with treatment and policy issues. Investigators, in contrast, often are part of these conversations even before they join the agency. As a result, investigators rarely valorize lawyers. According to the director of the agency, they are more likely to say, "Oh, another crop of lawyers for us to train." The advocacy director labels new lawyers in the agency "technicians" and says the social service staff "bring in the program policy piece." She wants investigators to be as knowledgeable about the facts and issues as possible "so that the attorney becomes dependent on them." Lawyers describe the relationship differently. While the legal director notes that being a lawyer in this agency "involves a great deal more sharing and dependency on other people than they would find in other places," he also sees lawyers as responsible for each case. A supervisory lawyer describes team members as "peers" but implies that it is the lawyer's responsibility to "involve" the investigators, "bring them in," and "keep them informed."

One of Valerie's concerns early in her tenure as director was healing dissension between lawyers and social service staff by explicit exhortation, by moving people's offices to avoid disciplinary ghettos, and by having more office parties. As we have seen, many of the interviews revealed disciplinary loyalties, with both legal and social service supervisors privileging their own subordinates. But though one may infer loyalties from the language and metaphors speakers use and from their responses to specific questions, all supervisors explicitly endorse the organizational myth that these two groups of professionals are equals: "that is, just stressed, stressed, stressed."

As we have seen, Jim did not accept the notion of equality. He says that the agency's problem is that the "social service staff swung the ax in that place.... They were the tail wagging the dog." Unsure of his role and anxious about his writing abilities, Brian was unwilling to challenge Jim. It is possible that no attempt could have succeeded. Dody was certainly a strong personality who knew a great deal about the intricacies of state programs for people with mental retardation and who had some experience in teams working on class-action suits, but Jim rarely followed her advice and never mentioned her during his interview. He does not seem to have perceived her as having anything worthwhile to offer.

The Expectation of Commitment

This organization has a very strong ethos of advocating on behalf of its clients and representing their wishes, not what others paternally deem best for them. Within the agency, in the words of the director, "You have got to be perceived as tough and zealous and competent and if you [are] not, Lord help you." Employees are asked to be creative risk takers. They must find ways to communicate with clients who may have difficulty understanding concepts or talking; they must develop strategies to work within a regulatory and legal system that is often less enlightened than professionals in the field would wish.

The stories that supervisors tell reveal that the agency's heroes are employees who are very committed to their clients and who work very hard because they want to. Valerie says, "You go to somebody and you say, 'What do you think we could do about this?' And they say, 'I do not know but I will think about it.' Three days later they say...' Well I have been up three nights in a row but I figured it out.'...and they do that because they wanted to do it." Karen says, "Here people sort of take pride in...their advocacy for clients, their zealousness, and the fact that we're not just regular state employees. That whatever the job takes, you know, people...have contests about how much time they put in." When I pointed out to her that some employees had been promoted who did not work excessive overtime, she modified her position slightly; "It's not just the hours, it's...caring about the people you work with, and caring about the clients and the results. And being result-oriented. And being responsible and product-driven."

Jim failed to produce an acceptable product and failed to demonstrate the visible commitment that the agency values. Lisa recalls, "He seemed to have lots of free time. I had the dart board in my office, and he spent hours on end throwing darts at the dart board." Karen perceived that "he was just going to put in the time with a state agency so he could retire."

Differences in the Organizational Environment

Even though the two groups worked at the same agency, they did not work in the same organizational environment. The first group's difficulties were exacerbated by sources of change and conflicts that were resolved by the time group 2 began work: almost everyone in the agency was negotiating new roles or reporting relationships; the attorneys were being asked to "work to a different standard"; and conflicts arose between Jim and his supervisors on topics unrelated to this collaborative project.

An enormous amount of change occurred during Valerie's first year as director. Although she had already served as acting director, she now had to deal with a new commission created to oversee the agency. She made several changes in the organizational structure of the agency, bringing in a new legal director and creating several new administrative and supervisory positions. The agency assumed responsibility for two new programs and hired fourteen new people. This dramatic increase in size led the agency to create more structure and more rules. Cheryl recalls saying at the time, "It's just crazy. I mean, everybody's trying to figure out their job all at once....I mean EVERYBODY was, from the director on down to the individual staff member. So there was a lot of...growth tension."

Continuing attorneys like Lisa had another challenge. Rick told the lawyers "they were going to have to learn how to litigate." Some of the attorneys disliked the prospect of more trial work; none appreciated the often explicit message that their knowledge was inadequate and their work deficient. Few of the attorneys had been at the agency long enough to have known Rick as a staff attorney four years earlier. He therefore was perceived as an outsider. The attorneys didn't know him, trust him, or see him as their advocate. Valerie recalls, "There was some real resentment. I think people thought we were mean."

Finally, the supervisors were in continuing conflict with Jim about other aspects of his job performance. Jim appears to have spent a lot of time talking to other disaffected employees; these conversations probably strengthened his conviction that the supervisors were unreasonable. He discounted their comments on his drafts in part because he saw the criticism as one more piece of a harassment campaign fueled by their desire for "control."

By the time group 2 was formed, a majority of the agency's employees had been in the same position and the same reporting relationship for at least a year; they were more comfortable with their roles. The people who had been unhappy with the organizational changes had left voluntarily for other positions. Bob and Nancy had been hired under the new regime, so they had been socialized to Rick's requirements for lawyers. And during the period of this case, none of the group members had serious conflicts with supervisors about other aspects of their performance. Group 2's task was challenging but, in retrospect, not as difficult as the one that group 1 had faced.

Relation of This Case Study to Previous Research

My findings duplicate other researchers' conclusions about group processes, the importance of internal audiences, and assimilation into discourse communities in the workplace. My findings challenge or extend earlier statements about the nature of legal writing, the nature of collaborative processes in the workplace, and the methods and contexts we should use in studying collaborative writing in the workplace.

Several researchers have discussed the importance of group dynamics in the success of student collaborative groups (Forman and Katsky; Goldstein and Malone), and my study demonstrates that this factor is also crucial to the success of collaborative teams in the workplace. Furthermore, the members of group 2 met all the characteristics of the "emerging profile of effective collaborative writers" suggested by Lunsford and Ede: "They are flexible; respectful of others; attentive and analytical listeners; able to speak and write clearly and articulately; dependable and able to meet deadlines; able to designate and share responsibility, to lead and to follow; open to criticism but confident in their own abilities; ready to engage in creative conflict" (66).

Carolyn Miller and James Porter (43) have suggested that audiences outside the organization may be less important than audiences inside the organization. The supervisors in this case were gatekeepers rather than decision makers; they could determine whether a document left the agency but not whether it was ultimately persuasive. In the taxonomy developed by J. C. Mathes and Dwight Stevenson, they were "immediate" rather than primary or secondary audiences (21). Nevertheless, they were the audience that writers had to please.

The conflicts that both Jim and Lisa experienced with the organization remind us that assimilation into a discourse community involves conforming to or at least seeming to accept its values, not merely intellectually mastering its code; this is a point Stephen Doheny-Farina makes in his account of the student intern who felt that she was asked to present information unfairly in a report for her organization.

This case study suggests that "legal writing" is a less monolithic genre than previous writers have implied. Law professor and rhetorician Theresa Phelps notes that "Different legal documents have dramatically different audiences" (366), but her taxonomy — presumably representing the documents written in most law firms — does not mention the possibility that a single document might have multiple audiences or multiple purposes. She refers to "*the* legal discourse community" (364; emphasis added), yet as this case suggests, the kind of writing that wins praise for a lawyer in one agency can be condemned in another.

The successful team in this case collaborated more thoroughly than have most of the workplace groups described to date. At the beginning, the entire group of team members and supervisors met several times to plan the document; the team of lawyers and social service staff assigned portions of the document to various team members, who then drafted as individuals. The four supervisors read the draft individually but discussed their comments with the team in one large meeting. The team then met at length to go through the draft and plan revisions. The individual who had drafted the section then made the revisions. (While Nancy was on maternity leave, Bob revised her sections.) When the team had time, it reviewed the document as a group, sometimes revising it further before presenting a new draft to the supervisors. This process was repeated. Finally, one person edited the draft for grammar and stylistic consistency. This group's process does not match exactly any of the patterns for collaborative writing identified in the surveys conducted by Barbara Couture and Jone Rymer, by Allen et al., or by Lunsford and Ede. The fact that this pattern has not been identified in previous research suggests both that the pattern may be an uncommon one and that surveys alone may not identify all the processes and organizational structures collaborative groups may use.

Finally, and perhaps most importantly, my study suggests that research on collaborative writing in the workplace cannot focus simply upon the group's activities but must consider the larger organizational context as well. Members of a collaborative team in the workplace usually know or know of each other before the project begins; they relate to supervisors as individual employees as well as in their role as team members. People are not neat compartments; their collaborative efforts will be enhanced or complicated by the images they have of each other and by their experiences with supervisors on other issues. Prejudices that predate a group's formation or conflicts on unrelated topics may reduce members' willingness to work together; preexisting friendships or unrelated successes may create a halo effect that makes it easier for group members to cooperate. The stresses caused by organizational changes and conflicts may do as much to explain the failure of some collaborative writing groups as the internal processes of the groups themselves.

Implications for Further Research

Failed collaboration carries monetary and psychic costs, both to the individual involved and to the organization. Even employees who succeed in other, individual endeavors may carry a heavy load of rage years after the experience of failure. Even organizations whose income is not reduced by failed collaboration experience "opportunity costs," for the time put into failed collaboration could have been spent in other, more productive ways.

In this case study, the organization, the participants, the task, and the time frame are all atypical. The agency has only one counterpart in each state; those agencies sometimes have different missions and different relationships among personnel. Few groups collaborate as completely as the successful team in this study. Complaints initiating class-action lawsuits constitute a genre that few writers are called on to produce. Few lawyers have the luxury of revising a document so extensively. Because of these differences, we need more research to determine whether the factors that led to successful collaboration in this case are limited to it or are common to most successful collaborative writing groups. The following aspects of that question seem to me the most interesting:

Group Members

- To what extent do the factors necessary for successful collaboration vary according to the participants' professional backgrounds, knowledge, values, or relationships?
- Are there people who cannot successfully collaborate?
- Anecdotal evidence suggests that some collaborative writing teams produce documents that their organizations judge acceptable even though individual members may be elitist or sexist or dislike each other. What strategies enable such groups to succeed? What is the cost to individuals and to the organization when a group produces a successful product by means of a flawed process?

Task

- Do the features necessary for successful collaboration vary according to the genre or the rhetorical complexity of the task?

Time Constraints

- Would additional or different processes have been needed for success under a deadline?

Organizational Values and Culture

- Does collaboration function differently in government and other nonprofit organizations than in businesses that must be concerned about the "bottom line"?

- How does collaboration function in strongly hierarchical organizations? Do hierarchical teams need different strategies to be successful than do teams using more dialogic methods of collaboration?

- Does successful collaboration depend in part on organizational stability? If not, what factors can allow a group to work effectively during shifts in organizational culture and management style?

Pedagogical Implications

Given the convincing data showing how common collaborative writing is in the workplace, it is essential that we at least discuss the topic with our students. We should make clear the variety of collaborative and cycling situations that can occur; we should admit the present fragmentary state of our knowledge about whether one method of organizing a group is better than another.

If students will be doing collaborative assignments, we also need to help them understand group dynamics and conflict resolution; we need to suggest ways that collaborative writing processes differ from individual writing and to model for them ways to achieve stylistic consistency in a document and to talk about the strengths and weaknesses in a colleague's draft.

The great variety of collaborative processes and products in the workplace makes it obvious that we cannot possibly prepare students for every collaborative challenge they may face. But writing teachers have never been able to prepare students for every individual writing challenge either. Teaching students to analyze a case rhetorically in terms of audience and purpose is an important first step, especially if we stress the likelihood that collaborative documents will have multiple audiences and multiple purposes. Helping students understand how to analyze the discourse communities and the organizational cultures in which they find themselves would be a useful addition. Perhaps most important, we should encourage our students to reflect on their own writing and group processes. Ultimately, success in any collaborative project, as in any individual project, depends on the ability to evaluate what is happening and to try alternatives if problems arise. Students who know how to think about their processes will best be able to collaborate effectively when they find themselves in a new situation where the old answers don't fit.

Works Cited

Allen, Nancy, et al. "What Experienced Collaborators Say about Collaborative Writing." *Journal of Business and Technical Communication* 1.2 (1987): 70–90.

Couture, Barbara, and Jone Rymer. "Interactive Writing on the Job: Definitions and Implications of 'Collaboration.'" *Writing in the Business Professions*. Ed. Myra Kogen. Urbana: NCTE, ABC, 1989. 73–93.

Cross, Geoffrey A. "A Bakhtinian Exploration of Factors Affecting the Collaborative Writing of an Executive Letter of an Annual Report." *Research in the Teaching of English 24* (1990): 173–202.

Deal, Terrence E., and Allan A. Kennedy. *Corporate Cultures: The Rites and Rituals of Corporate Life*. Reading: Addison-Wesley, 1982.

Doheny-Farina, Stephen. "The Individual and the Organization: The Relations of the Part to the Whole in Nonacademic Discourse." CCCC, Seattle, March 16–18, 1989.

Forman, Janis, and Patricia Katsky. "The Group Report: A Problem in Small Group or Writing Processes?" *Journal of Business Communication* 23.4 (1986): 23–35.

Goldstein, Jone Rymer, and Elizabeth L. Malone. "Using Journals to Strengthen Collaborative Writing." *Bulletin of the Association for Business Communication* 48.3 (1985): 24–29.

Gopen, George D. "The State of Legal Writing: *Res Ipsa Loquitur.*" *Writing in the Business Professions*. Ed. Myra Kogen. Urbana: NCTE, ABC, 1989. 146–73.

Lunsford, Andrea, and Lisa Ede. *Singular Texts/Plural Authors: Perspectives on Collaborative Writing*. Carbondale: Southern Illinois UP, 1990.

Mathes, J. C., and Dwight Stevenson. *Designing Technical Reports: Writing for Audiences in Organizations*. Indianapolis: Bobbs-Merrill, 1976.

Miller, Carolyn. Respondent. "The Ethics and Politics of Negotiating in the Workplace: Research, Theory, and Practice." CCCC Seattle, March 16–18, 1989.

Page's Ohio Revised Code Annotated. Title 51. Public Welfare. Ed. John L. Mason, Dale J. Hartig, and Delores A. Dunn. Cincinnati: Anderson, 1989.

Phelps, Teresa Godwin. "In Law the Text is King." *Worlds of Writing: Teaching and Learning in Discourse Communities of Work*. Ed. Carolyn B. Matalene. New York: Random, 1989. 363–72.

Porter, James E. "Intertextuality and the Discourse Community," *Rhetoric Review* 5 (1986): 34–47.

Schein, Edgar H. *Organizational Culture and Leadership*. San Francisco: Jossey-Bass, 1985.

4

Bakhtin, Collaborative Partners, and Published Discourse
A Collaborative View of Composing

Charlotte Thralls

Although most research on collaboration has explored the concept of joint authorship, current social theory suggests that all writing is essentially collaborative, even when that writing is attributed to only a single author. At present, however, theoretical support for this claim remains scattered throughout the literature in rhetoric and composition, leaving writing specialists without a clearly synthesized theoretical framework for explaining the range and significance of relationships than can exist among collaborators when texts are ostensibly produced by individual rather than plural authors. This essay suggests that Bakhtin's theory of language can provide that theoretical framework, allowing writing specialists to account for the collaborative impulses in all writing. The essay summarizes Bakhtin's theory of collaboration and then illustrates the collaborative process through an example of scholarly article production. The essay concludes by discussing how a collaborative perspective on composing modifies traditional pedagogic assumptions about authorship and context.

[I wish to thank Jimmie Killingsworth for so graciously allowing me to use drafts of his commentary (published in *The Journal of Business and Technical Communication*) as a case study in this article.]

Research, like Reither and Vipond's classification of collaborative forms, is beginning to show that collaboration is a complex and comprehensive activity that extends well beyond joint authorship. The

63

thrust of current research, however, remains focused on collaboration in only its narrowest sense: writing produced by two or more authors. This research attempts to describe the process of co- and group-authorship (e.g., Couture and Rymer; Doheny-Farina; Lunsford and Ede; Faigley et al.; Lay; Paradis, Dobrin, and Miller); to assess the effectiveness of joint authorship as a means of teaching writing (e.g., Blissland; Gebhardt; Jacko; O'Donnell et al.), and to address pedagogic strategies for incorporating joint authorship into academic writing assignments (e.g., Forman and Katsky; Goldstein and Malone; Louth and Scott; Morgan et al.; Scott).

In contrast to these studies, we have a much smaller body of theory and research to advance our understanding of collaboration as a more comprehensive activity than plural authorship. As theory, we have, for example, Bruffee's examinations of social construction, suggesting how social theory might serve as a theoretical basis for the collaborative impulses in all writing. We also have the concept of intertextuality, imported from poststructuralist literary theory, to help explain the collaboration inherent in all writing. As Porter has pointed out, intertextuality — the idea that texts contain traces of other texts — undercuts "the traditional notion of the text as the single work of a single author" (35). Even with the addition, however, of LeFevre's study of social theory and invention and Bartholomae and Petrosky's social theory of reading, we find that existing theory takes a piecemeal approach, with material pertinent to collaboration scattered throughout the literature on rhetoric and composition. As a result, we have no clearly formulated theory to explain the range and significance of relationships that can exist among collaborators, especially when texts are attributed to individual rather than plural authors. We have, as more practical research, a handful of studies that do address some of these relationships among collaborators. In separate studies, for example, Reither and Vipond, and Myers have examined collaboration in journal-article publication. These two studies have been invaluable in advancing the claim that all writing is collaborative, but neither study provides a detailed theoretical explanation to accompany its analysis of collaboration. These practical studies, then, when coupled with the fragmented state of existing theory, leave us without the combined theory and practical research that we need if we are to understand collaboration as an inherent condition for *all* writing activity.

The purpose of this essay, then, is to develop the claim that all writing is inherently collaborative. More specifically, this essay seeks to show how texts, whether individually or jointly authored, should be considered collaborative and to examine how this collaboration works. In this discussion, I will draw on Bakhtin's theory of dialogue, showing how this theory allows us to account for the collaboration implicit in an individually authored text. As practical illustration, I, like Reither and Vipond, and Myers, will use journal-article publication as my case study. I have selected a journal article for analysis because my former coeditorship of the *Journal of Business and Technical Communication (JBTC)* offered me a unique opportunity to observe firsthand the collaborative process involved in preparing an article for publication. By revealing details about the editors', reviewers', and author's roles in producing an article, I hope to provide a concrete picture of the collaborative partnership these parties form during the publication process.

Although my analysis will focus on this single example of collaboration, I hope to bring to light some fundamental characteristics of collaboration that can be generalized to any discourse-production situation. More specifically, I will suggest that, as instructors of writing, we should teach our students the collaborative activity inherent in all writing, rather than reserve instruction on collaboration to those situations involving plural authorship. I will further suggest that a collaborative view of composing can help students develop a more sophisticated understanding of the composing process.

My discussion will proceed, first, with a discussion of Bakhtin's theory of language, showing how this theory provides us with a way to explain the complex voices and relationships in published discourse. Then, this theory will be illustrated in an article written for publication by a single author. Finally, the essay will examine the pedagogic implications of defining collaboration, not merely as joint authorship, but as a collaborative partnership present in all discourse-production situations.

Bakhtin's Theory of Language and Collaboration

Bakhtin's theory of the *communication chain* provides a solid vantage point from which to begin to explore the sense in which collaboration is present in both individually and jointly authored texts. More specifically, Bakhtin's theory asserts that 1) all communication is an *active process* involving collaborative partnerships, and that 2) collaborative partners are linked through a chain of *responsive reactions*. Taken together, these theoretical premises can help clarify the centrality of collaboration in all writing activity.

Communication as a Collaborative Partnership

Bakhtin's theory of language asserts that communication is an active process. Although in his essay, "The Problem of Speech Genres," Bakhtin refers to this communication process as speech, he explicitly indicates that speech is meant to encompass both written and oral discourse. Thus, when Bakhtin asserts that speech communication is an "active process" because it involves both speakers and listeners, he refers equally to writers and readers (*Speech Genres* 69). Central to Bakhtin's view of speech communication is the active role of the *other* in the communication process. According to Bakhtin, "The word in language is half someone else's" (*Dialogic Imagination* 293). Language is never the purview of the individual only, but always an interaction of the individual with *others* because language is, in Bakhtin's words, "not a neutral media that passes freely and easily into the private property of the speaker's intentions; it is populated — overpopulated — with the intentions of others" (*Dialogic Imagination* 294). Because the role of these others is not merely to understand passively the speaker, but rather to prompt a speaker's response, active listeners are, for Bakhtin, "partner-interlocutors" (*Speech Genres* 66) in utterance formation. Utterances reflect these active partners and, thus, utterances are imbued with the voices of both speakers and respondents.

To explain this interaction among partners, Bakhtin broadly characterizes the utterance as "a link in a very complexly organized" communication chain (*Speech Genres* 69). Every utterance is linked to others through dialogue. This dialogue takes the form of responsive reactions as every utterance anticipates and responds to other utterances related to it by the "communality of the sphere of speech communication" (*Speech Genres* 91). This dialogue is, for Bakhtin, the most important feature of the utterance because in the utterance we see the responsive nature of language. To communicate is to engage dialogic partners. To speak — to write — demands collaboration with others in a communication chain.

Specific Links Among Collaborative Partners

In addition to providing us with a broad theoretical framework, grounded in language theory, that explains the collaborative partnership implicit in discourse, Bakhtin's communication chain gives us insight into the specific ways collaborative partners are linked in discourse production. According to Bakhtin, authors and respondents are linked in a communication chain in two ways: first, the utterance is linked to utterances that have *preceded* it in any given sphere; and, second, the utterance is linked to *subsequent* utterances.

In terms of its link to utterances that have *preceded* it, every utterance takes from other utterances the worldviews and meanings of other speakers and writers who have already "articulated, disputed, elucidated, and evaluated" (*Speech Genres* 93) an author's topic. An author's text, thus, is addressed not only "to its own object, but also to other's speech about it" (*Speech Genres* 94), for an author presupposes "not only the existence of a language system he is using but also the existence of preceding utterances — his own and others' — with which his given utterance enters into one kind of relation or another." An author's relationship to these preceding utterances surfaces in a text through various traces of others' worldviews and meanings. An author, for example, may directly mention and build upon the utterances of another. Or an author may employ only a single word that indirectly evokes the voice of a preceding partner, in which case an author is simply referring to previous voices "as though the interlocutor were already aware of them" (*Speech Genres* 91).

In addition to these direct and indirect references to preceding partners, an author's relationship to others is reflected in the actual forms of expression an author employs. According to Bakhtin, we (as authors) generally adopt from others various forms of expression "that are kindred to ours in genre, that is, in theme, composition, and style" (*Speech Genres* 87). These genres correspond to the language forms employed by different communication groups, such as scientific or literary communities, who adopt forms of expression that define meaningful communication within that sphere. Because certain forms are already in place when an author composes, these forms restrict possible expression, so an author communicating within a specific communication sphere naturally incorporates expressions typical of that sphere.

Utterances also are linked to *subsequent* utterances or addressees. According to Bakhtin, an author's utterance is "from the very beginning. . .constructed while taking into account possible responsive reactions" from which "it is actually created. . . . The entire utterance is constructed, as it were, in anticipation of encountering this response" (*Speech Genres* 94). These anticipated addressees, Bakhtin maintains, can take the form of a "more or less differentiated public," a "differentiated collective of specialists," groups of "contemporaries," "like-minded people," "opponents," or "someone who is lower, higher, familiar, foreign, and so forth" (*Speech Genres* 95). In the absence of a defined addressee, Bakhtin maintains, a respondent is "presupposed in the person of a normal representative of the social group to which the speaker belongs" (*Dialogic Imagination* 85).

Significance to Collaboration and Composing

Bakhtin's theory of the utterance is important to our understanding of collaboration and composing for several reasons. First, Bakhtin shows us that a writer's written communication cannot be viewed separately from a larger discourse chain. Every written utterance is a dialogic response to other utterances, making up a collaborative partnership. Second, Bakhtin shows us how a writer's voice is linked to collaborative partners. A text is both a response to certain others who have preceded a writer and a response to subsequent utterances that a writer anticipates as possible responsive reactions. Finally, Bakhtin shows us that the collaborative partnership inherent in written communication is reflected in a writer's text. A text is simultaneously filled with

> varying degrees of otherness or varying degrees of "our-ownness," varying degrees of awareness and detachment. These words of others carry with them their own expression, their own evaluative tone, which we (authors) assimilate, rework, and re-accentuate. (*Speech Genres* 89)

Because these dialogues between authors and collaborative partners permeate texts, a writer's written text may be viewed as a textualized representation of the entire collaborative chain.

Collaboration in Journal Article Publication

Journal articles published under the name of individual authors can serve as useful illustration of the collaborative partnerships tacitly present in all communication. Journal articles are the product of a collaborative chain involving many partners, including, for example, other scholars who have preceded an author on a given subject, as evidenced through a text's literature review, documentation, and problem statement. Partners also include addressees — colleagues, reviewers, editors, a journal's readership — whose responsive reactions an author anticipates. Taken together, these collaborative partners are part of a complex chain of communication reflected in an author's published manuscript. When we begin to unravel this collaborative chain, we find that an author's manuscript reflects a whole series of utterances among partners that lie behind this final draft. These utterances within utterances are like Chinese boxes, each utterance marking a dialogue among collaborative partners at some stage in the publication process. As a manuscript passes through different stages of review and revision, the dialogue that occurred among collaborative partners at any stage is retextualized in a following stage; this dialogue is then passed on to subsequent partners. The draft of an author's manuscript that reaches publication bears traces of these various dialogic partners and, thus, ultimately represents the entire collaborative chain. In the following discussion, I will elaborate on this collaborative chain by providing, first, a brief overview of the process and, then, an analysis of a specific case of published discourse.

Overview of the Process

Up to the point an author submits an article for publication, the collaborative process generally takes place between the author and colleagues who serve as readers. As Reither and Vipond have pointed out, these readers often serve as "immediate communities" who function within larger "disciplinary communities," and they collaborate with authors to help make an article "withstand the scrutiny of journal editors and reviewers, the official representatives of the discipline" (859). Often, however, the collaboration remains an internalized process within a writer's consciousness. In the presubmission drafts of an article, for example, this internalized collaboration might include a writer's interaction with researchers who have preceded her on a given subject. The collaboration likely includes, as well, a writer's attempt to interpret editorial policy and envision the journal's readership, in order to fit her voice successfully into the dialogue of published discourse.

Once the article is actually submitted to a specific journal, however, the collaboration moves beyond the author's internalized dialogue with collaborative partners to an external collaborative process involving real individuals with actual, embodied voices. At this submission stage, collaboration moves beyond the dialogue implicit in the author's individual utterances to become a collaboration involving a whole chain of utterances in dialogic partnership that constitute the verbal life of the publication process. This chain of communication involves three primary speakers — reviewers, editors, and author — who together are engaged in a complex multilayered dialogue, with each speaker in dialogue with the partner before her in the chain.

Reviewer Utterances

On the level of reviewer utterances, the reviewer's report is itself a collaborative utterance involving dialogic partners. These partners include voices that precede the reviewer's utterance, like authors and philosophies or books that have shaped the reviewer's worldview or disciplinary perspective. Or these partners may be addressees, like the editor, whose responsive reactions the reviewer anticipates.

Editor Utterances

On the editor's level, we see a collaboration between editors and reviewers and between editors and author. With reviewers, an editor's collaboration takes two forms: one is the conversation that takes place between the editor and each individual reviewer, as the editor interprets and assesses each reviewer's judgment of a manuscript. The second conversation is the one the editor must create between the reviewers. Because reviewers' utterances do not speak directly to one another, an editor creates a dialogue between these partners by comparing reviewers' judgments and comments. This dialogue between reviewers is then brought into further dialogue with the editor's own background and image of the journal, as the editor weighs the reviewers' judgments against her own judgments in order to decide whether a manuscript will be accepted or rejected, or whether revision of the author's manuscript will be requested. In the case of journals like *JBTC*, the existence of two editors of equal decision-making status, adds yet another dialogue to collaboration at the editorial level in that the editors have to engage in dialogue about their individual judgments of the manuscript and about their respective judgments of the reviewers' report.

Author Utterances

On the level of the author, the author engages in dialogue with the reviewers' reports, if they are made available, and with the editor's decision letter. If the author is asked and agrees to revise the manuscript, the author must first interpret these previous utterances and use this interpretation to reshape the manuscript, fitting it to the demands of the collaborative partners. If an author disagrees with some aspect of these demands, he may engage in further dialogue with an editor, via letter or telephone conversation, before revising the manuscript. Of course, if an author's manuscript is rejected by more than one journal and thus undergoes many reviews and revisions, the process is multiplied. Ultimately, however, the author's published manuscript will be the culmination of an entire chain of dialogues among collaborators. Because traces of this collaboration echo throughout the publication process, the author's manuscript will represent a retextualizing of the dialogue throughout the collaborative chain.

A Specific Case of Collaboration

To illustrate this collaborative chain, I wish to discuss an article published as a commentary, defined in *JBTC* as an opinion piece of interest to either academicians or practitioners in business and technical communication, as opposed to the results of research or a description of pedagogic practice. In the commentary, the author addressed the topic of metalanguage, the language, in his words, "used to talk about the language" used in professional communication. The author took the position that the ideal metalanguage for professional communication should be useful to both scholars and practitioners.

Although in the original version of the manuscript the author presented three claims to develop this point, I will limit my analysis to only one claim, the one that proved to be most controversial with reviewers and editors and, thus, a point of dialogue among significant partners throughout the collaborative chain. I also will focus my analysis on this dialogue as it emerged among collaborators between the first and third drafts of the author's manuscript because it is here that we see the strongest interaction among dialogic partners, which, in turn, prompted the most substantive revision in the manuscript. Let me begin with the reviewers as dialogic partners and move up the communication chain to editors and author.

Reviewers

The reviewers responded only to the first draft of the manuscript. In this first draft the author claimed that an ideal metalanguage for talking about business and technical writing should avoid terms that are "morally deep but technically shallow." Citing such examples as "user friendly" and "plain style," the author objected to the "hidden premises of theories" implicit in these terms, and the author called for a more neutral metalanguage, one that would use terms suggesting "a correspondence between conceptual meaning and grammatical or rhetorical structures."

In addressing this claim in their reports, each reviewer's judgment was shaped by a different dialogue each carried on with the author's manuscript. These dialogues, moreovers, were shaped to some extent by preceding theorists and researchers in each reviewer's disciplinary background. One reviewer strongly recommended publication; the other recommended the manuscript be rejected. The reviewer casting a negative judgment interpreted the author's claim as an assertion that metalanguage can and should be morally neutral, as evident in this excerpt from the reviewer's report:

> The problem of metalanguage is interesting and important, but the approach here is, I believe, wrongheaded. The writer makes several assumptions about language: he assumes that a morally neutral language exists; he assumes that moral language — whatever that is — is bad, which is, of course, a moral statement; he assumes that some language codes — the rhetoric or something like that — are better than others.... He seems to suggest here some sort of positivistic notion that language corresponds to something that can be described without the use of language itself.

That this excerpt is a dialogue with subsequent partners — editors and author — is clear; these partners are the intended addresses of the reviewer's report. Perhaps somewhat less obvious is the implicit dialogue with previous dialogic partners — those who share or have shaped the reviewer's own assumptions — that language cannot be morally neutral. Although these partners are not named here, a look at the reviewer's background and publications would reveal that antipositivist and anti-foundationalist theorists, such as Derrida, Rorty, and Wittgenstein, have heavily influenced the reviewer's perspective and, thus, in this case, shape the nature of the dialogue between reviewer and author.

The second reviewer, who strongly recommended acceptance with minor revision, praised the manuscript for "addressing an issue of great importance to practitioners and teachers of technical, as well as any kind of referential, writing." This reviewer's comments suggest that he viewed the author's text in an altogether different context with different collaborative partners than the first reviewer. For this second reviewer, the author's claim of a morally neutral language was both suitable and possible in referential or technical discourse. In his report and in three additional places in his margin notes on the manuscript, for example, the reviewer referred to referential language, advising the author to talk about the offending metalanguage in relation to the "precise, measurable, tangible" qualities expected of technical language. Because this reviewer's vocabulary and advice were compatible with a referential view of language, they suggest the nature of the dialogue implicit in his report.

If we return to Bakhtin's original premise, then, that any utterance is a response in dialogue with other utterances in a communication chain, we can see that each reviewer's report is itself a collaboration, linked to a larger communication chain — those preceding and subsequent voices that reverberate within the reviewers' reports. As these reports are then passed on to subsequent partners, the dialogues and collaborators multiply, as the reports enter into dialogue with other participants in the communication chain.

Editors

On the editorial level of the chain, the reviewers' reports spawned several collaborations: 1) the editors' dialogue with the two reports, 2) the editors' collaboration between themselves to arrive at a publication decision, and 3) the editors' dialogue with the author, created when the editors recast the results of preceding collaborations into a decision letter for the author, who, as subsequent partner, continued the collaborative chain.

Traces of these various editorial collaborations are reflected in excerpts of the editors' decision letter to the author:

We certainly appreciated the opportunity to review your essay, "How to Talk about Technical Writing: The Case Against Moralistic Metalanguage." We now have two reader's reports. Because these reviewers were divided in their judgment about the readiness of the essay for publication and because they both offered suggestions for revision, we would like to accept the essay, contingent on revision, for publication as a commentary in...(date and issue of journal).

Both reviewers felt you were discussing an interesting and important topic. One reviewer, however, was uneasy with the basic dichotomy established in your essay—that language is either moral or neutral—and questioned whether such a distinction is theoretically tenable. Your comment on page 10 of the essay ("...that metalanguage may also admittedly have a moral impact") suggests that you too have reservations about the possible existence of a morally neutral language. Your commentary, then, would seem to require either a fuller examination of your assumptions about a morally neutral metalanguage or some qualification of your basic thesis. In formulating your stance, you may wish to consider three questions raised by reviewer #1:

- Is a morally neutral language possible?
- Is it not a moral statement to say that moral language is bad?
- Are some language codes "better" than others? If so, why?

The collaboration *between* editors is reflected most directly in the plural "we" throughout the letter: Both editors' decision to accept the manuscript upon revision and the decision letter itself are the result of editorial collaboration. The dialogue the editors created *between reviewers* is reflected in expressions such as "both reviewers," used rhetorically to de-emphasize the reviewers' different judgments and to emphasize instead the reviewers' agreement about the need for additional revision. The collaboration *between editors and author* takes the form of the entire letter, as a direct communication between the two parties. As the editors comment on problems in the author's manuscript and suggest possible revisions, the dialogue between editors and author is filled with traces of the other collaborations in the publication chain. Perhaps most obvious is the editors' tendency to appropriate the language of the reviewer who objected to the author's claim, overtly linking the editors' communication to preceding collaborators.

Author

When the author received this decision letter and reviewer reports, he agreed to revise. This revised and published manuscript formed yet an additional collaboration or dialogue, then, serving as a responsive reaction to the various dialogic partners that preceded the author in the review and editing process, while, at the same time, serving as a projected dialogue with future partners — the readers of the journal.

Because space does not permit me to examine the entire revised draft of the manuscript, I will compare just one of the passages in the original and revised drafts that address the author's claim about a morally neutral metalanguage. In telephone conversations with the editors, the author indicated that it had never been his intention to claim language is morally/ideologically neutral, but instead to argue against metalanguage that moralizes — "be truthful," "be user friendly" — when such a metalanguage fails to tell technical writers how these qualities are to be achieved.

The second paragraph of the original manuscript, however, read like this:

> I am not really offering a how-to paper, but what if I were? What if my aim were to write a user friendly guide for how to talk about technical writing? I would have to begin on a negative note. My user friendly guide would have to warn the user against words like *user friendly*, loaded terms that involve value judgments of kinds of writing whose actual nature is not at all clearly delimited. *User friendly* and related terms like *honest, truthful*, and even *plain style* have meanings that are morally deep but technically shallow. They give you a way of talking about a result but not a way of achieving it or even describing it. They also involve talking about hidden premises of theories that, if presented outright, might be unacceptable to many teachers and practitioners.

Note here that the author introduces such examples as "user-friendly" before a clear statement of his claim. Note also that the claim itself is ambiguous, since words like "morally deep" and "hidden premises of theories" do imply the author's concern is with the moral/ideological dimensions of metalanguage.

In the final draft of the article, this second paragraph was revised, as the author's attempt to clarify his point in dialogic response to his most immediate collaborative partners — the reviewer who raised questions about the author's argument and the editors who communicated these concerns. Traces of the collaborative chain permeate the passage as the following revision of paragraph two shows:

> My first concern is to warn against moralistic terminology that says more about the character of the writer than about the language the writer uses. Note that I use the word moralistic, not moral, for all language in context is necessarily moral or ideological; a morally neutral language is a positivistic illusion. By moralistic, I mean language that consists of loaded terms involving value judgments about kinds of writing whose actual nature is not at all clearly delimited. *User*

friendly and related terms like *honest*, *truthful*, and even *plain style* have meanings that are morally deep but technically shallow. They give you a way of talking about a result but not a way of achieving it or even describing it technically. They also involve hidden premises of theories that, if presented outright, might be unacceptable to many teachers and practitioners.

In this revised draft, the author's topic — moralistic terminology — is clarified at the outset. The author now explicitly contrasts key terms — moral/moralistic. In addition, he offers an explicit disclaimer to clarify his claim that a metalanguage cannot be morally neutral. This clarification of intentions, which directly addresses earlier reviewer objections, echoes previous dialogues and shows the author entering a conversation with others in a chain of communication.

In tracing this collaborative chain in the production of an author's scholarly article, my intent has been to make explicit some of the collaborative voices behind discourse production in order to show the sense in which discourse is collaborative, even when produced under the name of an individual author. By framing this analysis within the context of Bakhtin's theory of the utterance, I have also attempted to show how we can account for the collaborative partners implicit in written discourse. Certainly, because my analysis has been limited to a single example of scholarly-article production, I do not wish to claim that all publication processes or individually authored texts are identical to the collaborative process I have described. The collaborative partners and exact interaction among them will vary depending on the particular context for a communication. I do believe, however, that the description of collaboration I have outlined here may be generalized to all discourse situations.

For example, a student writing an academic essay opposing abortion collaborates with others who have spoken or written, both pro and con, on the subject. The student also collaborates with subsequent partners, or actual readers, by anticipating these readers' responses. If the student paper is reviewed and evaluated by peers, and then evaluated by a teacher, the peer group (e.g., classmates) and instructor become additional collaborative partners. Each of these partners, in turn, brings to the collaboration previous collaborations with partners who have shaped each person's attitudes and expectations. Finally, the student's paper engages the academic community and certain discourse norms linked to this community. Although the names and specific roles of collaborative partners are different in a student paper and in a scholarly article, both writing situations suggest that, at any given stage of composing, an author's discourse is the product of dynamic interaction among collaborative partners, who, together with an author, form a communication chain.

Collaboration and Writing Pedagogy

To acknowledge that all discourse is a form of collaboration has important implications for writing pedagogy. The most obvious implication is that pedagogy should address the collaboration implicit in all composing activity, rather than equate collaboration with only co- or group-authored composing. This more comprehensive view of collaboration has the potential to provide needed continuity to writing courses that include both individual- and joint-composing assignments. In this final part of my discussion, however, I would like to examine two more specific implications: how a collaborative approach to composition affects traditional notions of 1) authorship and 2) context. I have selected these two issues because authorship and context are important points of controversy and even confusion in current writing pedagogy. By providing us with an alternate way of conceptualizing authorship and context, a collaborative view of composing can help address and resolve problems in this pedagogy.

Authorship

The view that all writing is a collaborative partnership calls attention to problems in two traditional representations of authorship — associated with the expressive and the social approaches to composition — and offers us a way to resolve conflict between these characterizations. On one end of the spectrum is the expressive view (Elbow, Macrorie, and Stewart), which characterizes authorship as an individual enterprise. By focusing on the individual writer, this view elevates individual creativity and personal development, subordinating, and sometimes ignoring altogether, the social context in which individual expression occurs. Because authorship so narrowly defined does not encourage students to consider their writing in relation to other voices and influences, the expressive view perpetuates, as Giroux has pointed out, a false notion of "private authorship." For Giroux, situating the individual at the center of authorship is to overlook the sense in which subjectivity is socially constituted and to "suppress questions of power, knowledge, and ideology" in the "existing social order" (3).

The social view, on the other hand, focuses on the social forces that limit and shape an author's expression. Taken to extremes, the social view may appear to disempower the individual, implying that authorial expression is completely determined in advance by social constraints on expression. This view of authorship is most apparent in professional communication textbooks (e.g., Anderson, Burnett), which emphasize the disciplinary and organizational contexts in which composing occurs. In *Technical Communication*, Burnett, for example, subordinates all writer-based activities (focus of content, selection of organization) to social forces — what she calls the "environment" (17).

Because the expressive approach, then, focuses on the individual authorial voice and the social approach focuses on cultural and institutional voices, the two approaches set up seemingly irreconcilable differences about what constitutes authorship. These extreme positions, however, may be reconciled by defining authorship as a collaborative partnership — a blend of individual and social voices.

A collaborative view of authorship allows us to recognize the social sphere of voices that inform and limit expression; individual utterances are never entirely original because individual consciousness and language use are socially constituted. At the same time, the collaborative perspective recognizes that the individual author can assert a voice. This assertion, as we have seen in the case of a scholarly article, occurs because an author "reaccents" or "retextualizes" the social voices of collaborative partners in a communication chain. In other words, an author, though adapting his article to the demands of others, has ultimate responsibility for textualizing the dialogue that takes place among collaborative partners. In narrative and certain other types of discourse, authors may engage in an even more radical interaction with collaborators than we have seen in scholarly article production. According to Bakhtin, authors can resist existing social forms, as for example in the novel, by deforming voices of preceding partners, to create innovative forms of expression. These innovative forms are never entirely purged of other voices, however, because preceding others make up the background voices to which an author responds.

A view of composing that accounts for the collaboration implicit in all writing avoids dichotomizing the individual and social dimensions of authorship. This more comprehensive understanding of collaboration, in turn, can help students avoid naive and oversimplified notions of themselves as writers. On the one hand, students can avoid viewing their writing as entirely "self" expression, free from the active influence of others. On the other hand, students can avoid viewing their writing as a predetermined formula that totally prescribes authorial expression. Finally, students may understand the varying authorial roles they may be asked to assume for different composing situations. Students may find, for example, that in a proposal written for a specific corporation, authorship may mean largely accommodation: fitting authorial utterance to the demands of one's collaborative partners. Students may find that in composing a novel or poem, however, authorship requires a writer to engage in conflict, mediating, and even writing against, collaborative voices.

Context

In addition to reconciling problems with traditional notions of authorship, a collaborative perspective on composing can foster for students a more sophisticated understanding of context, extending the narrow view of context implicit in much writing pedagogy. This restrictive view of context surfaces in current research and pedagogy on co- or group authorship and on audience. In both instances, context is characterized as the immediate and specific sphere in which a communication is composed and situated. Instruction on joint authorship, for example, tends to focus primarily on the interaction among team members who make up a writing group. Although this interaction among partners is important, coauthorship constitutes only one level of collaboration operative in a communication chain. Pedagogy that heavily emphasizes this aspect of the composing context may unintentionally encourage students to consider as collaborative partners only those persons who are physically part of a writing team.

Pedagogy that emphasizes audience analysis potentially creates a similar problem by equating context with the definable readers for a communication. Like joint authors, these specific readers are important active partners, but immediate readers also are only one layer of collaborative partners making up a communication chain. Writers who consider actual readers as their only collaborative partners may fail to recognize the larger context, which encloses the specific sphere of communication in which authors and readers interact.

Introducing students to the collaboration inherent in all their writing encourages them to consider partners that extend beyond coauthors and readers because a collaborative view of composing addresses the hierarchy of contexts implicit in any communication chain. Collaboration, more comprehensively understood than coauthorship, can bring to light two levels of contextual partners that Bakhtin's theory suggests are present in any composing situation. The first level is analogous to a speech act: Social context is a closed sphere of communication between a definable writer and reader. This level of context is a necessary condition for communication because it defines the actual conditions of an utterance within an immediate social situation. This level of context allows us to account for collaborative partners like team members and readers.

Immediate contexts are enclosed, however, within a second, larger contextual level. Bakhtin calls these larger contexts speech genres, "mandatory forms of utterances that are necessary for mutual understanding" (*Speech Genres* 80). Roughly comparable to the concept of discourse communities, speech genres are contexts outside immediate contexts. However, because these outer contexts define conditions for meaning for individual utterances between writers and readers, outer contexts are *imported into* specific contexts.

Both these immediate and outer context were evident in the earlier analysis of scholarly-article production. The specific and closed context for the text included editors, reviewers, and journal readers, who, as addressees, acted as collaborators whose responsive reactions the author attempted to anticipate. At the same time, however, these editors and readers operated within a larger context, or speech genre, which framed the style and organization of published discourse in professional communication. Both levels of context also come into play in the classroom and in organizational settings. In the case of a student's paper on abortion or a proposal for a major corporation, the outer context or speech genre would be the academic communities' and the corporation's discourse norms, respectively. In the scholarly article, the student paper, and the corporate proposal, outer contexts are at least as important as immediate contexts because outer contexts determine many of the discourse conventions that bind communities. Writers need to understand that both these immediate and outer contexts affect written texts. A collaborative view of composing helps foster this insight by bringing attention to the hierarchy of contextual partners that exist within any communication chain.

Conclusion

This essay has advanced the claim that all writing, whether authored by individuals or groups, is collaborative. In support of this claim, we have seen how Bakhtin's theory of the utterance might begin to help us account for the collaborative process in all writing, how this collaborative process works in, at least, some instances of scholarly article production, and how a collaborative view of composing can offer us a perspective for addressing certain problematic issues in writing pedagogy. As research, theory, and pedagogy continue to evolve on collaboration, we need to continue refining our understanding of collaboration and composing, and to further explore the collaborative partnerships that, as Bakhtin shows, define knowledge and expression.

Works Cited

Anderson, Paul V. *Technical Writing: A Reader-Centered Approach*. San Diego: Harcourt Brace Javanovich, 1987.

Bakhtin, Mikhail M. *Speech Genres and Other Late Essays*. Trans. Caryl Emerson and Michael Holquist. Austin: U Texas P, 1986.

———. *The Dialogic Imagination*. Trans. by Caryl Emerson and Michael Holquist. Austin: U Texas P, 1981.

Bartholomae, David, and Anthony Petrosky. *Facts, Artifacts and Counterfacts: Theory and Method for a Reading and Writing Course*. Portsmouth, N.H.;

Boynton/Cook, 1986.

Blissland, J. H. "Peer Evaluation Method Promotes Sharper Writing." *Journalism Educator* 34.4 (1980): 17–19.

Bruffee, Kenneth A. "Collaborative Learning and the 'Conversation of Mankind.'" *College English* 46 (1984): 635–52.

———. "Social Construction, Language, and the Authority of Knowledge: A Bibliographical Essay." *College English* 48 (1986): 773–90.

Burnett, Rebecca E. *Technical Communication*. 2nd. ed. Belmont: Wadsworth, 1990.

Couture, Barbara, and Jone Rymer. "Interactive Writing on the Job: Definitions and Implications of Collaboration." *Writing in the Business Professions: Research, Theory, Practice*. Ed. Myra Kogen. Urbana: NCTE, ABC, 1989. 73–93.

Doheny-Farina, Stephen. "Writing in an Emerging Organization: An Ethnographic Study." *Written Communication* 3 (1986): 158–85.

Ede, Lisa, and Andrea Lunsford. "Why Write…Together." *Rhetoric Review* 1 (1983): 150–57.

———. "Collaborative Learning: Lessons from the World of Work." *Journal of the Council of Writing Program Administrators* 9.3 (1986): 17–26.

Elbow, Peter. *Writing Without Teachers*. New York: Oxford UP, 1973.

———. *Writing with Power*. New York: Oxford UP, 1981.

Faigley, Lester, et al. *Assessing Writers' Knowledge and Processes of Composing*. Norwood: Ablex, 1985.

Forman, Janis, and Patricia Katsky. "The Group Report: A Problem in Small Group or Writing Processes?" *Journal of Business Communication* 23.4 (1986): 23–35.

Gebhardt, Richard. "Teamwork and Feedback: Broadening the Base of Collaborative Writing." *College English* 42 (1986): 69–74.

Giroux, Henry. *Theory and Resistance in Education*. South Hadley: Bergin and Garvey, 1983.

Goldstein, Jone Rymer, and Elizabeth L. Malone. "Using Journals to Strengthen Collaborative Writing." *Bulletin of the Association for Business Communication* 48.3 (1985): 24–28.

Jacko, Carol M. "Small Group Triad: An Instructional Mode for the Teaching of Writing." *College Composition and Communication* 29 (1978): 290–92.

Lay, Mary M. "Interpersonal Conflict in Collaborative Writing: What We Can Learn from Gender Studies." *Journal of Business and Technical Communication* 3.2 (1989): 5–28.

LeFevre, Karen Burke. *Invention as a Social Act*. Carbondale: Southern Illinois UP, 1987.

Louth, Richard, and Ann Martin Scott, eds. *Collaborative Technical Writing: Theory and Practice*. Association of Teachers of Technical Writing Anthology Series. Lubbock: ATTW, 1989.

Lunsford, Andrea, and Lisa Ede. *Singular Texts/Plural Authors: Perspectives on Collaborative Writing*. Carbondale: Southern Illinois UP, 1990.

Macrorie, Ken. "To Be Read." *English Journal*, 57 (1968): 686–92.

Medvedev, P. N., and Mikhail M. Bakhtin. *The Formal Method in Literary Scholarship: A Critical Introduction to Sociological Poetics*. Trans. Albert J. Wehrle. Baltimore: Johns Hopkins UP, 1973.

Morgan, Meg, et al. "Collaborative Writing in the Classroom." *Bulletin of the Association for Business Communication* 50.3 (1987): 20–26.

Myers, Greg. "Texts as Knowledge Claims: The Social Construction of Two Biologists' Articles." *Social Studies of Science* 15 (1985): 593–630.

O'Donnell, Angela M., et al. "Cooperative Writing: Direct Effects and Transfer." *Written Communication* 2 (1985): 307–15.

———. "Effects of Cooperative and Individual Rewriting on an Instruction Writing Task." *Written Communication* 4 (1987): 90–99.

Paradis, James, David Dobrin, and Richard Miller. "Writing at Exxon ITD: Notes on the Writing Environment of an R&D Organization." *Writing in Nonacademic Settings*. Ed. Lee Odell and Dixie Goswami. New York: Guilford, 1985. 281–307.

Porter, James E. "Intertextuality and the Discourse Community." *Rhetoric Review* 5 (1986): 34–47.

Reither James A., and Douglas Vipond. "Writing as Collaboration." *College English* 51 (1989): 855–67.

Scott, Ann Martin. "Group Projects in Technical Writing Courses." *Technical Writing Teacher* 15 (1988): 138–42.

Stewart, Donald C. "Prose with Integrity: A Primary Objective." *College Composition and Communication* 20 (1969): 223–27.

5

The Androgynous Collaborator
The Impact of Gender Studies on Collaboration

Mary M. Lay

Collaborative writing is affected by the community in which it is produced, whether that community is the classroom or the business and industrial setting. Interpersonal dynamics within the group or team often determine the success of the collaborative product, and the gender of the collaborators contributes to those interpersonal dynamics. Psychological and social barriers exist that may inhibit male sex-typed collaborators from learning the group maintenance skills that enhance effective collaboration. This essay describes androgynous behavior that overcomes those barriers and appreciates the nurturing and bonding skills that define the traditional female role, skills previously undervalued in the business arena. The essay reviews the work of gender studies scholars that have studied androgyny and ends with a demonstration of how student collaborators have considered androgynous strategies.

Since the early 1980s, when Kenneth Bruffee stressed the notion that knowledge is socially constructed, composition specialists have emphasized collaborative learning and writing. Texts, said Bruffee, are "constructs generated by communities of like-minded peers" ("Social Construction" 774), whether their construction is influenced by internalized "human conversation" within the writer or by the classroom mechanisms such as peer review ("Collaborative Learning" 639; see also "Writing and Reading" 161). In turn, business and technical communication scholars point out that much of the writing that students encounter after graduation is team or collaborative, and that not only the opinions of individual writers, editors, illustrators, and technical experts but also overall company policy and image contribute to the written product (see, for example, Allen et al.; Anderson; Doheny-Farina; Faigley and Miller). Students who seek careers within business and industry must be ready to function within these writing teams. However, while these technical and business communication scholars acknowledge and demonstrate the influences of community, they too seldom know the interpersonal aspects that affect how these communities are formed and maintained, what causes them to flourish or fail. Moreover, only two recent studies hint that the gender of community members might affect the collaborative process (Lay; Lunsford and Ede 133–36).

To teach students how to relate as collaborators, instructors need to understand why and how humans form relationships, how these relationships grow and are maintained, and what conflicts threaten their existence. To enter into a relationship is to acknowledge that one is part of a community. Whether the relationship lasts a class period, as students critique each other's essays, or exists for years, as professional writers periodically update corporate documentation, the written product is affected by the interpersonal relations within the community or group. Marilyn Cooper notes that collaborative connections are much like a web, "in which anything that affects one strand of the web vibrates throughout the whole" (370). Because the gender of the collaborators may help determine the interpersonal dynamics within the group, gender studies provide an essential source for understanding and strengthening interpersonal relationships between collaborators.

Scholars of small group behavior have documented that many females use group maintenance strategies such as self-disclosure and reflective listening to encourage close interpersonal relations while males may focus on task completion (see, for example, Aries 12; Baird 192). Within business and industry, both strategies are certainly necessary; however, traditionally "female" bonding skills have been undervalued in the business arena. If collaborators can be made to feel comfortable with group maintenance strategies, then collaboration will be enriched and an effective written communication more easily produced. This essay contrasts female and male bonding to locate the roots of relational attitudes and skills and suggests that collaborators need to be androgynous, capable of calling upon a range of collaborative strategies that have been traditionally reserved for either males or females. Unlike many past explorations of androgyny, in which the female entering the business world was encouraged to adopt such "male" strategies as assertiveness and competitiveness, this essay proposes that traditional female skills should be acquired by all collaborators. To encourage androgyny, educators and business leaders must be aware of the psychological sources of gender typing within childhood and how these types may be reinforced or challenged socially in adulthood.

Female Bonding

Psychologist Nancy Chodorow proposes that women place such emphasis on relationships because of their identification with the primary parent in their life — the mother — during the pre-Oedipal stage. "Because of their mothering by women," Chodorow concludes, "girls come to experience themselves as less separate than boys, as having more permeable ego boundaries. Girls come to define themselves more in relation to others" (93). Boys, who later withdraw from the mother and identify with the father, separate and distinguish themselves as individuals, often through competition within a hierarchical system. A member of the object relations psychological school, Chodorow locates the source of gender-typing within the traditional family structure.

Jane Flax, building upon Chodorow, links the way boys relate to their mothers and fathers to their frequent inability to nurture as adult males. Flax believes:

> The girl, unlike the boy, cannot repress the female part of herself and totally reject the mother, because it is precisely at this stage that she is coming to an awareness of her own femaleness, that is, her gender. The boy's repression of the female aspect of himself is one of the reasons men find it hard to be nurturant as adults. To be nurturant would threaten their sense of identity, which is in part built upon being not like mother. Furthermore, it could revive the pain accompanying the boy's original acts of repression as well as the terror of the all-powerful infantile mother. (178)

Because of the way children are raised and gender identity established, men may have a real psychological stake in *not* becoming nurturers or close collaborators. And, according to Flax, the lack of female influence may be one of the attractions of the workplace: Men's "fear of returning to the mother's control may be an unconscious motive for keeping women out of the workplace, and especially out of positions of authority over men" (181).

Furthermore, Carol Gilligan, a specialist in the education of women, finds that in adulthood women's need to connect becomes the source for an ethic of care often in opposition to a more publicly esteemed masculine ethic of objectivity (43). Extending the findings of Chodorow and Gilligan, sociologist Mary Field Belenky and her coauthors focus on women's "bonds of attachment," leading to a strategy of "connected knowing," as women understand others through common experiences (178, 118). Thus women, because of their identity with the primary nurturer within the family, are often experts at initiating and maintaining relationships, on acknowledging and preserving community. Many men may carry their suspicion of such values into the collaborative process and strive for individual recognition that can lead to intragroup conflict.

Although in recent years men have become more involved in the parenting of children, until that involvement equals that of women, the ways in which young girls and boys develop psychological gender identity are unlikely to change radically, say Chodorow and Gilligan. Therefore, men have different goals within relationships.

Male Bonding

Some readers might suggest that men do form close relationships, particularly in long-term friendships and on sports teams. In the past women have been encouraged to study sports to learn team strategies in business (see, for example, Harragan; Hennig and Jardim). However, sociologists, psychologists, and cultural anthropologists distinguish between men's and women's goals within friendship. "Women seem to look for intimate confidantes, while men seek partners for adventure," notes social psychologist Drury Sherrod (217). Intimacy and disclosure within friendships are not as important to men as are acceptance and companionship. Both Sherrod and cultural anthropologists Hammond and Jablow attribute these characteristics of friendship between men to the dynamics of the workplace, in which men compete with other men. While men may cooperate with each other, this cooperation still occurs within a competitive atmosphere that "excludes" emotional closeness (Hammond and Jablow 256). As a result, men often act within roles, the role of father, the role of worker, the role of husband, the role of friend.

Psychologists Spence and Helmrich note the importance of distinguishing between role taking and role playing for men. In role taking, behavior is congruent with self-concept, while in role playing men may perform behaviors that are contradictory to self-concept. People engage in role playing to avoid social penalty or "to respond in line with value systems about correct sex-role behavior," say Spence and Helmrich (15). Even if men may long for closeness with their colleagues, they may feel that closeness makes them socially vulnerable.

Clinical psychologist Richard Ochberg identifies one way men may maintain distance: "Psychodynamically, the sense of acting in roles promises each man a resolution to his ambivalent wish to be wholly engaged and at the same time safely dispassionate" (185). However, it is the public man, one expert in competition, who matures within his role (or gets better at it), while the private man remains an "emotionally detached, efficient provider" (Ochberg 177). If, according to these scholars, many men then do not seek or achieve intimacy within friendships, what about intimacy and bonding between male athletes—

that team or collaborative effort on the playing field that women entering the business arena have been encouraged to imitate?

Upon interviewing male athletes, sociologist Michael Messner found that many males join sports teams in order to become as close to others as gender image will permit. According to Messner, the young male, "who both seeks and fears attachment with others, thus finds the rulebound structure of games and sports to be a psychologically 'safe' place in which he can get (nonintimate) connection with others within the context that maintains clear boundaries, distance, and separation from others" (198). He is soon disappointed. Part of athletic participation is the drive for public success and recognition, limited to the very few. Messner concludes that athletic participation "exacerbates" males' inability to have close relationships, for "*success* in the sports world involves the development of a personality that amplifies many of the most ambivalent and destructive traits of traditional masculinity" (208, 201). The successful athlete, Messner finds, must "develop a goal-oriented personality, that encourages him to view his body as a tool, a machine, or even a weapon utilized to defeat an objectified opponent. He is likely to have difficulty establishing intimate and lasting friendships with other males because of low self-disclosure, homophobia, and cut-throat competition" (201).

Offering perhaps a more optimistic view, psychologist M. Brinton Lykes proposes that men are indeed concerned with relationships but view them in ways different from women. Women tend to evaluate their abilities "in terms of making or sustaining connection and doing good for others"; for many men, "relationships, described as part of one's obligations or commitments, are evaluated in terms of one's 'ability' or 'skill in interacting with others'" (358–9). If men and women realize these differences, Lykes believes that individualism and collectivity can be viewed less in opposition and more in relation, as an "ensemble of social relations" (357).

These studies indicate that many men do maintain more distance than women might within personal friendships, among professional colleagues, and between athletic team members, the areas in which men have greatest opportunity to collaborate. More barriers than incentives exist for men to become androgynous collaborators. One way to change this behavior is to redefine masculine and feminine roles or even resist the terms "masculine" and "feminine" themselves.

Definitions of Masculinity, Femininity, and Androgyny

Psychological androgyny can be simply defined as "the blending of positive masculine and feminine characteristics within a given person" (Cook 2). It does not represent physical bisexuality or hermaphroditism.

Derived from the Greek words for man and woman, androgyny connotes flexibility, or the "capacity in a single person of either sex to embody the full range of human character traits, despite cultural attempts to render some exclusively feminine and some exclusively masculine" (Secor 139). Carolyn Heilbrun brought the term to the attention of literary scholars in the 1960s, when she confirmed that androgyny "suggests a spirit of reconciliation between the sexes; it suggests, further, a full range of experience open to individuals who may, as women, be aggressive, as men, tender; it suggests a spectrum upon which human beings choose their places without regard to propriety or custom" (*Toward a Recognition* x-xi). Collaborators who adopt both traditional female and male strategies might then be called androgynous.

Androgyny provokes controversy, of course. Some scholars remind us of historical interpretations, such as Jung's *anima* (the contrasexual or feminine side of man) and the *animus* (woman's contrasexual masculine side), which were used to oppress rather than appreciate women. Jung found that men could ignore their "feminine" traits as they projected those traits outside of themselves upon real women and gave the females in their lives the job of completing the missing half of the men's lives. Literary scholar Daniel Harris interprets Jung as encouraging men to find their *anima* but suspecting that the woman who explored her internal *animus* "violated her true identity" (180). Harris rejects Jungian androgyny "not only because it fosters the oppression of women, but because, even as it offers a stunning critique of our present deprivations, it reinforces the very dependence on women which keeps us, the oppressors, from nurturing a richness and a warmth in our own lives..." (181).

Psychologist June Singer also attacks past applications of androgyny: "The man's *anima* helps *him* to produce his creative work. The woman's *animus* is supposed to inseminate the man's *anima*, which thereupon inspires *him* to produce *his* creative work. Fortunate, but rare indeed, is the woman whose active creative *animus* is furthered by the tender nurturing of a man's *anima*" (35). Thus androgyny has been used to externalize and project traditional gender traits in a way that will disadvantage women; it can reinforce the notion of two distinct gender identities, regardless of how many individuals possess both. As a result, some scholars suggest that "fully human" or "non-sex-typed" are more appropriate terms than androgyny, terms that better avoid binary opposition and stereotyping.

Psychologist Ellen Cook offers a list of these "masculine" and "feminine" traits of binary opposition:

> *Masculine*: aggressive, independent, unemotional, objective, dominant, competitive, logical/rational, adventurous, decisive, self-confident, ambitious, worldly, act as a leader, assertive, analytical,

strong, sexual, knowledgeable, physical, successful, good in mathematics and science, and the reverse of the feminine characteristics
listed below.

Feminine: emotional, sensitive, expressive, aware of other's
feelings, tactful, gentle, security-oriented, quiet, nurturing, tender,
cooperative, interested in pleasing others, interdependent, sympath-
etic, helpful, warm, interested in personal appearance and beauty in
general, intuitive, focused on home and family, sensual, good in art
and literature, and the reverse of the masculine characteristics above
(4).

In assigning these features to men and women, to masculinity and
femininity, one could indeed contribute to polarization. And it
would be fairer, rather than labeling all men aggressive, independent,
unemotional, and so on, to consider men who strongly display these
traits as "masculine-typed." However, the real trick is to propose
androgynous behavior in a new sense, one that not only values traditional female traits but also redefines traditional gender skills, and in
doing so, frees both genders to choose strategies applicable to situation
rather than gender role. Although psychologist Jean Baker Miller
resists the term androgyny, in her "new psychology for women," she
redefines traditionally masculine traits such as autonomy: "Women are
quite validly seeking something more complete than autonomy as it is
defined for men, a fuller not a lesser ability to encompass relationships
to others, simultaneous with the fullest development of self" (95).
Again, the androgynous collaborator would value the assertion and
leadership skills that enable a group to complete a task as well as the
bonding skills that allow a group to settle interpersonal conflict.

Accordingly, communication theorist Sandra Bem, whose early
studies of gender roles applauded androgynous individuals, most recently
suggests that a sex-typed person be identified not on the basis of the
"masculine" or "feminine" traits he or she possesses but upon whether
his or her self-concepts and behaviors are "organized" according to
gender, whether "a person has a generalized readiness to classify
perceptions into one of the two classes and then act advisedly based on
this processing" ("Gender Scheme" 354). A sex-typed person may
think of himself or herself as masculine or feminine and model behavior
accordingly. Which traits then are termed masculine or feminine does
not matter; as Bem states, "Many non-sex-typed individuals may describe themselves as, say, dominant or nurturant without implicating
the concepts of masculinity or femininity" ("Gender Scheme" 356). What
does matter, says Bem, is that society teaches children "the substantive
network of sex-related associations that can come to serve as a cognitive
scheme" ("Gender Scheme" 362). If in focusing on androgyny we
somehow reaffirm traditional definitions of masculine and feminine in

order to promote blending, then we fall short of examining the way gender organizes our world.

Cook offers another way to avoid perpetuating stereotypes while exploring androgyny. Traits that have been traditionally labeled masculine become part of "instrumentality" or the "coordination and adaptation of the family system's needs with the outside world" and "a goal orientation and general insensitivity to the responses that others have to the person's behavior." Traits traditionally assigned to females are "expressiveness" or "maintenance and regulation of the family's emotional needs and interactions within itself" and "a sensitivity to others' responses and a concern with interpersonal relationships." To be instrumental, one must be independent and self-reliant; to be expressive, one nurtures (4; see, also, Spence and Helmrich 4–5, 16).

Or traditional masculine traits become part of "agency," according to Cook, where one is concerned with the "maintenance of the organism as individual," and engages in "assertive activity, differentiation, self-protection, self-expansion, an urge toward mastery, and forming separations from others." Traditional feminine traits become "communion" or the "integrated participation of the organism with a larger whole," and require skills in "selflessness, relationships, contact, cooperation, union with others, and openness" (5).

In calling for *androgynous* collaborative strategies in the classroom or the business world, I recognize that the family structure has not evolved enough to eliminate identification of girls with mother and boys with father during the pre-Oedipal and Oedipal stages. However, we can concentrate on changing the social values that devalue women's skills. Thus I agree with Heilbrun, as she defended the term androgyny in the 1970s: "But it seems to me that the word androgyny is better able to startle us, to penetrate our age-old defenses, and make us aware of the need to give up stereotyped roles and modes of behavior... Androgynous means that one need not be male to be a priest, or female to be a nurturer" ("Further Notes" 147). The word or at least the spirit of androgyny can serve this same purpose when one studies collaborative strategies. Again, an androgynous collaborator then would not only bring to the collaborative process the ability to complete a task, to assert an opinion, and to engage in conflict over ideas, but would preserve the group so that the task could be completed.

Adult Gender Identity

Let us assume then that effective collaborators are androgynous, not bound by gender identity. And again the purpose of reasserting androgyny, as psychologist Linda Olds puts it, is to open up "positive qualities of each sex role for both sexes, with a particular concern for not losing the positive qualities traditionally assigned to women (for example, compassion, less competitiveness), but allowing men to assume these characteristics too" (64). In the area of collaboration, men have much to gain from adopting androgynous behavior. However, as we have seen, resistance may be so strong, particularly for the masculine-typed collaborator that all social sources of that resistance must be understood.

In her early work on gender role behavior, Sandra Bem concluded that sex-typed males and females complete tasks well that call for behavior "congruent with their self-definition," but "androgynous subjects would do well regardless of the sex role stereotype of the particular behavior in question" ("Sex Role Adaptability" 635). (Bem specified that androgynous individuals possessed a high degree of both masculine and feminine traits as opposed to "undifferentiated" individuals who measured low on both the masculinity and femininity scale.) However, as we have seen, male collaborators may resist learning the interpersonal strategies that affect group maintenance, because the "feminine" is not only threatening to masculinity but also undervalued within society. As Olds states, "Since the dominant value system in the United States extols the masculine traits in its citizens, it is perhaps not surprising that deviation from the norm in the masculine direction would be more tolerated than deviation in the feminine direction" (9). The challenge of androgyny really lies in disassociating collaborative strategies from gender identity.

If the best solution seems to be freeing collaborative strengths from gender labels, we must understand why gender stereotyping is preserved within the *adult* world. We must add to our understanding of how boys and girls find identity within the family three more features of gender typing in adulthood: we must understand within the individual the urge to *project*, within the classroom and workplace the image of *scientific objectivity*, and within our culture as a whole the *power of the patriarchy*.

Projection

According to Olds, projection is a "self-defensive process in which one attributes to other persons or to the environment those characteristics in oneself which one is unable to own or accept" (15–16). In striving for self-identity and self-understanding, humans tend to see themselves in terms of *self* and *other*. What the self does not have, the other must. Or what the self does have, but is unacceptable or dangerous to reveal and therefore must be denied, is assigned to the other.

In a society that undervalues the "feminine," individual men would deny, hide, or project their "feminine" traits onto women. "Dichotomous thinking" or polarization, according to Olds, "can be seen to foster the psychological process of projection by reinforcing the tendency to understand oneself in terms of polar opposites, where one end of the polarity is affirmed as typical of oneself and the other end is disowned. It is these disowned, undeveloped dimensions which are most likely to be projected onto others, either in hate or love" (15–16). If androgynous behavior were the standard, rather than masculine behavior, projection of disowned traits upon the other sex would instead be lessened. Group maintenance and nurturing would be considered traits of the androgynous collaborator, as would be assertion of opinion and rationality. Thus all collaborators might be convinced that they could maintain self-identity and still bond with group members.

The Myth of Scientific Objectivity

Often reinforcing projection within the individual is the myth of scientific objectivity. While many composition theorists and instructors recognize that knowledge is communal and social, a result of agreement among subjective individuals, the myth of scientific objectivity promotes gender stereotyping within the classroom and workplace. This myth, associated with scientific positivism, proposes that truth can be discovered through the experimental or scientific method if the individual is free from cultural bias. Although Thomas Kuhn and other philosophers of science have asserted that scientific "discoveries" reflect cultural values, from which the individual is never free, the cultural myth of scientific objectivism still contributes to polarization and sex-typed behavior.

As Ruth Bleier states, "Science is an integral part, expression, and product of a culture's complex set of ideologies, and it has ideological commitments to certain social beliefs, values, and goals. These commitments are, on the one hand, a source of its great strength and value, and, on the other, the source of its oppressive power" (57). The image that some hold of science dismisses the impact of community on scientific knowledge. Building on the work of Kuhn and other philosophers of science, feminists such as Bleier recognize that science is "a set of social practices engaging individuals who are specifically located within cultural categories, each person having a history, beliefs, and a world view" (63). Moreover, this description of communal science somewhat matches Bruffee's description of learning as collaborative, and texts as "constructs generated by communities of like-minded peers" (SC 774).

However, many who hold science in esteem or are in positions of power in the classroom and workplace still perpetuate the myth of objectivity. And as Bleier and Evelyn Fox Keller assert, those perpetuating the myth often organize the world in binary oppositions, nature/culture, female/male, emotional/rational. Thus for many, science, that discipline so powerful in academic and industrial circles, is strongly linked with masculinity. Despite the fact that scientists themselves collaborate and must initiate and maintain relationships with their peers, much of the world views science as objective, rational, logical, and therefore masculine.

Moreover, if science, according to the myth, is logical, objective, and masculine, its subject, nature, is subjective, emotional, and feminine. Keller speculates that capitalism contributes to this view of science. The scientific revolution

> ...did both respond to and provide crucial support for the polarization of gender required by industrial capitalism. In sympathy with, and even in response to, the growing division between male and female, public and private, work and home, modern science opted for an even greater polarization of mind and nature, reason and feeling, objective and subjective; in parallel with the gradual desexualization of women, it offered a deanimated, desanctified, and increasingly mechanized conception of nature. (63–64)

If Keller is correct, our economic systems, the values reflected within business and industry in those settings for collaborative writing, are organized in a way that promotes traditional "masculine" traits. One solution, Keller believes, is a recognition of dynamic objectivity to displace mythical static objectivity. If objectivity, says Keller, is the "pursuit of a maximally reliable understanding of the world around oneself," then dynamic objectivity "actively draws on the commonality between mind and nature as a resource for understanding," "grants to the world around us its independent integrity," and makes use of subjective experience and "our connection with that world" (116). Rather than separate the subject from object as in static objectivity, dynamic objectivity promotes an androgynous scientific approach. Subject/object, mind/nature, logic/feeling are equally valid and valued. If that most powerful discipline, science, can be seen as subjective as well as objective, "feminine" as well as "masculine," then androgynous behavior might be recognized in other areas of collaboration.

The Power of the Patriarchy

Finally, in attempting to encourage androgyny within collaboration, one must not only confront polarization within self-identity and the myth of scientific objectivity within academic and industrial work, but also the very power of the patriarchy within our culture. To value what has been labeled a "feminine" ability to relate, men must relinquish what appears to be power and control.

The patriarchy, according to Flax, "has a material base in men's control of women's labor and reproductive power and a psychological base as a defense against the infantile mother and men's fear of women" (188, fn 5). The patriarchy is that system "in which men as a group oppress women as a group," says Flax (188, fn 5). Gender, therefore, is not neutral, and to recognize gender is to acknowledge that "men and women are not valued equally, that, in fact, men are socially more esteemed than women" (Flax 173). Those who promote androgyny must realize that women who enter the public world and adopt "masculine" traits to seek success might feel this transformation inappropriate to their gender. However, men who adopt "feminine" traits are not only shattering their gender identity but also associating with the powerless of society. Androgyny then not only disrupts gender identity but also threatens those who have any vested interest in conventional attitudes about gender.

As noted before, men often just don't see any benefits in becoming more "feminine." Young boys taunt their more "feminine" peers, the military frequently degrades the male recruit by labeling him "feminine," and adult men, according to Cook, may "perceive changes in sex roles as promising only reverse discrimination and increased competition, more domestic responsibilities, heightened sexual demands, and uncertainties about previously predictable etiquette" (174). It is extremely difficult, then, to convince men of the advantages of being expressive and nurturing—particularly within that arena of competition, hierarchy, and masculinity, the workplace.

Moreover, Lykes finds those without power in a community tend to have strong group associations, regardless of whether they are women, people of color, or working class people; they may "experience group solidarity or some sense of the 'giveness' of 'being-in-relation,' for their survival as a group may seem possible only in relationship" (364). Those without power would more readily see self as "social individuality," while the powerful experience "autonomous individuality," reinforcing in males psychological preference for separation (364).

Since society so rewards traditional masculinity, some scholars warn that until cultural values and the power structure change, androgynous behavior may instead threaten satisfaction and happiness. Empirical studies of self-esteem have generally followed one of three models, according to Whitley: the traditional congruence model that proposes that psychological well-being is "fostered only when one's sex role orientation is congruent with one's gender"; the androgyny model that proposes that "well-being is maximized when one's sex role orientation incorporates a high degree of both masculinity and femininity"; and the masculinity model that proposes that "well-being is a function of the extent to which one has a masculine sex role orientation" (765).

Some studies, such as those conducted by psychologist Jones and his colleagues, find that masculine-identified, not androgynous, males *and* females were most flexible, adaptive, and competent. However, Jones and his associates admit, "In a society that prefers the former to the latter, it becomes reasonable to conclude that individuals high in agentic tendencies [assertiveness; decisiveness; intellectuality versus nurturance; responsiveness; and emotionality] will not only be more successful within the context of such a society's values, but such persons will be more confident due to a history of differential application of social rewards" (311). In our present culture, traditional masculinity is not only accepted but rewarded. Thus, psychologists such as Taylor and Hall warn that promoting androgyny within a masculine-biased power structure might foster "a kind of false consciousness that problems entailed in current sex-role definitions have psychological rather than social structural solutions" (359). Until social values change, promoting changes in the family structure and psychological gender identity of boys and girls will have little impact and might cause dissonance.

Finally, historian Barbara Ehrenreich offers a more optimistic view about changing these social values as she traces over four decades the emergence of and the rebellion against the traditional breadwinner model of male maturity, the married man with the steady job. Ehrenreich identifies such social changes as the "ethnicization" of homosexual men, or homosexuality as a specific condition rather than an "inherent possibility" in all men, as freeing men from traditional gender roles, so that "straight men were free to 'soften' themselves indefinitely without losing their status as heterosexuals" (128, 130). Ehrenreich believes that changes in cultural gender image, initiated by everything from the media to the medical community, can free or restrict men to nurture and bond.

Despite all these social barriers, to add to psychological and familial forces, some psychologists and sociologists (as well as communication theorists such as Bem) have found what they consider androgynous men. Given the obstacles with the parenting and family structure and the strength of the patriarchy, how and why have these male subjects achieved androgyny? How have these men overcome their fear of femininity and found means of achieving closeness and bonding?

The Androgynous Male

Singer proposes that everyone is already androgynous, that we need "only to let ourselves be ourselves" (273). Others, of course, propose that it is more difficult than that; achieving androgyny, according to Olds, "does indeed appear to be a developmental, gradual process that is grounded in life history, critical incidents, and significant personality patterns and preferences" (80). What are some of those incidents and patterns?

Olds finds that androgynous men describe their mothers as "strong, bright, and independent," and that they were closer to their mothers than to their fathers during childhood (82). Also during childhood, androgynous men were "quiet, unassertive, and introspective" in contrast to masculine-identified men (84). Androgynous men report times when they wondered what it would be like to be the other sex; during childhood and adolescence they preferred academic achievement to athletics and were dissatisfied with the lack of closeness between men; they had positive contacts with their mothers and had female friends and during adulthood envied women's ability to expres their emotions (86, 89, 92, 71). These men appear to have allowed traditional feminine traits to emerge.

More important to any study of collaboration, however, in Olds's conclusion that "the development toward androgyny appears to be facilitated by work environments which provide opportunities for collaboration and exposure to competent women peers and models of equal status" (104). What women appear to bring to the workplace is a new mode of collaborative or cooperative leadership, which appears to be both a strength of traditional femaleness and an invitation to men to become androgynous (Baird and Bradley 109; Olds 252). Any increase in the number of women in the workplace provides more potential models for collaboration, and certainly addresses the warnings of psychologists such as Taylor and Hall that changes in psychological gender image must be accompanied or even preceded by changes in the social structure.

The Androgynous Female

The essential invitation to androgyny that women can extend to men comes from a demonstration that nurturing is compatible with self-growth in the family, classroom, and workplace. This notion was expressed in the 1970s by Jean Baker Miller and Jane Flax, and most recently by philosopher and women's studies scholar Sara Ruddick and psychologists Toni Bernay, Judith Jordan, and Janet Surrey.

Bernay calls for a "reconstruction of femininity" that "encompasses both aggressive and nurturant psychic and emotional trends as legitimate and valued dimensions of feminine identity" (75); to do otherwise is to deprive women of all aspects of self and social roles. Jordan and Surrey's "new model" involves an "oscillating self-structure" in which women can "move from one perspective to another as the needs of a relational situation arise" (92). This model does not involve a breaking down of relational ties to promote autonomy, according to Jordan and

Surrey, but instead a "dynamic process of growth," in which each person in a relationship is "challenged to maintain connection and to foster, allow, and adapt to the growth of the other" (96). Ideally, females can initiate and promote group maintenance while maintaining autonomy and self-growth.

Ruddick's work on maternal thinking is perhaps the most optimistic of the recent work. Ruddick bases her work on a practicalist view — that thinking derives from the activities in which humans engage. She proposes that there is a system of maternal thinking, much as there is scientific thinking, managerial thinking, and so on, in which mothers set goals and strategies as they engage in preservation, fostering of growth, and training of their children (13–14). In addition, Ruddick proposes that maternal thinking promotes nonviolent peacekeeping (or renunciation of violence, resistance to the violence of others, responsible reconciliation by naming "crimes" and those responsible, and peace-keeping or finding ways to avoid battles) (161). While it would be tempting to say that if women could be the ultimate peacemakers within society they surely could demonstrate well how to collaborate, Ruddick's book is so utopian that for the moment it serves only as another example of how women's patterns of thinking and responding are legitimate and valuable.

The Androgynous Collaborator

Collaborators must enter into relationships with others and maintain those relationships in such a way that interpersonal conflict does not disrupt the thinking and writing process. The studies reviewed in this essay demonstrate that masculine-typed collaborators may find these group maintenance strategies difficult and even threatening. Collaborators may best accept interpersonal strategies if these strategies are disassociated from gender role. Scholars and instructors need to reinforce the notion that autonomy is compatible with nurturance, that individuality can be maintained within relationships.

Given an understanding of the psychological and social forces for and against gender-typing, how do we promote androgynous behavior during classroom and workplace collaboration? Strategies termed "androgynous" or "feminine" may meet with immediate resistance.

Self-reflective exercises, particularly journal and log keeping, encourage collaborators to externalize and assess attitudes and behaviors among collaborators. The very act of writing about collaboration is one immediate way to reflect upon and possibly change attitude and behavior. Janet Emig asserts that writing is a better form of learning than talking (124), and Toby Fulwiler considers the journal the "natural format for self-examination" (25). Others, using Fulwiler's method, document that even in math and science courses, journal keeping allows students to express and resolve frustrations, to reach insight not only into subject matter but also into their own feelings and sense of self (see BeMiller 362 and Meese 345).

Technical and business communication scholars have suggested that students and technical writers keep journals or logs during collaboration. They encourage students to express feelings within the journals (Morgan et al. 25–6) and conclude that journal keeping helps "the individual student develop interpersonal and group communication skills by enforcing contemplation of the team experience," especially since the instructor's written responses in the journal encourage this self-examination (Goldstein and Malone 114). The instructor usually reads student journals periodically and upon request, such as when a group or group member has difficulty during the collaborative process. Instructor comments are kept confidential, which allows the instructor to act as "coach," rather than evaluator. Initial journal entries, instructor comments in these entries, and student responses to instructor comments create a dialogue. If journals receive credit or a grade, students' efforts and thoroughness should be assessed, and instructors should find means other than the journal to have students formally evaluate their group members. As yet, those promoting journal keeping during collaboration recommend only an initial form or mode of response. Better yet for the development of androgynous strategies would be for collaborators to progress through a series of specific responses within their journals. Also these responses need not even mention androgyny or feminine/masculine but instead be provoked by the reader or instructor using non-gender-linked terms. The responses can also be supported by activities that a whole class or department can engage in (see suggestions for community wide exercises in Lay 13–26).

The following journal entries were taken from my professional writing class that consisted of 33 students, 21 of whom were male, who worked in 8 collaborative groups of from 3 to 5 students for a 14-week semester. The entries demonstrate how instructors or managers could help collaborators begin to accept androgynous collaborative strategies. Much like Goldstein and Malone as well as Morgan and her colleagues, I suggest to the students that they address in their journals not what happened in each group meeting, but why it happened. For example, they should focus on how and why a particular decision was reached, how a conflict was resolved, what caused them to work well together or not so well on any portion of the project, what skills productive team members seemed to have, and finally, what they, as collaborators, could do to enhance the process.

In the beginning of the semester, collaborators should focus on commonalities among group members; I ask them to delay any task completion until they have discovered with whom they are working. Discovering what they have in common, what characteristics and values they might share, allows them to appreciate and even tolerate the differences that inevitably emerge during the collaborative process. Those who are comfortable with self-disclosure find this preliminary period useful, and by the end of the collaborative process, most team members appreciate building a sense of community. As one student related, "I think all the chatting we did at the beginning of our meetings really got everyone going and made the ideas flow a lot easier. All in all, I feel everyone was a good collaborator because we all had a steady flow of ideas, regardless of how many times we got 'shot down.'" This student's teammates achieved a union with each other, and this openness allowed them to express thoughts and weather criticism.

Midway through a collaborative project, collaborators should reflect upon how they might be perceived within their team. These speculations often help them realize what information they have shared and what impressions they might be making, but also what they have hidden. Many students accurately describe how their colleagues see them; for example, one student wrote, "I think that my group members might think I am too grade oriented sometimes. I have to try to make others do their best work," and his team members described him in their journals as "uptight" or "tense." However, feelings that are hidden from the group but at least revealed within the journal can be validated by the very act of writing about them (and often by the instructor's or reader's comments on them). One team member revealed in his journal: "Probably they think that because I am a foreigner, I don't know much about American advertising. They think I'm just book-smart and not very creative. Lots of my input is not taken seriously and after a while, I stop giving it, but I have had lots of experience with American culture." This student came to the decision by the end of the semester that the best collaborator was the one who was really interested in others' opinions, who had a degree of *expressiveness* or "sensitivity to others' responses" (Cook 4).

Also, by speculating about team members' impressions of them, collaborators can realize what roles they try to play, especially those roles that are incongruent with feelings; as one student said, "My feelings were hurt by having only part of the group there when the decision was made to exclude my idea and use Chad's. However, I didn't want my group to see me as a 'sore loser.'" This student's image of himself as tough competitor didn't permit him to express what he was really feeling. By focusing on the difference between roles and feelings, collaborators take the first step toward eliminating this incongruence.

While team members reflect upon their own images, they gain insight by describing a colleague within their journals, concentrating not only on that team member's behavior but also speculating about his or her motivation. To do this, they must listen reflectively to their colleagues. They also begin to take responsibility for helping that colleague overcome any interpersonal traits that interfere with the collaborative process, and so realize they can improve the interpersonal dynamics within the group. For example, one student commented: "Marshall seems more aloof all the time; I am trying to aim more discussion his way to see if he'll participate more." By taking responsibility for team members' needs, collaborators again engage in what Cook labeled *expressiveness* and are now ready to recognize difference among their team members.

In focusing on other team members' behavior and motivation, collaborators also discover that they have a choice of strategies. As one student revealed, "Instead of always trying not to 'step on Chad's toes,' I have decided to give him the subtle signal to 'relax.' This should allow us to reach a mutual agreement on the subject." This flexibility frees collaborators to adopt Jordan and Surrey's *oscillating self-structure*, the ability to move from one perspective to another, depending on the changing needs within the team.

Upon reflecting on the collaborative process itself within their journals, team members learn to balance group maintenance with task completion skills. Most collaborators want every team member to participate fully and on time so that the group project will receive praise, and in the beginning of the semester, students are concerned with who is the group leader. The leader appears to be the one with power; as one student said, "I know I'm perceived by my group as the leader. Often I am the deciding factor in group decisions." However, collaborators learn that instrumentality may push the group to complete the task, but the team relationship should become equally important. A collaborator with the "leader" quoted above concluded, "The word 'group' means helping one another out. The reason Ken is a good collaborator is his ideas are very solid. The bad thing about Ken's collaboration is that he is very impatient with others. He pushes his own ideas too much and doesn't listen to others."

At the very least, students begin to appreciate that avoiding interpersonal conflict enhances the collaborative process. Early in the semester, one student believed that she had to choose between honesty and hurting her team members' feelings: "The most difficult thing about collaborating is when I am afraid of alienating people and thus am not always fully honest." By working to strengthen interpersonal ties, her group was able to allow for open discussion. Her team member expressed the rewards of working in a group that had overcome interpersonal conflict: "We would all throw out ideas for slogans, ads, commercials, plans, and so on, and would either accept or reject these plans on the spot. This, to my amazement, is the sign of an effective group."

Thus, by reflecting on the importance of interpersonal skills within their groups, collaborators begin to see the difference between interpersonal conflict and substantive conflict or conflict over ideas. Traditional masculine strategies not only permit but often urge collaborators to argue over ideas, to objectify and "win out" over their collaborators. Those collaborators who identify strongly with traditional feminine values may resist volatile debate over ideas, particularly if feelings are hurt and relationships threatened. The androgynous collaborator recognizes the difference between interpersonal and substantive conflict; for example, one student commented, "Chad and I have a conflict between personalities, not ideas. To handle it, I have tried to understand and accommodate his way of working in order not to have a bigger conflict." One such potentially disruptive conflict was managed in a group, when a collaborator discovered a strategy that would avoid publicly hurting a team member's feelings but would point out how the team member failed the group: "I can't run the risk of Ken getting mad at the group because his ideas are quite impressive. But I also felt it was important to let him know that I was dissatisfied with his effort. So I went through the project and pointed out the areas that needed improvement; the areas were all those Ken worked on. This way Ken knew we were all dissatisfied but it wasn't done in a way that personally attacked him." Again, the androgynous collaborator distinguishes between productive and nonproductive debate and appreciates different styles and needs of team members.

As they reflect within their journals, students then discover that the collaborative process is complex. Conflict can be either productive or unproductive depending upon whether the conflict is about ideas or over personalities. Strong leadership may disrupt the collaborative process, and listening may be more essential than asserting an opinion. Thus, as students externalize and examine their feelings within their journals, they often discover new interpersonal strategies that free them from previous roles, including gender roles. As one student said, "Many times I write these thoughts in my journal, then solve problems in a way that no one gets hurt. Keeping a journal helps me notice patterns and then monitor situations in our group." The insight and flexibility collaborators achieve in their journals take them beyond gender-typed behavior and values and toward androgynous collaborative strategies.

These sample journal entries represent only one way that allows collaborators to experience androgynous strategies. The main part of this essay presented the psychological and social barriers to androgyny, the debate over whether the promotion of androgyny may reinforce or shatter binary opposition, and the analyses by gender scholars of related areas such as science. However, the pressure to recognize how traditionally feminine behavior and values can enhance the public area, the world of business and industry, is increasingly obvious in our classrooms and journals as well.

Instructors of business and technical communication, such as Tebeaux, propose that there are differences in the way women and men approach professional writing tasks and that studying these can help writers achieve "androgynous language skills" (38–9). Lunsford and Ede urge scholars to investigate further the two modes of collaboration the respondents to their industrial surveys described, the hierarchical and dialogic modes of collaboration (133–36). While Lunsford and Ede resist contrasting these modes and so contributing to binary opposition, they recognize that most respondents who described the dialogic mode, in which the "group effort is seen as an essential part of the production — rather than the recovery — of knowledge and as a means of individual satisfaction within the group" were women (133). Journalist Sally Helgesen interviewed prominent women managers to find a successful management style that includes "appreciation of diversity" and "a concern for the wider needs of the community" (xx). In any conscientious effort to prepare students for future collaborative work assignments, technical and business communication instructors have turned from prescriptive models to heuristic case studies to help students become flexible. Part of that flexibility must be what Jordan and Surrey call "oscillating self-structure," moving from one perspective to another. The androgynous collaborator, freed from gender-typed roles, can best do that.

Works Cited

Allen, Nancy, et al. "What Experienced Collaborators Say About Collaborative Writing." *Journal of Business and Technical Communication* 1.2 (1987): 70–90.

Anderson, Paul V. "What Survey Research Tells Us About Writing at Work." *Writing in Nonacademic Settings.* Ed. Lee Odell and Dixie Goswami. New York: Guilford, 1985. 3–83.

Aries, Elizabeth. "Interpersonal Patterns and Themes of Male, Female, and Mixed Groups." *Small Group Behavior* 7.1 (1976): 7–18.

Baird, John E., Jr. "Sex Differences in Group Communication: A Review of Relevant Research." *Quarterly Journal of Speech* 62 (1979): 179–92.

Baird, John E., Jr., and Patricia Hayes Bradley. "Styles of Management and Communication: A Comparative Study of Men and Women." *Communi-*

cation Monographs 46.2 (1979): 101–11.

Belenky, Mary Field, et al. *Women's Ways of Knowing*. New York: Basic, 1986.

Bem, Sandra. "Sex Role Adaptability: One Consequence of Psychological Androgyny." *Journal of Personality and Social Psychology* 31 (1975): 634–43.

———. "Gender Scheme Theory: A Cognitive Account of Sex Typing." *Psychological Review* 88 (1981): 354–64.

BeMiller, Stephen. "The Mathematics Workbook." *The Journal Book*. Ed. Toby Fulwiler. Portsmouth, NH: Boynton/Cook, 1987. 359–66.

Bernay, Toni. "Reconciling Nurturance and Aggression: A New Feminine Identity." *The Psychology of Today's Woman: New Psychoanalytic Visions*. Ed. Toni Bernay and Dorothy W. Cantor. Cambridge, MA: Harvard UP, 1986.

Bleier, Ruth, "Lab Coat: Robe of Innocence or Klansman's Sheet?" *Feminist Studies/Critical Studies*. Ed. Teresa De Laurentis. Bloomington: Indiana UP, 1986. 55–66.

Bruffee, Kenneth A. "Collaborative Learning and the 'Conversation of Mankind.'" *College English* 46 (1984): 635–52.

———. "Social Construction, Language, and the Authority of Knowledge: A Bibliographical Essay." *College English* 48 (1986): 773–90.

———. "Writing and Reading as Collaborative or Social Acts." *The Writer's Mind: Writing as a Mode of Thinking*. Ed. Janice N. Hays, et al. Urbana: NCTE, 1983. 159–69.

Chodorow, Nancy. *The Reproduction of Mothering: Psychoanalysis and the Sociology of Gender*. Berkeley: U of California P, 1978.

Cook, Ellen Piel. *Psychological Androgyny*. New York: Pergamon Press, 1985.

Cooper, Marilyn. "The Ecology of Writing." *College English* 48 (1986): 364–75.

Doheny-Farina, Stephen. "Writing in an Emerging Organization: An Ethnographic Study." *Written Communication* 3 (1986): 158–85.

Ehrenreich, Barbara. *The Hearts of Men: American Dreams and the Flight from Commitment*. New York: Anchor/Doubleday, 1983.

Emig, Janet. "Writing as a Mode of Learning." *College Composition and Communication* 28 (May 1977): 122–28.

Faigley, Lester, and Thomas Miller. "What We Learn from Writing on the Job." *College English* 44 (1982): 557–69.

Flax, Jane. "The Conflict between Nurturance and Autonomy in Mother-Daughter Relationships and within Feminism." *Feminist Studies* 4 (1978): 171–89.

Fulwiler, Toby. "The Personal Connection: Journal Writing across the Curriculum." *Language Connections: Writing and Reading across the Curricu-*

lum. Ed. Toby Fulwiler and Art Young. Urbana: NCTE, 1982. 15–31.

Gilligan, Carol. *In a Different Voice: Psychological Theory and Women's Development*. Cambridge, MA: Harvard UP, 1982.

Goldstein, Jone Rymer, and Elizabeth L. Malone. "Journals on Interpersonal and Group Communication: Facilitating Technical Project Groups." *Journal of Technical Writing and Communication* 14 (1984): 113–31.

Hammond, Dorothy, and Alta Jablow. "Gilgamesh and the Sundance Kid: The Myth of Male Friendship." *The Making of Masculinities: The New Men's Studies*. Ed. Harry Brod. Boston: Allen and Unwin, 1987. 241–58.

Harragan, Betty Lehan. *Games Mother Never Taught You*. New York: Warner, 1977.

Harris, Daniel A. "Androgyny: The Sexist Myth of Disguise." *Women's Studies* 2 (1974): 171–84.

Heilbrun, Carolyn G. "Further Notes Toward a Recognition of Androgyny." *Women's Studies* 2 (1974): 143–49.

———. *Toward a Recognition of Androgyny*. New York: Norton, 1964.

Helgesen, Sally. *The Female Advantage: Women's Ways of Leadership*. New York: Doubleday, 1990.

Hennig, Margaret, and Anne Jardim. *The Managerial Woman*. New York: Pocket, 1976.

Jones, Warren H., Mary Ellen Q'C. Chernovetz, and Robert O. Hansson. "The Enigma of Androgyny: Differential Implications for Males and Females?" *Journal of Consulting and Clinical Psychology* 46 (1978): 298–313.

Jordan, Judith V., and Janet L. Surrey. "The Self-in-Relation: Empathy and the Mother-Daughter Relationship." *The Psychology of Today's Woman: New Psychoanalytic Visions*. Ed. Toni Bernay and Dorothy W. Cantor, Cambridge, MA: Harvard UP, 1986. 81–104.

Keller, Evelyn Fox. *Reflections on Gender and Science*. New Haven: Yale UP, 1985.

Kuhn, Thomas. *The Structure of Scientific Revolution*. Chicago: U of Chicago P, 1970.

Lay, Mary M. "Interpersonal Conflict in Collaborative Writing: What We Can Learn from Gender Studies." *Journal of Business and Technical Communication* 3.2 (1989): 5–28.

Lunsford, Andrea, and Lisa Ede. *Singular Texts/Plural Authors: Perpectives on Collaborative Writing*. Carbondale: Southern Illinois, UP, 1990.

Lykes, M. Brinton. "Gender and Individualistic vs. Collectivist Bases for Notions about the Self." *Journal of Personality* 53 (1985): 356–83.

Meese, George. "Focused Learning in Chemistry Research: Suzanne's Journal." *The Journal Book*. Ed. Toby Fulwiler. Portsmouth, NH: Boynton/Cook, 1987. 337–47.

Messner, Michael. "The Meaning of Success: The Athletic Experience and the Development of Male Identity." *The Making of Masculinities: The New Men's Studies*. Ed. Harry Brod. Boston: Allen and Unwin, 1987. 193–209.

Miller, Jean Baker. *Toward a New Psychology of Women*. Boston: Beacon, 1976.

Morgan, Meg, et al. "Collaborative Writing in the Classroom." *Bulletin of the Association for Business Communication* 50.3 (1987): 20–26.

Ochberg, Richard L. "The Male Career Code and the Ideology of Role." *The Making of Masculinities: The New Men's Studies*. Ed. Harry Brod. Boston: Allen and Unwin, 1987.

Olds, Linda E. *Fully Human: How Everyone Can Integrate the Benefits of Masculine and Feminine Sex Roles*. Englewood Cliffs: Prentice-Hall, 1981.

Ruddick, Sara. *Maternal Thinking: Toward a Politics of Peace*. Boston: Beacon, 1989.

Secor, Cynthia. "The Androgyny Papers." *Women's Studies* 2 (1974): 139–41.

Sherrod, Drury. "The Bonds of Men: Problems and Possibilities in Close Male Relationships." *The Making of Masculinities: The New Men's Studies*. Ed. Harry Brod. Boston: Allen and Unwin, 1987.

Singer, June. *Androgyny: Toward a New Theory of Sexuality*. Garden City, NY: Anchor, 1977.

Spence, Janet T., and Robert L. Helmrich. *Masculinity and Feminity: Their Psychological Dimensions, Correlates, and Antecedents*. Austin: U of Texas P, 1978.

Taylor, Marylee E., and Judith A. Hall. "Psychological Androgyny: Theories, Methods, and Conclusions." *Psychological Bulletin* 92 (1982): 347–66.

Tebeaux, Elizabeth. "Toward an Understanding of Gender Differences in Written Business Communication: A Suggested Perspective for Future Research." *Journal of Business and Technical Communication* 4.1 (1990): 23–43.

Whitley, Bernard E., Jr. "Sex Role Orientation and Self-Esteem: A Critical Meta-Analytic Review." *Journal of Personality and Social Psychology* 44 (1983): 765–78.

6

The Sociological Imagination and the Ethics of Collaboration

John Schilb

The controversy over Paul de Man's "collaborationist" war-time journalism serves to remind us that "collaboration" may occur in various ethical contexts, which writing students ought to examine. More precisely, when we have our students "collaborate" with one another in our classrooms, and prepare them to "collaborate" in their workplaces, we should encourage them to study how their activities connect to struggles for freedom in the larger world. A useful guide for such a pedagogy is C. Wright Mills's 1959 book *The Sociological Imagination*, which calls for scholars to extend themselves beyond the "situations" of various "milieux" and analyze larger social structures. Students who face ethical conflicts with their superiors in the workplace should take these conflicts as an opportunity for engaging in the kind of inquiry Mills advocates.

Over the last several years, composition specialists have explored the practices and benefits of "collaboration." Recently, literary theorists have also focused upon the word. Yet they have done so in a radically different context: the discovery of "collaboration" in the wartime journalism of the late Paul de Man, America's leading exponent of deconstruction. As it turns out, de Man not only worked for Nazi-controlled newspapers in his native Belgium, but also wrote columns endorsing the invaders and affirming their anti-Semitism. Consider the by now notorious statement he made in his March 4, 1941, *Le Soir* article "The Jews in Contemporary Literature": "one sees that a solution to the Jewish question that would aim at the creation of a Jewish colony isolated from Europe would not entail, for the literary life of the West, deplorable consequences. The latter would lose, in all, a few personalities of mediocre value and would continue, as in the past, to develop according to its great evolutive laws" (quoted in Derrida 142).

Did Paul de Man fully support the Nazis? Should he have revealed this episode in his history later on? What, if anything, does it imply about his later theory? These questions have rocked literary circles, leading the University of Nebraska Press to publish the unearthed documents and another volume of responses to them. The thirty-seven essays comprising the latter take various positions, but almost all use the term "collaboration" or forms of it to label de Man's conduct.[1]

The Two Meanings of "Collaboration"

We may feel these references to "collaboration" in the essays about de Man have nothing to do with our own calls for it. When we teach students to "collaborate," we hardly urge them to collude with oppressive regimes. Indeed, the *American Heritage Dictionary* defines "collaborate" in two very different ways: "1. To work together, especially in a joint intellectual effort. 2. To cooperate treasonably, as with an enemy occupying one's country." Given its alternately bright and ominous connotations, the term seems to exemplify what Freud had in mind when he spoke of "the antithetical meaning of primal words" (353). Naturally, we credit our teaching practices with the first meaning.

The second, however, could function in our classes as a heuristic. Indeed, students need to consider this second meaning if they are truly to address the moral implications of their own "collaborative" acts. I do not claim that "collaboration" always yields dire consequences. When Donald Stewart chides its advocates for ignoring the wartime history of the term ("Collaborative" 66), he unfairly implies that "collaboration" inevitably proves nefarious, not analyzing how its ethical nature may shift with context. I do feel, however, that writing students should examine the various ethical contexts in which "collaboration" occurs. In particular, they should ponder how their own "collaborations" might be perceived beyond their immediate setting. Note the case of Paul de Man again. He "collaborated" with fellow staff members at *Le Soir* in the sense of "working together" with them, but he also "collaborated" with the Nazis by not defending other Belgians they victimized. I propose that we have our own students consider how their "collaborations" might be seen by others as being distant from the darker sense of the word or as sliding toward it. More precisely, when we have our students "collaborate" with one another in our classrooms, and prepare them to "collaborate" in their workplaces, we should encourage them to study how their activities connect to struggles for freedom in the larger world.

Problems with Composition's Present
Approach to Collaboration

I take the occasion here to propose this kind of writing course because I feel we have yet to ponder much what the ethics of "collaboration" in our sense might be. We often presume it will admirably challenge classroom arrangements that privilege the teacher's authority and the misleading image of the isolated writer. Indeed, it has this potential. We have just started, though, to examine the range of ways that collaboration might affect students' moral development. For example, only at the end of his classic 1984 article "Collaborative Learning and the 'Conversation of Mankind'" does Kenneth Bruffee even allude to "the many possible negative effects of peer group influence: conformity, anti-intellectualism, intimidation, and leveling-down of quality" (652).

Recent articles by Greg Myers, John Trimbur, Donald Stewart, David Smit, and Bill Karis have begun to redress this imbalance, noting above all how consensus may amount to compliance with unjust power. Moreover, in their new book *Singular Texts/Plural Authors: Perspectives on Collaborative Writing*, Andrea Lunsford and Lisa Ede ruefully observe that most of the professional "collaborators" they interviewed "seemed generally unconcerned with questions of power and ideology" (137). Concerned themselves with these issues, Lunsford and Ede also criticize the "hierarchical mode" of collaboration they found in professional workplaces, a style in which "the realities of multiple voices and shifting *author*ity are seen as difficulties to be overcome or resolved" (133). They contrast this with a "dialogic" mode in which the participants "generally value the creative tension inherent in multivoiced and multivalent ventures" (133). Given that "collaboration" in the professional workplace has often depended upon the homogeneity of white males in particular, Lunsford and Ede ask, "What...will result when such a context changes, when the professional work scene is populated much more by women and people of color?" (138). The kind of writing course I propose would follow Lunsford and Ede in examining how various modes and contexts of "collaboration" impinge upon women, people of color, and other historically victimized groups—not only when they join a workplace, but also when they experience its public effects.

In essence, I am arguing for a *sociological* approach to collaboration that many writing teachers have yet to adopt. Admittedly, composition specialists have studied for several years now "the social construction of knowledge," to use a familiar phrase. But most of this work has accepted the academy and the workplace as "discourse communities" into which students need to be "initiated," instead of radically scrutinizing the effects of their practices and raising the possibility of altering at least some.[2] Note how Bruffee's influential 1986 bibliographic essay on "social construction" downplays social *criticism*, altogether omitting feminists, Marxists, Foucauldians, Afro-American theorists, and Third World theorists who have dramatically challenged the academy and other institutions. In fact, when he later elaborated his arguments by declaring himself one of the "middle-of-the-road or liberal social constructionists" and by scorning "radical left-wing cognitivists" who "turn to 'action' and 'struggle' to force change in people's 'interests'" ("Kenneth Bruffee Responds" 714), Bruffee suggested that his version of "social construction" seeks to *displace* serious questioning of the social order. Particular case studies of "collaboration" emphasize how it helps students contribute to already entrenched disciplines, not raising the prospect of shaking them. When researchers of "collaboration" move outside the academy, they usually stick to firms and bureaucracies very much at home in a late capitalist world. Overall, "social construction" has taken on a decidedly reformist air, in line with the traditional "service" ethos of composition teaching.

I hasten to add that the concept of "social construction" is not in itself a reactionary ploy. It does constitute a significant advance over the unduly individualistic models of the composing process that predominated in the seventies. Its advocates sincerely want to help students navigate the world. Moreover, the term *can* spur us to undertake wide-ranging analyses of the networks in which acts of collaboration take place and have their effects. If we are to grasp the ethics of collaboration, however, we need to recognize that our traditional "service" ethos still curtails our intellectual range, whatever new successes and vocabularies now adorn it. If, to use the title of Karen Burke LeFevre's book, we now consider "invention as a social act," we need to consider all the issues that are *engendered*, not resolved, when we invent "the social" as a rubric for scholarship and teaching. In particular, we should resist equating "the social" with simply demarcated visions of the academic and professional "discourse communities" that immediately surround us.[3] Instead, we should struggle to locate them in larger constellations of power. While certainly this kind of analysis is difficult and debate-ridden, we risk merely validating business as usual if we avoid it.

Consider how a recent article on collaboration swerves from exploring issues posed by the concept of "the social" and thereby winds up embracing the disciplines. In "Writing and Collaboration," James Reither and Douglas Vipond begin by contending that "the case for writing's social dimensions no longer requires arguing — it can be assumed" (855). Nevertheless, they do not go on to elaborate what "the social" might entail. Instead, they explicitly dodge this task, declaring "the term's ambiguity is perhaps unresolvable" and it "implicates too little by way of concrete activity" (856). Yet it is precisely by keeping the term "social" ambiguous and by not adjudicating various theories of it that writing specialists have felt free to concentrate upon certain "discourse communities" and marginalize others. Deeming social analysis too challenging is what has traditionally encouraged them merely to reform the *technē* of the classroom.

Furthermore, Reither and Vipond do cultivate a particular vision of "the social" as they proceed with their substitute focus: "Much academic writing is certainly 'bad,' probably because it functions merely to demonstrate competence. Still, it manages well enough to get done the legitimate business of academics, which is to construct and advance knowledge claims in scholarly venues. And, of course, academic writing is the discourse form that counts in academia, for teachers and students alike" (856). Here the authors simply "assume" that academics have a "legitimate business," that they mainly produce knowledge, and that what "counts" for them is a civic good. This position does "require arguing," however, since other theorists have set forth quite different perspectives. Pierre Bourdieu and Jean-Claude Passeron, for example, have emphasized how schools mainly function to reproduce social class, by restricting to children of the upper strata information and experience that aid cultural mobility. Michel Foucault has stressed how the disciplinary practices of the human sciences control people more than they liberate them by emphasizing values, methods of inquiry, and self-conceptions that encourage tacit comformity to the social order. Edward Said has shown how academic subjects like "Orientalism" have reinforced colonial systems by failing to treat native "Others" as genuinely human participants in the study and advancement of their lives. And of course, scholars in women's and minority studies have repeatedly critiqued the discourses that "count" for various fields. Reither and Vipond are especially misleading when they identify "academic writing" as a single "discourse form." By evoking "academic writing" as textual artifact, they slight the institutional processes involved in defining its nature and "legitimacy." By implying that it has a uniform identity, they minimize debates launched by feminist, minority, and other scholars over what its genres, protocols, and topics should be. Ultimately, "academic writing" might be worth defending; however, we must link collaboration with more explicit anatomies of "the social" if we are truly to assess the principles, practices, and structures of our schools.

Mills's Sociological Imagination and A Pedagogy for Collaboration

To elaborate the questions about collaboration I think writing courses should raise, I will focus upon a particular teaching scenario and apply to it ideas that C. Wright Mills articulates in his 1959 book *The Sociological Imagination*. Invoking a text from thirty years ago might

seem odd in a volume devoted to "*new* visions of collaborative writing."
Yet Mills's effort to define "the sociological imagination" seems relevant
to a field now struggling to understand how its objects of study are
"socially constructed." In fact, Mills believed his discipline was insuf-
ficiently analyzing the structure of "the social" because it was failing to
steer a middle course between a Scylla and Charybdis that loom in
composition studies today: abstract "Grand Theory" and narrow empirical research. He also saw the growing ability of managerial elites to
ensure that intellectual work supports them, thus anticipating pressures
that writing teachers and their students now face. Worried in general
that his was "a time of uneasiness and indifference" (11) because
Americans failed to understand how their lives related to larger con-
figurations of power, Mills identified a political apathy that many
writing teachers find in their classes today, and pointed toward the sort
of inquiry that could mitigate it.

The teaching scenario I will draw upon as I relate Mills's ideas to
collaboration appears in LeFevre's book. Generally, the book endorses
collaboration and other activities that acknowledge the social nature of
composing. The specific passage that follows does not deal with collaboration per se, but certainly points to sociological questions and ethical
quandaries it can pose. Although I will suggest that LeFevre treats
such matters superficially, I aim not to assess a particular scholar but to
develop a pedagogy that theorists of collaborative writing in general
have yet to foster:

> In recent years, the increase in older adults returning to college
> campuses has no doubt helped to make us less naive about invention.
> These students' work experiences give rise to writing problems that
> cannot be solved by suggestions that they need only express what is
> hidden deep within, or that they are free to include in their writing
> any ideas or information they may have. It would be naive to expect a
> student who writes for a hospital newsletter to add details about, say,
> the problems of the hospital's current system of storing x-rays, when
> her article must be approved by a public relations director who does
> not want the existing system to appear too inefficient even though it is
> about to be replaced. Or consider the case of an engineering student
> who tells a writing tutor that his advisor will not allow him to draw
> certain conclusions in his thesis because the agency sponsoring the
> research would discover that the work was essentially completed and
> would cut off funding. It would be beside the point for the tutor to
> suggest that this student try free writing or tagmemics to come up
> with new material for his conclusion. A writing teacher who critiques
> a technical writer's article about innovations in computer documen-
> tation may sense that specific details or quotations from company
> authorities would improve it. But if the company employing the
> writer must approve the article before she can publish it, and if their

policy is never to reveal specifics, she will not solve this problem by looking within and inventing as she pleases. Diplomacy is the rudder of invention.

Given such situations, what is a writing teacher or tutor to do? That is difficult to say. We can help writers to articulate their concerns and perceptions of the constraints they face. We can talk about ways they might test the accuracy of their perceptions, or work around their constraints, or discuss problems with those responsible for creating and enforcing certain rules and policies. The writers and their supervisors may or may not try to change the status quo. What we cannot do is act as if these problems do not exist, as if people's jobs are not at stake, as if invention means asking the journalist's five W's and an H without taking into account the very real implications that these choices have for writers in their social contexts. (133–34)

In reviewing LeFevre's book, Donald Stewart criticizes her reference to the engineer's plight, discerning "an implied moral relativism" symptomatic of the whole volume (109). To me, "relativism" does not seem the most appropriate charge here, given that LeFevre clearly believes the engineer faces a moral difficulty. I think Stewart rightly intuits, though, a certain flatness in her discussion of ethics. Perhaps unintentionally, LeFevre winds up broaching the subject only to keep it within strict bounds. For one thing, she unduly limits here the range of coaching models that writing teachers can adopt: the only alternative she presents to the teacher who counsels "diplomacy" is an instructor bent upon reciting heuristic formulas rather than addressing students' actual feelings. More important, she implicitly restricts the notion of "social contexts" to the students' immediate job sites, focusing upon what Mills called "milieux" instead of looking to the overall structures of power that embed these milieux. That is, she treats the "situations" she cites merely as localized "writing problems" that may or may not be "solved," rather than as opportunities for students to analyze how writing in the workplace can bear upon a variety of broader public concerns. Indeed, Mills associates a focus upon "situations" with what he calls "liberal practicality": "an occupational incapacity to rise above a series of 'cases'" and "construct the whole" (88). His criticism serves to remind writing specialists that study of "the rhetorical situation" should encompass larger societal frameworks.

Especially when geared to career preparation, a course in collaborative writing should insistently bring up incidents like those LeFevre cites so that students will examine the various contexts and implications of their group behavior. One possibility is for them to re-create composing episodes that occurred during events of pronounced social consequence. Years ago, for example, I had a Technical Writing class produce the kinds of memoranda, reports, policy statements, and correspondence that circulated during the Three Mile Island crisis, encouraging them to "re-enact" and probe the ethical decisions made during it. As LeFevre's passage indicates, students nowadays can probably analyze a host of less apocalyptic dilemmas in their own jobs. The point, however, would be not to remain at the local level of such conflicts, but to use them as a catalyst for broader social inquiry. In Mills's words, the course would exploit these conflicts as occasions for studying "the intersections of biography and history within society" (7), "the ways in which personal troubles are connected with public issues" (185). Exigencies that students face in working for hospitals, research institutes, and computer companies would therefore be tied to "substantive problems" (75) faced by numerous people in the contemporary world.

Far from abandoning efforts to delineate "the social," Mills proposed a set of questions about it that students could refer to as they widen the context for their collaborative acts:

> (1) What is the structure of this particular society as a whole? What are its essential components, and how are they related to one another? How does it differ from other varieties of social order? Within it, what is the meaning of any particular feature for its continuance and for its change?
>
> (2) Where does this society stand in human history? What are the mechanics by which it is changing? What is its place within and its meaning for the development of humanity as a whole? How does any particular feature we are examining affect, and how is it affected by, the historical period in which it moves? And this period—what are its essential features? How does it differ from other periods? What are its characteristic ways of history-making?
>
> (3) What varieties of men and women now prevail in this society and in this period? And what varieties are coming to prevail? In what ways are they selected and formed, liberated and repressed, made sensitive and blunted? What kinds of "human nature" are revealed in the conduct and character we observe in this society in this period? And what is the meaning for "human nature" of each and every feature of the society we are examining? (6–7)

Writing teachers may deem these issues too formidable for their students to handle. They could take comfort, though, from Mills's belief that social problems ultimately require interdisciplinary perspectives, and that research into them "is not best done as the sole specialty of one person" (121). In other words, the course might emphasize collaborative approaches not only to writing but also to the analysis of its various social contexts. Faculty in other disciplines might be invited to join this inquiry, and the students themselves could work as partners in it. More important, the course need not demand of students that they definitively answer all of Mills's questions. He himself ultimately associated "the sociological imagination" not with command of particular data but with certain "qualities of mind" (21). I submit that it *is* necessary for them to see these issues as worth grappling with, in their classroom talk and in at least some of their writing projects, even as they more directly confront "situations" on the job.

Although I will not try to address Mills's questions exhaustively here, let me suggest considerations that might emerge for the particular students LeFevre mentions. The writer for the hospital newsletter might ponder Mills's observation that "It is when new centers of power, not yet legitimated, not able to cloak themselves in established symbols of authority, arise, that there is a need for new ideologies of justification" (97). Of course, in one sense the institution of the hospital is hardly new. But over the last several years, many have taken on a new administrative scope and complexity. Also, many find themselves engaged in new struggles for "power," "authority," and "justification," given the overall economy and politics of health care in America. When poor communities need hospitals but cannot make them profitable, when richer communities spawn a competitive market of health care options, when insurance companies and Medicare seek greater control over hospital expenses, public relations assumes a much greater importance for the hospital as a managerial enterprise. While additional approaches to her problem are possible, I suggest encouraging the student to analyze and report to the class on this larger state of affairs behind her supervisor's concern. She would inquire into the forces, agents, and institutional relationships driving "those responsible for creating and enforcing certain rules and policies." I would especially urge her to think about whose interests might ultimately be served, and whose interests might ultimately be threatened, when she collaborates with her supervisor and the hospital as an institution. I would press her as well to consider what about the American health care system needs to be transformed so that particular hospitals practice candor and uphold other civic goods like equal access to medical technology. Expanding her notion of "the status quo," such inquiry would follow Mills's recommendation that social scientists "study the structural limits of human decision in an attempt to find points of effective intervention, in order to know what can and what must be structurally changed if the role of explicit decision in human history-making is to be enlarged" (174).

The engineering student could use his painful experience to develop a related insight of Mills: that scholars themselves increasingly risk being compromised by their dependence upon funding agencies. More specifically, he could be encouraged to research general patterns of funding in his field, identifying the kinds of projects they support, the kinds they marginalize, and the ultimate beneficiaries of both.[4] Similarly, the student writing about computer documentation could explore how this technology does get circulated and what groups suffer lack of access to it.

I have suggested that Mills presciently identified trends that the sociological imagination must confront today. Indeed, he even used the currently popular word "post-modern" (166) when he described the emerging world order, associating this term with the increasing centralization of power in bureaucratic organizations. A writing teacher drawing upon Mills's ideas, though, might want to supplement them with present theories of "postmodernism." With respect to computers, for example — a development whose scale Mills could not have fore-seen — David Harvey in *The Condition of Postmodernity* and Jean-François Lyotard in *The Postmodern Condition* point out how electronic modes of transmitting and storing information enable multinational firms to consolidate their power even more. Along with Gayatri Spivak and Fredric Jameson, Harvey has also generally sketched out the present phase of capitalism better than Mills could have, evoking a global economic context that students engaged in professional collab-oration should ponder. Mills himself observed, "It is perhaps one defining characteristic of our period that it is one in which for the first time the varieties of social worlds it contains are in serious, rapid, and obvious interplay" (150). These three contemporary theorists more specifically observe that multinationals have remained strong partly because their harshest effects now transpire far away from the American academy, as well as from the service and information industries currently predominating here — which include public relations, engineering, and computer firms along with others that may hire our students as writers. Harvey, Spivak, and Jameson emphasize that many international com-panies seek to reduce production costs by displacing their sweatshops to the Third World, exploiting primarily a female labor force there. It thus takes determined effort for American intellectuals and their students to grasp what materially supports their country's managerial class and their own professional labor. But understanding the ethics of their work and others' requires that the effort be made.

I can imagine LeFevre or other writing teachers agreeing with my proposal for extending a class's perspectives on collaboration, yet reminding me that LeFevre's hypothetical students still face an im-mediate dilemma in their workplace that no sociological imagination will remove. Given that the relevant changes in social structure are unlikely to happen right away, they probably will have to adopt some stance toward their supervisors. But even though negotiation with them may turn out to be morally and practically efficacious, simply declaring that "diplomacy is the rudder of invention" leaves other courses of action unexplored. For one thing, the students could choose to resign in protest. Even if they ultimately remain, they ought to consider just what circumstances would compel them to leave. Also, they ought to see if they can collaborate with anyone else at work in expressing their concerns to their supervisor, a possibility that LeFevre curiously fails to mention.

Furthermore, the students should identify just what actions would address the problems of social structure they have come to recognize, even if they are not immediately able to eradicate them. Mills believed that "what are required are parties and movements and publics having two characteristics: (1) within them ideas and alternatives of social life are truly debated, and (2) they have a chance really to influence decisions of social consequence" (190). In short, people need to collaborate with others in the public sphere if they are to produce genuine social change. Unfortunately, writing specialists have neglected to study how collaboration has historically operated in progressive movements, including ones that have dramatically transformed the workplace. In his time, Mills lamented that

> The American university system seldom if ever provides political education; it seldom teaches how to gauge what is going on in the general struggle for power in modern society. Most social scientists have had little or no sustained contacts with such sections of the community as have been insurgent; there is no left-wing press with which the average academic practitioner in the course of his career could come into mutually educative relations. There is no movement that would support or give prestige, not to speak of jobs, to political intellectuals, and the academic community has few if any roots in labor circles. (99)

Unbeknownst to him, Mills was writing on the eve of a turbulent era that would see particular movements emerging with new force, engaging academics among others. Now, years after that era, the professoriate and its students perhaps need Richard Ohmann's reminder that

> Critical intellectuals...work in different sites and in different ways and will have to elaborate and sophisticate those ways enormously before gaining the power to challenge seriously the centers of ideological and social power. That will not happen apart from a gathering of oppositional forces comparable to what took place in the sixties. But critical intellectuals will play a role in that gathering—are playing a role in it—albeit not on the star system. They are doing so *collaboratively*, both within the university and in relation to movements outside it. (256) (my emphasis)

As examples of progressive collaborations with significant public impact, Ohmann cites feminism, black studies, critical legal studies, Physicians for Social Responsibility, the antiapartheid movement, and protests against United States intervention in Central America. Whether or not a course in collaborative writing endorses them, at least it should help the class learn how they deploy collaboration beyond workplace "diplomacy" to achieve larger social change. Becoming aware of the principles and strategies they represent is, I think, necessary today for developing the sociological imagination and the ethics of collaboration.

Coda

I have argued that collaboration needs to be studied in context, and that it can be used for good or ill. Nevertheless, in suggesting how writing theory has unduly simplified its ethical aspects, I may have seemed generally suspicious of its value. I have cited Ohmann partly to counter this impression. I want to go further, though, by returning to the Paul de Man case and pointing out how collaborative writing might have enhanced the volume of responses to it.

Consciously or not, the preface to the volume tries to deflect charges that its editors have acted like de Man's wartime superiors, demanding "collaboration" in the negative sense: "We made clear to our contributors that we had no interest in monitoring what they wrote; they were told that they could write on any aspect of the subject, at any length, and that their texts would be printed as they were received, without editorial intervention on our part" (vii-viii). Yet the book unfortunately resists "collaboration" in the other sense: none of the thirty-seven essays that follow stem from multiple authors. Indeed, I know of only one coauthored entry in the whole controversy over de Man (see Brenkman and Law). By not encouraging at least some respondents to work with one another, the book misses, I think, an opportunity to foster genuinely dialectical inquiry into its important topic. Instead, it unrolls a procession of isolated voices, bent upon expressing their personal analyses and positions. For all the new vocabulary that many of its contributors wield, operating here is a classic image of the literary intellectual as a cranky individual seer. I cannot help but feel that if their traditional "service" ethos has made writing specialists embrace collaboration uncritically, so the professional ideology of literary studies has prevented its scholars from exploring how they could stimulate one another through dialogue or shared insight. It may be too simplistic to propose that each field move toward the other. But juxtaposing the perspectives of both is perhaps a way to begin examining the ethical complexity of collaboration in schools, workplaces, and the larger world.

Notes

1. The two meanings of "collaboration" also surfaced in the Spring 1989 issue of *Critical Inquiry*, in a debate over the Arab-Israeli conflict. When Robert Griffin accuses PLO groups of assassinating certain Arab leaders

interested in compromise (614), Edward Said responds that "surely even he must be aware that the UN Charter and every other known document or protocol entitles a people under foreign occupation not only to resist but also by extension to deal severely with *collaborators*" (641) (my emphasis). Meanwhile, even though they advocate "Jewish self-determination," Daniel and Jonathan Boyarin add that "we would wish to *collaborate* with Edward Said and others in tracing the path toward Israeli-Palestinian equality and reconciliation as one facet of the global effort to overcome the heritage of imperialism" (633) (my emphasis).

2. The notion of "initiation" stems from Patricia Bizzell's 1982 review article "College Composition: Initiation into the Academic Discourse Community." It should be noted that Bizzell has subsequently revised her thinking, finding that the term "initiation" obscures the power relations between students and the academy. See her forthcoming essay "Marxist Ideas and Composition Studies."

3. For a critique of composition's excessive reliance upon the term "community," see Joseph Harris's "The Idea of Community in the Study of Writing." For an analysis of how the demarcation of "communities" might reflect the political interests of the observer, see Daniel Cottom's *Text and Culture*, especially pp. 58–59.

4. For an incisive critique of how social scientists have turned to governmental funding agencies, see Alvin Gouldner's *The Coming Crisis of Western Sociology*.

Works Cited

Bizzell, Patricia. "College Composition: Initiation into the Academic Discourse Community." *Curriculum Inquiry* 12 (1982): 191–207.

———. "Marxist Ideas and Composition Studies." *Contending with Words: Composition and Rhetoric in a Postmodern Age*. Ed. Patricia Harkin and John Schilb. New York: MLA, forthcoming.

Bourdieu, Pierre, and J. C. Passeron. *Reproduction: In Education, Society, and Culture*. Beverly Hills: Sage, 1977.

Boyarin, Daniel, and Jonathan Boyarin. "Toward a Dialogue with Edward Said." *Critical Inquiry* 15 (1989): 626–33.

Brenkman, John, and Jules David Law. "Resetting the Agenda." *Critical Inquiry* 15 (1989): 804–11.

Bruffee, Kenneth A. "Collaborative Learning and the 'Conversation of Mankind.'" *College English* 46 (1984): 635–52.

———. "Kenneth Bruffee Responds." *College English* 49 (1987): 711–16.

———. "Social Construction, Language, and the Authority of Knowledge: A Bibliographical Essay." *College English* 48 (1986): 773–90.

Cottom, Daniel. *Text and Culture*. Minneapolis: U of Minnesota P, 1989.

Derrida, Jacques. "Like the Sound of the Sea Deep Within a Shell: Paul de Man's War." Trans. Peggy Kamuf. Hamacher, Hertz, and Keenan: 127–64.

Foucault, Michel. *Discipline and Punish: The Birth of the Prison.* Trans. Alan Sheridan. New York: Vintage/Random, 1979.

Freud, Sigmund. *The Interpretation of Dreams.* Trans. James Strachey. New York: Avon, 1965.

Gouldner, Alvin W. *The Coming Crisis of Western Sociology.* New York: Basic, 1970.

Griffin, Robert J. "Ideology and Misrepresentation: A Response to Edward Said." *Critical Inquiry* 15 (1989): 611–25.

Hamacher, Werner, Neil Hertz, and Thomas Keenan, eds. *Responses: On Paul de Man's Wartime Journalism.* Lincoln: U of Nebraska P, 1989.

Harris, Joseph. "The Idea of Community in the Study of Writing." *College Composition and Communication* 40 (1989): 11–22.

Harvey, David. *The Condition of Postmodernity: An Enquiry into the Origins of Cultural Change.* Cambridge, MA: Basil Blackwell, 1989.

Jameson, Fredric. "Postmodernism, or the Cultural Logic of Late Capitalism." *New Left Review* 146 (1984): 53–92.

Karis, Bill. "Conflict in Collaboration: A Burkean Perspective." *Rhetoric Review* 8 (1989): 113–26.

LeFevre, Karen Burke. *Invention as a Social Act.* Carbondale: Southern Illinois UP, 1987.

Lunsford, Andrea, and Lisa Ede. *Singular Texts/Plural Authors: Perspectives on Collaborative Writing.* Urbana: Southern Illinois UP, 1990.

Lyotard, Jean-François. *The Postmodern Condition: A Report on Knowledge.* Trans. Geoff Bennington and Brian Massumi. Minneapolis: U of Minnesota P, 1984.

Mills, C. Wright. *The Sociological Imagination.* 1959. New York: Oxford UP, 1980.

Myers, Greg. "Reality, Consensus, and Reform in the Rhetoric of Composition Teaching." *College English* 48 (1986): 154–74.

Ohmann, Richard. "Graduate Students, Professionals, Intellectuals." *College English* 52 (1990): 247–57.

Reither, James A., and Douglas Vipond. "Writing as Collaboration." *College English* 51 (1989): 855–67.

Said, Edward W. *Orientalism.* New York: Vintage/Random, 1979.

———. "Response." *Critical Inquiry* 15 (1989): 634–46.

Smit, David W. "Some Difficulties with Collaborative Learning." *Journal of Advanced Composition* 9 (1989): 45–58.

Spivak, Gayatri Chrakravorty. *In Other Worlds: Essays in Cultural Politics.* New York: Methuen, 1987.

Stewart, Donald. "Collaborative Learning and Composition: Boon or Bane?"

Rhetoric Review 7 (1988): 58−83.

―――. Rev. of *Invention as a Social Act*, by Karen Burke LeFevre. *Rhetoric Review* 6 (1987): 107−11.

Trimbur, John. "Consensus and Difference in Collaborative Learning." *College English* 51 (1989): 602−16.

7

Exploring the Value of Face-to-Face Collaborative Writing

Priscilla S. Rogers
Marjorie S. Horton

This essay presents a case for the value of *face-to-face* collaborative writing; that is, collaboration in which co-authors are physically present in the same room and interact directly to plan, draft, and revise a document. We begin by suggesting that face-to-face collaborative writing activities involve individuals in the kind of "talk about talk" that Kenneth Bruffee deems necessary for learning to write. We then illustrate potential benefits of face-to-face collaborative writing by reviewing the oral and written texts generated by one of the nineteen writing groups we observed. Analysis of these texts suggests that face-to-face collaborative writing allows groups to understand their rhetorical situation, examine their language choices, consider the ethical dimensions of their decisions, and reappraise their decisions in greater depth than could be achieved if any aspect of the writing were completed individually. In light of these benefits, we recommend face-to-face collaborative writing for several professional situations. Finally, we discuss the pedagogical implications of our thesis.

A group is struggling to write a memorandum. They have worked together for almost an hour.

Carol says twice: "This isn't working. It's taking forever." The others ignore her comment. They continue discussing the memo. Several minutes pass.

Ed: "I think we're taking way too long on one sentence."

Alex: "Everyone pick a topic and write on it."

120

The group divides the memorandum sections among themselves. They begin to write individually.

This scene is real; although, in our experience it is not unique. It is a scene we have observed often in the course of our research at the Center for Machine Intelligence (CMI), an Electronic Data Systems research center. As part of an empirical study of collaborative writing with computer technology (see Horton et al. for a preliminary report), we observed nineteen groups, each working in two conference room environments at CMI. In one environment, each group had access to collaborative computer technology (a shared public computer with a large projection screen and individual computers with monitors); in the other environment, each group had access to traditional writing tools (a flip chart, individual notepads, and pens). In both settings, groups were given two hours to plan, draft, and revise a memorandum in response to a politically sensitive business situation.

These groups often had difficulty with various aspects of the face-to-face collaborative writing experience, particularly drafting. "It's like giving blood," said one group member. Research findings confirm our observations. Writers interviewed by Lunsford and Ede found face-to-face collaboration useful for brainstorming, organizational planning, information gathering, and revising, but felt drafting and editing were better done individually, except under special circumstances. Ten of the fourteen groups studied by Allen et al. "reported that actual words-on-paper drafting was always an individual effort" (77). "Frustrating" is a word group members commonly use to describe face-to-face collaborative drafting (Allen et al.; Forman and Katsky; Lunsford and Ede).

The apparent resistance writers have to face-to-face collaborative writing, particularly collaborative drafting, may partially explain why it is not a major topic in pedagogical materials and research studies. There may be other reasons as well. Adams and Thornton found that academics prefer writing individually and, when they do collaborate, it is usually on projects "too large to complete alone" (78). The fact that writers typically collaborate on longer documents may partially account for the little attention the subject of face-to-face collaborative writing has received. (Allen et al.). Drafting books and long reports face-to-face may require an unreasonable amount of time and energy. Moreover, face-to-face joint authorship may not be considered because writers find it difficult to arrange group meetings (Fleming). Only one group of professional writers Allen et al. studied composed "together on a fairly regular basis word by word, sentence by sentence" even though they had neighboring offices (79). Although these collaborators had written together for over fifteen years, they typically began their face-to-face collaborative writing sessions with a working draft one of them had composed individually. As Fleming writes, "it may be difficult to move away from the notion of individual composing as ideal" (78).

The purpose of our essay is to present a case for the value of face-to-face collaborative writing; that is, collaboration in which coauthors are physically present in the same room and interact directly in every aspect of the writing process. In the past, collaborative writing has been defined very broadly to encompass writing projects in which more than one person contributes (Couture and Rymer). These contributions may range from mere discussion before or after a document is written by an individual, to the much rarer truly multiple authorship. In contrast to this broad definition of collaborative writing, we focus on the fully collaborative enterprise involving coauthors who plan, draft, and revise a document in a face-to-face context.

We build a case for the value of face-to-face collaborative writing in several ways. We begin by suggesting that face-to-face planning, drafting, and revising put into practice the kind of "talk about talk" that Bruffee deems necessary for individuals to learn the discourse of a community. We extend this idea by proposing four benefits groups may gain through face-to-face collaborative writing and illustrate these benefits by reviewing portions of the written and spoken texts generated by one of the groups we observed. We further suggest several specific professional contexts in which face-to-face collaborative writing may bring highly desirable results. Finally, we discuss the pedagogical implications of our thesis.

Face-to-Face Collaboration to Operationalize Bruffee's Theory of "Collaborative Learning"

Bruffee believes that learning results from social interaction and is therefore inherently collaborative. He draws on the experimental work of Vygotsky, who suggests that we learn through *internal* dialogue. Vygotsky found that children solved problems by talking aloud to themselves. Adults employ the same dialogical thinking process, Vygotsky conjectured; however, adults turn it inward. Consequently, Vygotsky argued that human thought is actually public or social conversation internalized.

Bruffee extends Vygotsky's notion to the *external* world when he posits that "any effort to understand how we think requires us to understand the nature of conversation; and any effort to understand conversation requires us to understand the nature of community life that generates and maintains conversation" ("Collaborative Learning"

640). In other words, we learn to think better as we learn to converse better, or as we "talk about talk" ("Writing and Reading" 164–5). In this way, learning is not an individual activity, but a social or collaborative activity, involving the establishment and maintenance of knowledge within a community. Moreover, individuals *learn* the discourse of a community through writing. "Writing always has its roots deep in the acquired ability to carry on the social symbolic exchange we call conversation," Bruffee explains ("Collaborative Learning" 641–642). Writing then is collaborative by nature, and "talk about talk" is a necessary part of learning how to write.

The idea that writing is inherently collaborative raises an interesting question for Bruffee: "What do we do with the fact that we normally write and read alone?" ("Writing and Reading" 167). Bruffee suggests that students be taught to imagine social exchange and to audibly or inwardly talk through the writing task. He and other composition specialists also propose a variety of methods to get individuals to converse about their writing, including editing groups and work-in-progress sessions (Foley), tutoring and peer advisory groups (Copeland and Lomax). Fleming suggests the usefulness of face-to-face collaboration for planning, drafting, and revising; however, she focuses on ways groups can divide tasks or respond to texts individually written.

We propose face-to-face collaborative writing as an instrumental way to address Bruffee's concern that writers be explicitly introduced to the collaborative nature of writing. Face-to-face collaborative writing prompts writers to voice internalized dialogue. Through face-to-face collaborative writing, individual writers may bring to the surface, in a very natural and revealing way, the conversation gone underground since childhood, which Vygotsky describes. Like the child who solved her problem by talking aloud, individuals may find solutions by actually voicing their thoughts in face-to-face collaborative writing sessions. Face-to-face collaborative planning, drafting, and revising, we believe, allow individuals to externalize the "inward talking-through" that Bruffee suggests is a necessary part of learning to write, because face-to-face collaborative writing involves individuals in *explicit* discussions about text, or "talk about talk." Few other group activities involve individuals so intensely in the definition, selection, and arrangement of language as face-to-face collaborative writing.

Potential Benefits of Face-to-Face Collaborative Writing

The value of face-to-face collaborative writing extends beyond individual writers, however. We suggest that *groups* may often benefit from face-to-face collaborative writing. We explore these benefits, first with examples from our group observations and second by describing several professional contexts in which face-to-face collaborative writing may bring desirable results.

Benefits Observed in Groups

We find that in face-to-face collaborative writing sessions groups achieve at least four significant benefits. Our analysis of the spoken and written texts suggests that groups 1) understand their rhetorical situation, 2) examine language choice, 3) consider the ethical dimensions of their decisions, and 4) reappraise their group decisions in greater depth than could be achieved if any aspect of the writing were divided among group members and completed individually. Face-to-face planning, drafting, and revising involve group members in complex discussions about the nature of their situation and task, including dialogue about fundamental questions such as: What are the facts? What do they mean? What do our actions mean? Do we want to tell the truth? The spoken and written texts generated by the groups we studied provide many examples illustrating these benefits.

We have selected examples from one group's response to a task we call the Nelson Hardware Case (Appendix A). For the Nelson Case, the group assumed the role of personnel directors who were accused by their subordinate managers of implementing a new and undesirable hiring policy. As personnel directors, they recently hired new managers from outside the Nelson organization and fired two longtime managers. Now they must explain their actions in an internal memorandum to their subordinate managers.

The examples presented below are from our most experienced group. Prior to participating in our study, this group worked together for over a year on a variety of projects, including long written reports and oral presentations. The group had four members, whom we will call Cliff, Don, Leticia, and Rajiv.

Understanding the Rhetorical Situation

Our observations suggest that, through the face-to-face collaborative writing process, groups evolve a shared understanding and produce documents that possess a *group* voice. These benefits derive from group analysis of the rhetorical situation, an activity that enables groups to discover what they know and what they do not know, what they want to say, and how they want to say it.

Our group's discussion of Nelson's hiring policy illustrates this potential benefit. Rapid company expansion led them, as personnel directors, to hire new managers from outside the Nelson organization, an action

that insiders — their employees and intended readers of the memorandum — regarded as a sudden, and unsettling, shift in policy.

Rajiv: They're threatening to go to competitors, ah, so there really is
some kind of guarantee that we have to give. They're beyond the
worried stage. They're climbing already.

Cliff: Yeah....

Leticia: Employee morale is low and sales are down. [They] are
threatening to leave.

As the writing session proceeded, the group tried to determine the
meaning of their hiring actions. What had they done in their haste to
fill the many new managerial positions prompted by sudden company
expansion? Did they still endorse Nelson's long-held policy to hire old-
time employees? Or, were their subordinates right? Had they, by their
actions, actually implemented a "new hiring policy"?

Leticia: You know, they don't understand the policy at all....
[Long pause. Individual group members study their individual notepads.]

Leticia: I think a misconception is that a new hiring policy will ultimately hurt the company, they think, instead of benefiting the
company and that's like a real big misconception.

Don: That's something they're saying. A new hiring policy isn't really
a new one. I don't, I don't rec....

Rajiv: No, because in the old days we never had to fill twenty positions.
We never had to, to find that many people. Maybe this is a new
stage, a new evolution of the exact same policy we always had. So
there is no new hiring policy.

Cliff: You're sure this isn't new?...[We] were like family before.

Rajiv: And we still agree with that....

Leticia: But look, the well-known company policy was to consider
present employees *first* for any promotion.

Rajiv: Yeah, we still do that....But it was a lot easier when we were
finding one new store manager for the old guy retiring out in
Waterloo.

Leticia: Exactly.

Sixteen minutes into the session the group agrees that there is "no new
hiring policy."

Cliff: You think that...there is no new hiring policy?

Don, Leticia & Rajiv: Uh huh.

Cliff: That's the main point?

Don & Rajiv: Yeah.

Cliff: Okay.

Cliff, Don, Leticia, and Rajiv's brainstorming lists on their individual notepads, written during initial group planning, reflect this decision (Figure 7.1). Rajiv wrote "No new hiring policy"; Don modified his reference to the policy to read "new hiring policy — not really"; Leticia added and circled the phrase "is no new" in the margin by her entry; and Cliff crossed out the words "no new."

Despite this apparent agreement among group members that Nelson's hiring policy had not changed, references to "the *new* policy" persisted. Select portions of dialogue demonstrate the continued "talk about talk" that was required for the group to come to a shared understanding of their actions regarding the policy.

Twenty-two minutes into the session:

Rajiv: Ah, I think the new hiring policy should go first, maybe, or growth process first and then new hiring policy.

Twenty-six minutes into the session:

Don: Couldn't we say something like, "We'd like to take this opportunity to address"

Cliff: ". . .your concerns."

Don: ". . .the concerns and rumors that have been circulating concerning our. . .new hiring policies."

Cliff: ". . .our hiring policy."

Twenty-eight minutes into the session:

Leticia reading the draft: "We'd like to begin. . . .We'd like to begin the year with an explanation of the hiring procedure for 1990." Something like that. . . .

Rajiv: No, that would say that there's a *new* hiring policy.

Leticia: Yeah, that's true.

Rajiv: This is our hiring policy for 1990.

Thirty-four minutes into the session:

Cliff: Is it hiring? Is it hiring policy or is it kind of a promotion policy?

Rajiv: Both. They want it to be a promotion policy and they hate it when it's a hiring policy. See?

Cliff: Yeah. . . .

Don: We can say *recruiting* policy. . . .

Rajiv: Hiring *and* promoting. . . .

Figure 7.1
Individual Group Members' Brainstorming Lists

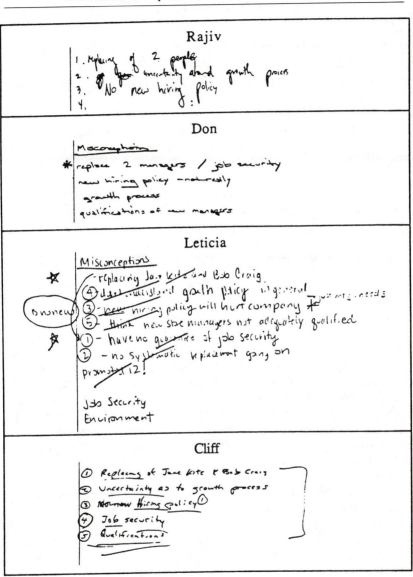

Don: Okay: . . .

Leticia reading the draft: "We'd like to take this opportunity to address the serious concerns many of you have regarding the hiring and promotion decisions."

Forty-one minutes into the session drafting continues:

Leticia: "As in the past, our hiring policy...."

Cliff: "As always...."

Leticia: "As always...."

Rajiv: Yeah.

Leticia reading from the draft: "Our hiring policy is to consider present employee qualifications first."

A lengthy discussion about the reasons why they hired from the outside followed. Finally, fifty-two minutes into the session the group arrived at the joint position that appeared in their final memorandum.

Leticia reading the memorandum draft: "We'd like to take this opportunity to address the serious concerns that many of you have regarding job security and Nelson's hiring and promotion decisions....As always our hiring policy is to consider present employee qualifications first for available positions...."

Clilff: I love it!

Rajiv: Yeah, Okay.

Cliff: I love it! [Laugh]

Following this reading, the hiring policy was referred to as the "*new* hiring policy" only once. During the remaining hour, occasional rereadings of the memorandum draft reinforced the group's shared understanding of their actions: There is no new policy and Nelson's old-line employees will continue to be considered first for new positions.

As we have seen, just minutes into the collaborative writing session, the group agreed that their hiring actions did not mean they were operating under a new policy. But the fact that group members continued to refer to the policy as "new" suggests the tentativeness of their initial agreement in the early minutes of their collaborative writing session. Additional "talk about talk" was required for the group to reach a shared understanding of the hiring policy. We speculate that if the group had collaborated face-to-face for only a portion of the process, perhaps just to plan or to revise, or if the group had divided the task and worked individually, with only occasional face-to-face interaction, they may have failed to address such fundamental questions or to reach this group understanding of their situation. As the dialogue indicates, the group came to understand their actions as they struggled together to articulate them for their readers, and much of this struggle occurred as the group was drafting.

Examining Language Choice

Face-to-face collaborative writing also allows groups to consider language choice and to develop a group vocabulary for talking about key issues in a way that would be difficult to replicate through individual efforts. To illustrate, we recall our example group's search for language to explain the fact that, as personnel directors, they had replaced two longtime store managers. Managers remaining with the company found this replacement disconcerting and some were threatening to resign — as one manager said: "As long as Nelson's is going to bounce me in the near future, I might as well leave while I can make a good connection" (Appendix A). Consequently, part of the collaborative writing group's task involved designing a written message that would allay this fear. Given the political sensitivity of the situation, their group's choice of language would be critical.

In discussing this issue, members of the collaborative writing group used the word "replace" over fifty times and some form of the word "fire" (as in "when you fire somebody," or "they were fired") fourteen times during their two-hour writing session. Ultimately, however, the group selected neither of these words for their final memorandum, which reads: "As you may be aware, two store managers were recently *let go*" (Appendix C). Group members arrived at the descriptive words "let go" through several minutes of fast and furious brainstorming, which occurred as they drafted the last paragraph of their memorandum.

Leticia: "Store managers were recently...."

Cliff: "Recently." How do you say fired? Recently, um....

Rajiv: Relieved of their duties.

[Cliff laughs]

[All laugh]

Cliff: Terminated.

Leticia: Do we want to say *that* to store managers?

Don: Maybe we do have to be blunt about it though.

Cliff: Were recently let go.

Leticia: Recently two store managers were replaced.

Rajiv: They were, um, um, um.

Cliff: They were released; were replaced.

Don: No, but they weren't replaced. They were *fired* and replaced.

Cliff: Okay. Okay. They were released. They were let go.

Rajiv: Let go.

Cliff: Canned.

[Laughter]

Cliff: Dropped.

Don: Given the pink slip.

Rajiv: Kicked in the teeth.
[Laughter]

Leticia: Were let go.

Cliff: Were let go.

Don: Were left out in the cold.
[Laughter]

Rajiv: Left to starve.

Leticia: Oh, mean!
[Laughter]

Leticia reading what she's written into the group draft: "As you're aware, two store managers were let go."

It would require a vivid imagination for an individual writer to entertain an internalized dialogue rivaling the interactive energy and fast-paced piggybacking of one idea upon another that we see in this group interaction. This and the previous example about Nelson's hiring policy illustrate the kind of interaction about language choices one may expect to find when groups write together face-to-face. Such group discussions about language, we suggest, can push groups to reach consensus about decisions and can prompt the creation of group documents that more accurately reflect those decisions. After face-to-face writing sessions, individual group members are also more likely to employ the same vocabulary when discussing key issues with individuals inside and outside the organization. In this way, face-to-face collaborative writing experiences enable group members to present a more uniform and consistent message, which is a highly desirable result, particularly in some professional situations as we suggest later in this essay.

Considering Ethical Issues

Discussions about language that dominate face-to-face collaborative writing sessions also facilitate group awareness and understanding of the ethical issues involved in a particular situation. We have often seen groups evaluate the truth of their words in face-to-face collaborative sessions. Groups also raised questions of ethical importance about the necessity or expediency of including or excluding content, questions such as: How much or how little should be said? In what manner should we say it? To what extent should we address our readers' concerns? Some groups engaged in explicit discussions about the morality of their decisions. Face-to-face writing sessions promote deliberate evaluation of these issues, which may not otherwise occur.

Moreover, dissension about language that we observed within groups suggests that face-to-face collaborative writing may reveal important differences among individual group members on issues ranging from simple misunderstandings about purpose to deep-seated differences about policy. In many situations group recognition and resolution of such differences are important, if not essential. In such cases, in order for the group to work smoothly and to concur on the final collaborative product, face-to-face collaborative writing may prove effective. After observing practices of individual writers at Exxon, Paradis, Dobrin, and Miller reported that writing made employees "evaluate their work, their attitudes, and their relationships with colleagues" (293). In this way, their documents became a means of self-analysis. Many of the groups we observed engaged in this kind of analysis which frequently involved discussions of ethical issues.

Face-to-face collaborative writing may also help groups recognize and take responsibility for their ethical decisions. Jaksa and Pritchard contend that a serious problem in the group decision-making process "is the tendency for individuals not to accept responsibility for decisions made in a group" (118). Shirking responsibility may be more difficult when the decision-making process must result in a signed document — sometimes even a document bearing a group signature has personal consequence. Moreover, it is widely understood that there is an inherent accountability when such documents become part of company archives (Paradis, Dobrin and Miller).

The fact that face-to-face collaborative writing prompts groups to address the ethical implications of their decisions is implicit in the hiring policy example offered earlier in this essay — to reach consensus about the nature of Nelson's hiring policy, the group had to discuss the nature of the truth and how to share that truth with their readers: a fact that does not escape their notice. As Rajiv said at one point, "We just want to clarify what the truth is." In the example offered below, we find group members keenly aware that their language choices have ethical consequences. This example involves a friendly argument between Cliff and Rajiv about the honesty of using "may" rather than "will" to describe their intentions regarding the hiring of outside managers.

Cliff: Do you want to say "have to"? I sort of like *may* . . . . You don't want to sound like we're always gonna have to.

Rajiv: How about just get rid of the *have*? [Let's say] *will* be brought in.

Cliff: Nooooooooo. . . . You don't want to say for sure, for sure.

Rajiv: For sure it happened. We might as well be real. I mean, it's going to happen.

Cliff: But *may* assures that it may happen. It's *not will*.

Rajiv: It *will* happen.

Leticia: [May] is more reassuring. . . .

Rajiv: It's lying. It's misleading.

Cliff: It's not *very* misleading.

Rajiv: I think it's very misleading. [Will] is at least very straightforward. Maybe it's too blunt. . . .

Cliff: It's too blunt.

Rajiv: . . .'cause you and I and she and him know that it's going to be *will*.

Cliff: Yeah, but employees want . . . *may*. [Outsiders] *may* have to be brought in on occasion. . . . *Will* is just a little too much. . . .

[Brief discussion of whether to mention the number of outsiders hired]

Cliff drafting aloud: "As expansion continues, new people *may* have to be."

Rajiv: No. . . . *Will* be hired. . . . If this says *may* and I were reading it I would definitely just crumple it up and, I mean, maybe, yeah right, of course we're *going* to hire new people.

At this point the discussion diverged, but the group quickly returned to the controversy.

Cliff: Let's go back to the *may*.

Rajiv: Let's change the *may*.

[Cliff laughs]

Rajiv: You [referring to Leticia who is scribing] left it as *will*. We want it as *may*. [Laughs]

Cliff drafting aloud: "As the expansion continues, new people *may* be. . . ."

Rajiv: Why don't we just make it one word, "maybe." "Maybe hired" [Laughs]. . . . We know very well that we're going to need outside people.

Don: We don't know *how*. . . .

Rajiv drafting aloud: "New people *will* be hired to supplement the already. . . ."

Cliff: Okay. What do you think, Don? New people *may* be?

Rajiv: *May* be or *will* be?

Don: I, I actually think that I agree with Cliff.

Rajiv: Okay.

Leticia: Okay.

Rajiv: Okay.

[All laugh]

In the final memorandum both "may" and "will" are used: "may" appears first, as if to buffer the fact that hiring outsiders will continue; "will" appears in the paragraph that immediately follows (Appendix C).

The idea to use both "will" and "may" was first voiced by Leticia; however, Cliff suggested the phrase "virtually all people that have and *will* be hired will be... placed in newly created... stores." Interestingly enough, it was Cliff who argued so vehemently for the use of "may" in the earlier paragraph. During the drafting of this final paragraph, however, the use of "will" never became an issue — perhaps the group was feeling time pressure or Cliff was drafting in the spirit of compromise.

Using the evidence from the group's transcript, one might argue that, despite their lively discussion, the group evaded the issue in order to preserve group cohesiveness. The fact that in face-to-face collaborative writing sessions groups raise ethical concerns and craft language reflecting decisions regarding those concerns, does not guarantee that groups will ultimately act ethically, or, in this case, generate documents that are in the best interests of their constituency. Groups may use face-to-face collaborative writing sessions to generate documents that manipulate readers. As Janis suggests, any improvement in the group decision-making process "can be used for evil as well as for good" (274). Jaksa and Pritchard suggest that groups may experience an "illusion of morality" by generating vague statements proclaiming the inherent goodness of their groups or their companies (115). This "illusion of morality," they contend, allows groups to avoid serious discussion of the ethical implications of their decisions. Some may interpret our example group's selection of the words "let go" to describe the replacement of the two managers as a case in point.

Moreover, Janis suggests that individual values may be compromised or never surface because of groupthink. This may be especially true in the corporate setting where individual success is often attributed to one's ability to connect one's personal identity with the company (Tompkins and Cheney). Such pressures to "fit in" may stifle the kind of discussions about ethical issues that we have observed.

Despite these pitfalls, Janis remains optimistic that improved group decision-making techniques will be put to *good* use. Similarly, we hope that the benefits to be gained from face-to-face collaborative writing are used for good.

We add one further consideration. Deal and Kennedy contend that "values are not *hard*, like organizational structures, policies, and procedures, strategies, or budgets. Often they are not even written down" (21). But we contend that documents reveal an ethic or the underlying motives of the writers who compose them. For example, in business a more accurate reading of a company's ethic may be discovered in documents generated in the course of day-to-day activities rather than in a company's written ethical code. In such daily, functional documents one may discover a use and arrangement of language that suggests, as Burke noted, a rhetoric of motives. As group members confront their choices in face-to-face collaborative writing sessions, such motives may be brought to light.

Reappraising Group Decisions

The face-to-face collaborative writing process also affords a kind of reappraisal that allows groups to confirm and solidify their ideas. When groups write face-to-face, it is common for them to review intermittently what they have written by reading text aloud or by scanning text on the public computer screen. Among the groups we observed, these reviews were often extensive, as when Rajiv requested, "Okay, read this from the top." Sometimes such reviews were brief, as when Cliff asked Leticia to "read the last paragraph." The repeated hearing and, in the case of the public computer screen, seeing of text, may solidify group commitment to positions established in the course of their collaboration.

Benefits in Professional Contexts

The benefits derived from face-to-face collaboration are already recognized in several professional contexts. For example, juries are entrusted with great decision-making power and asked to deliberate face-to-face to determine the guilt or innocence of a defendant (Kalven and Zeisel). Consider, for example, the judge's directions to the jury in Reginald Rose's screenplay titled *Twelve Angry Men*. The judge says: "Now it's your duty to sit down and separate the facts from the fancy." Later a juror remarks: "Here's the facts. What do they mean?" These are the same significant questions we have seen groups address in face-to-face collaborative writing sessions.

Face-to-face collaboration is also important in the field of medicine. As Cicourel's ethnographic analysis of diagnostic teams reveals, physicians depend on social interaction to exchange observations about a patient's medical condition and to assess the credibility of these observations. Abercrombie also found that face-to-face collaboration enhanced the development of medical students' diagnostic skills.

Similarly, Daft and Lengel propose that in business, high-level managers need the richness of face-to-face communication for the kinds of problem-solving and decision-making situations they routinely face, in which uncertainty and equivocality are high. Daft and Lengel argue that face-to-face interaction enables participants to test definitions of problems and to get feedback about whether their perspectives are shared. It can also be critical for reaching consensus and buy-in. Along the same lines, Finholt, Sproull, and Kiesler argue that "when decisions have important implications for the future or when they need active support by every member of the group, we want the decision makers to be sensitive to all the information available and to personify this sensitivity in face-to-face discussion" (296).

The extent to which face-to-face collaborative writing is employed in these professional contexts is unknown; however, our observations suggest that the argumentation, negotiation, and consensus reaching inherent in the face-to-face writing process can enhance group communication and decision making. To illustrate, consider the potential benefits of face-to-face collaborative writing in two critical management situations: managerial communication during a company crisis and communication to newly hired employees.

Suppose a group of executives needs to issue a press release in response to a company crisis — recall the Exxon oil spill or Johnson and Johnson's Tylenol case. In such situations executives should expect that their every word will be scrutinized, interpreted, and reinterpreted by the media and the public. These executives may expect phone calls and requests for interviews. The consequences of telling different versions of the facts or sending mixed messages are clearly not desirable in such situations. In fact, the very reputation and future of a company may depend in part on the ability of company leaders to *determine together* what the situation means and how they want to talk about it. It may be critical for executives to "speak with one voice." Our example group's decision regarding their hiring policy supports this conclusion.

Another example of benefits to be gained through face-to-face collaborative writing revolves around educating new group members. The discussions about language occurring in face-to-face writing sessions may facilitate the initiation of new members into an existing group, a notion Bruffee suggests ("Writing and Reading"). Here the example of a newly hired MBA comes to mind. It is not unusual for entry-level employees to draft documents for their supervisors. Typically, this leads newly hired employees to company files where they may find documents to emulate or, better still, boilerplate documents that provide the basic format and key language for an initial draft. The document may evolve through the resulting collaborative draft-review-revise process between new employees and supervisors. Paradis, Dobrin and Miller observed Exxon supervisors using a "document-cycling process as a mechanism to promote employee self-education" (299). We speculate that the immediacy of the face-to-face collaboration may facilitate, perhaps even hasten, the learning process.

Summary of Benefits

Analysis of dialogue from the collaborative sessions we studied suggests that groups derive at least four significant benefits through face-to-face collaborative writing: 1) understanding their rhetorical situation, 2) examining their language choices, 3) considering the ethical dimensions of their decisions, and 4) reappraising their decisions. In light of these benefits, we recommend face-to-face collaborative writing for some professional contexts, such as corporate crisis situations requiring managers to present a unified message, and business situations involving the education of new employees.

Face-to-Face Collaborative Writing and Pedagogy

Our arguments for the value of face-to-face collaborative writing have significant implications for writing pedagogy. Face-to-face collaborative writing experiences foster a depth of discussion about semantics, grammar, syntax, tone, argumentation, audience, and situation that might not be achieved otherwise. Writing collaboratively in a face-to-face context also provides the opportunity for students to strengthen their audience analysis skills as individual group members play out the roles of both reader and writer throughout the collaborative process. Moreover, the social exchange or "talk about talk" recommended by Bruffee is not left to the imagination of the individual writer, but becomes explicit.

Face-to-face collaborative writing experience may also prepare students for professional life. Recent surveys (Couture and Rymer; Faigley and Miller) and ethnographic studies of business writing (Doheny-Farina) indicate that face-to-face collaboration on writing tasks is quite prevalent, although face-to-face drafting is not. Perhaps drafting in this manner is not often pursued because writers do not know how to write together. Through classroom instruction we can provide students an opportunity to work face-to-face on each aspect of writing — planning, drafting, and revising — and to experience directly the benefits as well as the frustrations. Moreover, what we learn from these classroom experiences may allow us to develop techniques to improve such collaborations.

What kinds of writing tasks are most appropriate and potentially most effective for face-to-face collaborative assignments? One kind of assignment is a management memorandum addressing a politically sensitive situation, such as defending or disputing a corporate policy under consideration. We used this kind of task in our study of collaborative writing groups, modeling real business situations that would warrant a group writing effort. Included in each case was information about the group's role, the motivation for the memorandum, and the receiver. Suggestions for developing such face-to-face collaborative tasks are outlined in Appendix D.

We might also create writing tasks that present ill-structured problems, which require students to "take an active role in delimiting and defining the boundaries of their task" (Carey, et al.). Defining and redefining collaboratively throughout the writing process may prompt coauthors to analyze a rhetorical situation more thoroughly, as they work to develop a shared interpretation and response. The negotiations required to complete such tasks may also strengthen students' critiquing skills (Daiute).

Finally, students we have worked with expressed a desire to learn more about how to write in face-to-face collaborative contexts, including learning more about group processes. For example, one student suggested that writing instruction include training in "group dynamics and group writing struggles"; another suggested groups analyze a videotape of their initial collaborative session before going into subsequent sessions. All in all, it is clear that students both appreciate and benefit from face-to-face collaborative writing sessions requiring them to originate and complete a document.

Conclusion

Our observations suggest that through face-to-face collaborative writing sessions groups come to understand their rhetorical situation, examine language choices, consider ethical issues, and reappraise group decisions so that they ultimately develop an authentic *group voice*. Throughout their collaborations, we have seen groups develop a shared vocabulary and an understanding of the situation about which they are writing through the "talk about talk" inherent in collaborative writing. This kind of talk includes argumentation, negotiation, and consensus reaching about language and underlying rhetorical and ethical issues.

By suggesting the value of face-to-face collaboration, we do not intend to diminish the importance of other styles of collaboration.

However, we do believe that for certain situations, such as company crises and employee education, and for particular kinds of documents, such as corporate policy statements and crucial memoranda, the face-to-face approach enables groups to reap benefits that could not be achieved otherwise. These benefits stem from the fact that face-to-face collaborations create "living" documents; that is, documents generated through group input and consensus at every stage with the potential for far greater group ownership and commitment to both the process and the product.

Our analysis of the value of face-to-face collaborative writing suggests that further research is needed to identify the particular kinds of writing tasks for which this approach is best suited and to evaluate, in a more systematic way, the short- and long-term benefits. To determine the short-term benefits, we might assess the written and spoken texts groups generate in face-to-face environments; to determine the long-term benefits we might undertake longitudinal studies exploring ongoing working relationships as they develop through face-to-face working contexts. Among other things, we may discover that one reason writers have avoided face-to-face writing, particularly drafting, in the past is that the writing tools designed for individuals have not supported collaboration well. However, with the emergence of new technologies, such as computer-supported meeting rooms, collaborative writing groups may find face-to-face collaboration more efficient and satisfying (Elwart-Keys and Horton).

Paradis, Dobrin and Miller's research on individual writing in the workplace suggests that writers see the task of writing as one of "transferring and archiving information" rather than as a highly social process through which collaborators learn more about each other and develop significant professional relationships (282). Like Paradis, Dobrin and Miller, we believe this is unfortunate. However, we have seen that groups, when given the opportunity to write together face-to-face, begin to recognize that writing is much more than the mere recording and dissemination of facts. Rather, working together in this manner helps them make sense of their experience and relationships.

We close as we began, with a scene from one of our collaborative writing groups. However, in contrast to the opening scene, this scene affirms at least one of several potential benefits groups may experience through face-to-face collaborative writing.

[After the group has been drafting together for a while]

Cindy: Why don't each one of us take one of the points, and write on it and then combine them?

Abe: 'cause what happens is, everybody's diction is different and it sounds like everyone is trying to throw separate things together.

Cindy: Yeah, but even still it'll go a lot quicker. I mean then we can correct it as it gets up there ["up there" refers to the large public computer screen].

Jane: If we do it that way everyone has different writing styles and we have to put it all into the same writing style so we're going to sit and argue about it anyway, how it should sound.

Cindy: Okay.

[The group continues drafting together]

Appendix A: Nelson Hardware Case

Background

As Directors of Personnel, you make all the major managerial hiring decisions for Nelson's Hardware, a chain of hardware stores in the Midwest. Founded in 1966, Nelson's is a strong organization, which consists of eighty-two stores in Wisconsin, Illinois, and Michigan. In 1984, Nelson's merged with a large home supplies distributor, James & Turney (J&T). At that time, J&T supplied funds and mandated expansion. As a result, Nelson's grew quickly. This year alone, Nelson's opened twenty-two new stores.

Until the merger with J&T, Nelson's workers were like family. The well-known company policy was to consider present employees first for any promotions. Store managers were regularly recruited from within the company. With rapid expansion, however, you recently recruited ten managers for new stores from outside the company. After much consideration, you also replaced two old-line managers, Jane Kitz and Bob Craig, with outsiders. As longtime Personnel Directors you all support Nelson's policy of promoting from within; however, none of you is overly concerned about outside recruiting when no old-line employees qualify for advanced positions.

Rumors Among Old-Line Employees

In recent months, all of you have become aware that the old-line employees deeply resent your outside recruiting. You've recently received a memo from four of Nelson's most experienced store managers. They said the "new hiring policy" was hurting the company. They outlined three objections to hiring outsiders.

1. New store managers are being hired from outside the company without due consideration of old-line employees.

2. Old-line store managers have no job security and are being systematically replaced by outsiders. (For instance, Jane Kitz and Bob Craig were recently replaced.)

3. Store managers hired from outside are not adequately qualified because they do not understand the company's history and they do not know Nelson's employees.

In your recent directors' meeting you've discussed the fact that you have a serious communication problem. Old-line employees have misconceptions about the company's growth and your hiring practices. You've all heard store managers making statements like, "As long as Nelson's is going to bounce me in the near future, I might as well leave while I can make a good connection." Employee morale is low and sales are down. Several store managers are threatening to move to competitors.

Instructions

Write a persuasive memorandum in favor of your current hiring practices to all store managers. Assure these managers that they are not being overlooked or replaced. Make up details as needed to support your statements.

Use the traditional memorandum heading: "To:, From:, Subject:, Date:" Write with clarity and direction; avoid vague and official sounding vocabulary. You have two hours to complete this memorandum. Use as much of this time as you need.

Feel free to fully use the facilities and equipment provided, but leave the case and all notes, drafts, computer files, and software.

Appendix B: Sportech Case

Background

As the Sales Management Team for Sportech, Inc., you oversee the selling of all Sportech products and services. Founded in 1961, Sportech is a small but competitive company that produces and sells sport training equipment. Over the years, Sportech has developed a reputation for quality products backed by an excellent sales and service staff. Growth and competition in the health and fitness industry have contributed to Sportech's profits. Additionally, much of the company's success is attributed to the knowledge and skill of Sportech's sales staff.

As you know from personal experience, potential members of Sportech's sales staff are required to complete successfully Sportech's rigorous, four-week Sales Training Program (STP). Potential sales personnel join the company with excellent athletic backgrounds, but almost no formal sales and communication training. STP is designed to develop interpersonal and selling skills. Sales trainees learn everything from opening a conversation with a prospective client to closing a sale.

As the Sales Management Team, you attribute much of your sales division's effectiveness to the STP. Moreover, the success of new sales personnel brings increased profits to the entire sales staff under Sportech's profitsharing plan.

Proposal to Eliminate the Sales Training Program (STP)

At a recent meeting, Sportech's Executive Committee, headed by the company's new president Sue Walker, announced their decision to "cut the fat out of Sportech." Speaking for the Committee, Walker stated, "We must focus our resources on state-of-the-art technology and eliminate nonessential, costly programs such as the STP. Walker outlined three reasons why the STP should be eliminated:

1. Sales techniques are best learned through immediate and direct experience with Sportech products and customers.
2. Sportech's Sales Management Team can provide effective on-the-job training for new sales personnel.
    The Sales Management Team can set aside time to train new personnel in reporting procedures and sales techniques.
3. STP is not cost- or time-effective, and Sportech's resources are needed for new technological developments if the company is to remain competitive.

After the meeting you expressed your concerns, as members of the Sales Management Team, about the decision to drop the STP. Walker seemed to interpret your concerns as a challenge to her leadership. "We developed this resource redistribution plan after months of thorough analysis," she said. "All members of Sportech's Executive Committee support it; however, if you disagree you may outline your objections in a memorandum." You support Walker's innovative leadership. At the same time you believe STP is essential for Sportech's continued success.

Instructions

Write a persuasive memorandum in favor of the STP to the Executive Committee. Defend STP as essential to Sportech's continued success. Make up details as needed to support your statements.

Use the traditional memorandum heading: "To:, From:, Subject:, Date:" Write with clarity and direction; avoid vague and official sounding vocabulary. You have two hours to complete this memorandum. Use as much of this time as you need.

Feel free to fully use the facilities and equipment provided, but leave the case and all notes, drafts, computer files and software.

Appendix C: The Group's Final Memorandum

(This is an exact copy of the memorandum written by the group. Errors have not been corrected.)

To: All Store Managers

From: Directors of Personnel

Subject: Hiring and Promotion Policies

Date: November 19, 1989

We'd like to take this opportunity to address the serious concerns many of you have regarding Nelson's hiring and promotion decisions and job security.

Since 1984 and our merger with James & Turney, we have been growing rapidly. In the last year alone, we have opened 22 new stores, creating many new management positions. As always, our hiring policy is to consider present employee qualifications *first* for available positions. We believe that our employees know the companys history and know their employees giving them valuable qualifications for managing Nelson's new stores. In the past year, we have promoted 12 people from within to store manager, more than ever before in Nelson's history. Unfortunately we don't always have enough people ready to assume managerial roles especially in times of rapid expansion. As expansion continues, qualified people may be hired to fill these newly created positions.

We would like to stress that there is *no* systematic policy for replacing existing managers with outside people. Virtually all outside people that have and will be hired will be placed in management position for our new stores.

As you may be aware, two store managers were recently let go. It was a difficult decision reached after careful consideration. We view this as an infrequent occurrence because we have faith in the quality of our managers.

We expect continuing expansion in the future and we will need your continued excellent performance to grow in the years ahead.

Appendix D: Suggestions for Face-to-Face Collaborative Writing Tasks

In developing the collaborative writing tasks, we discovered criteria that contribute to their pedagogical effectiveness. We list these criteria below and illustrate them by using features of the Nelson Hardware Case.

1) Use a case that creates a real-world situation about which the students can write. In the Nelson Hardware Case, a detailed scenario giving a history of the company, its hiring practices, and the current crisis is provided.

2) Provide the writers with a group identity; for example, by making them all members of a committee or team that must respond to a critical situation. In the Nelson Hardware Case, the group is placed in the role of Directors of Personnel. This group identity is mentioned several times to reinforce the idea.

3) Set up an urgent situation that requires a group response, such as a politically sensitive issue that is best handled by a group. For example, if the expected audience is diverse, with varying perspectives and interpretations, a diversity of writers may be in a stronger position to anticipate and address audience needs and expectations. A group response may also be more compelling and show more company commitment than a response from a single individual. In the Nelson's Hardware Case, the urgent situation is the employee morale problem and declining sales.

4) Incorporate some of the organizational and individual concerns that require a *group* writing effort. We speculate that collaborative tasks are chosen for many different organizational reasons, for example, when the impact of the document is expected to be significant, when the message content is controversial or unwelcome, when organizational or employee buy-in is necessary, when different perspectives or factions must be represented, and of course, when the scope of expertise required extends beyond the individual level. Individuals within an organization may choose to form a group to write a document to give the document greater credibility or weight, to protect individual writers, and also to distribute the work among individuals with different areas of expertise. In the Nelson Hardware Case, a group writing effort is warranted given the potential impact of the memorandum on employee morale and retention.

5) Clearly articulate "the audience" by describing who will receive the document and what their interests are. The Nelson Hardware

Case includes a review of the employees' memorandum to the Directors of Personnel, outlining the employees' concerns, and also includes employees' statements and threats about leaving the company.

6) Center the case around conflict between the group of writers and the group of readers. This conflict will be helpful in engaging group members in the task. The Nelson Hardware Case involves conflicting interpretations of the recent hiring and personnel decisions.

7) Require a persuasive response to the situation presented. A collaborative approach is advantageous for persuasive documents because writers can test their arguments on the other group members. In the Nelson Hardware Case, a persuasive document is needed to mollify the disgruntled employees and motivate them enough to bring sales back up.

8) Require a short document—a memorandum, press release, etc. The literature on collaborative writing in the classroom indicates that the typical project is a long document, such as a report, which group members may feel compelled to divide among themselves. The Nelson Hardware Case requires a memorandum.

9) Provide a time constraint. Time constraints reflect the reality of the workplace. The Nelson Hardware Case was designed to be completed in two hours.

We found both of the cases we developed with these criteria in mind to be compelling and challenging for groups. Students engaged in much spirited discussion about the cases throughout their collaborative sessions. They rarely discussed non-task-related ideas. Feedback from the student groups completing the collaborative writing tasks as part of their course requirement also reveals they found both the group writing and group dynamics challenging.

Works Cited

Abercrombie, Minnie Louie Johnson. *The Anatomy of Judgment: An Investigation into the Processes of Perception and Reasoning.* London: Hutchinson, 1960.

Adams, Pauline Gordon, and Emma Shore Thornton. "An Inquiry into the Process of Collaboration." *Language Arts Journal of Michigan* 2 (Spring 1986): 25–28.

Allen, Nancy, et al. "What Experienced Collaborators Say About Collaborative Writing." *Journal of Business and Technical Communication.* 1.2 (1987): 70–90.

Bruffee, Kenneth A. "Collaborative Learning and the 'Conversation of Mankind.'" *College English* 46 (1984): 635–52.

———. "Writing and Reading as Collaborative or Social Acts." *The Writer's Mind: Writing as a Mode of Thinking.* Ed. Janice N. Hays, et al. Urbana: NCTE, 1983, 159–169.

Burke, Kenneth. *A Rhetoric of Motives.* Berkeley: U of California P, 1969.

Carey, Linda, et al. "Differences in Writers' Initial Task Representations." *A Rhetoric of Doing.* Ed Stephen Witte et al. Carbondale: Southern Illinois UP, 1989.

Cicourel, Aaron V. "The Integration of Distributed Knowledge in Collaborative Medical Diagnosis." *Intellectual Teamwork: Social and Technological Foundations of Cooperative Work.* Ed. Jolene Galegher, Robert E. Krout, and Carmen Egido. Hillsdale, NJ: Lawrence Erlbaum Associates, 1990. 221–42.

Copeland, Jeffrey S., and Earl D. Lomax. "Building Effective Student Writing Groups." NCTE Committee on Classroom Practices in Teaching English, *Focus on Collaborative Learning: Classroom Practices in Teaching English.* Urbana: NCTE, 1988. 99–104.

Couture, Barbara, and Jone Rymer. "Interactive Writing on the Job: Definitions and Implications of Collaboration." *Writing in the Business Professions.* Ed. Myra Kogen. Urbana: NCTE, ABC, 1989. 73–93.

Daft, Richard L., and Robert H. Lengel. "Organizational Information Requirements, Media Richness and Structural Design." *Management Science* 32 (1986): 554–71.

Daiute, Colette. "Do 1 and 1 Make 2?" *Written Communication* 3 (1986): 382–408.

Deal, Terrence E., and Allan A. Kennedy. *Corporate Cultures: The Rites and Rituals of Corporate Life.* Reading, MA: Addison-Wesley, 1982.

Doheny-Farina, Stephen. "Writing in an Emerging Organization: An Ethnographic Study." *Written Communication* 3 (1986): 158–85.

Elwart-Keys, Mary, and Marjorie Horton. "Collaborative Writing in the Capture Lab: Computer Support for Group Writing." *Bulletin of the Association for Business Communication* 53.2 (1990): 38–44.

Faigley, Lester, and Thomas P. Miller. "What We Learn from Writing on the Job." *College English* 44 (1982): 557–69.

Finholt, Tim, Lee Sproull, and Sara Kiesler. "Communication and Performance in Ad Hoc Task Groups." *Intellectual Teamwork: Social and Technological Foundations of Cooperative Work.* Ed. Jolene Galegher, Robert E. Kraut, and Carmen Egido. Hillsdale: Lawrence Erlbaum Associates, 1990. 291–325.

Fleming, Margaret B. "Getting Out of the Writing Vacuum." NCTE Committee on Classroom Practices in Teaching English, *Focus on Collaborative Learning.* Urbana: NCTE, 1988. 77–84.

Foley, Marie. "Revising Response Groups." NCTE Committee on Classroom Practices in Teaching English, *Focus on Collaborative Learning*. Urbana: NCTE, 1988. 117–122.

Forman, Janis, and Patricia Katsky. "The Group Report: A Problem in Small Group or Writing Processes?" *Journal of Business Communication* 23.4 (1986): 24–35.

Horton, Marjorie, et al. "The Impact of Face-to-Face Collaborative Technology on Group Writing." *Proceedings of the Twenty-Fourth Annual Hawaii International Conference on System Sciences*. Los Alamitos: IEEE Computer Society. 1991.

Jaksa, James A., and Michael S. Pritchard. *Communication Ethics: Methods of Analysis*. Belmont: Wadsworth, 1988.

Janis, Irving L. *Groupthink*. 2nd ed. Boston: Houghton, 1982.

Kalven, Harry, Jr., and Hans Zeisel. *The American Jury*. 2nd ed. Chicago: U of Chicago P, 1971.

Lunsford, Andrea, and Lisa Ede. *Singular Texts/Plural Authors: Perspectives on Collaborative Writing*. Carbondale: Southern Illinois UP, 1990.

Paradis, James, David Dobrin, and Richard Miller. "Writing at Exxon ITD: Notes on the Writing Environment of an R&D Organization." *Writing in Nonacademic Settings*. Ed. Lee Odell and Dixie L. Goswami. New York: Guilford, 1985. 281–307.

Tompkins, Phillip K., and George Cheney. "Account Analysis of Organizations: Decision Making and Identification." *Communication and Organizations: An Interpretive Approach*. Ed. Linda L. Putnam and Michael E. Pacanowski. Beverly Hills: Sage, 1983. 123–46.

Twelve Angry Men. Screenplay by Reginald Rose. Directed by Sidney Lumet. Orion-Nova/UA, 1957.

Vygotsky, L. S. *Mind in Society: The Development of Higher Psychological Processes*. Ed. Michael Cole. Cambridge: Harvard UP, 1978.

8

Computer-Based Conversations and The Changing Nature of Collaboration

Cynthia L. Selfe

Some of the most promising applications of computers in communication classrooms have been those that support collaborative writing tasks in practical ways. But, if we know **how** to use computers in encouraging groups to brainstorm, to create multiauthored drafts, and to exchange critiques, our theoretical understanding of **why** computers work well as forums for collaboration is less clear. One explanation is that computer-based collaboration takes place under constraints that differ from those governing face-to-face collaboration and that this differing set of constraints may support different and productive kinds of collaborative learning. For example, collaborative groups using electronic exchanges, unlike groups that meet face-to-face, do not depend on visual cues about age, ethnicity, sex, and status. In electronic exchanges, moreover, there are no interruptions; and collaborators can use pseudonyms to identify their contributions if they wish. These characteristics of electronic collaboration, in contrast to the characteristics of face-to-face exchanges, may allow group members to experiment more freely with exploring differences in individual approaches to problems, writing tasks, and issues.

Increasingly during the last decade, composition teachers and researchers have come to recognize the value of collaboration in creating realistic writing tasks for their students. Collaborative activities are used to illustrate for students how written communication is socially constructed; they are also used to provide writers with experience in the complexities of negotiating meaning within and among texts, and

147

among readers and authors of texts (Bruffee; Lunsford and Ede; Hawkins; NCTE Committee on Classroom Practices in Teaching English; among many others). Supporting this growing emphasis on collaborative writing is an emphasis in industry on cooperation and community consensus as tools for increasing productivity and the related use of team efforts for writing tasks (Bruffee, "Conversation"; Myers; Trimbur).

However, if we know generally that designing and implementing productive collaborative ventures for use within a classroom can make for productive teaching and learning, we cannot always identify more specifically those strategies or approaches that make collaborative activities work well or effectively. As Kenneth Bruffee ("Conversation") points out,

> ...many teachers are unsure about how to use collaborative learning and about when and where, appropriately, it should be used. Many are concerned also that when they try to use collaborative learning in what seems effective and appropriate ways, it sometimes quite simply fails. I sympathize.... Sometimes collaborative learning works beyond my highest expectations. Sometimes it doesn't work at all. (636)

In exploring the "when" and "where" of collaboration, teachers have begun to experiment with computers and computer networks as alternative forums for writing tasks involving groups, peer critiquing, and information exchange. Among the claims made for these forums are the following:

> Computer-based exchanges of written discourse are often marked by patterns of individual involvement that differ from those marking face-to-face discourse. Individuals who do not contribute equally in face-to-face discussions (given factors of age, race, gender, handicap) often contribute more equally to on-line discussions because access to the "floor" in such discussions, given the nature of electronic environments, is afforded in an unlimited way to all participants. Individuals can take their time in formulating a response, and are not interrupted as they respond. (Batson; Bump; Cooper and Selfe; Faigley; Kiesler, Siegel, and McGuire; Pfaffenberger; Spitzer, 1986, 1989, 1990).

> Given the potential for egalitarian involvement by participants, computer-based collaborative ventures can support power structures that differ from those characterizing face-to-face discussions. In online discussions, cues of gender, age, race, and socioeconomic status are limited and, as a result, so is the privilege characterizing hierarchical hegemonies based on these factors. (Batson; Bump; Butler; Faigley; Hiltz; Kiesler, Seigel, and McGuire; Cooper and Selfe)

Such claims appeal especially to composition teachers who hope to provide opportunites for student-centered collaborative writing that involve members of their classes in active learning situations centering on written discourse. Often, these teachers are looking for nontraditional strategies for involving those individuals who might be considered — or consider themselves — marginally engaged in traditional academic forums and in the making of meaning within a classroom community. On-line conferences seem to offer alternative spaces for academic discussions and exchanges, forums that can encourage new patterns of student involvement because they offer different conversational power structures than those characterizing collaboration in the forum of a traditional classroom setting.

Exploring collaboration as it takes place in computer-supported writing environments may also help readers address some of the challenges of collaborative work in general. During the same period we have come to recognize the value of collaborative learning and writing in our classrooms, we have also come to realize that such writing assignments produce a unique set of problems that ought to concern us as teachers. I shall name just a few: finding a means of accurately and equitably assessing productivity and individuals' efforts (Hawkins; Weiner); designing effective collaborative projects and implementing them within the constraints of traditional classrooms (Duin; George, "Working"; Hawkins; Myers); dealing with the changing politics of learning within collaborative groups of various compositions (George, "Politics"; Trimbur); and redefining our conceptions of authorship, ownership, and authority in connection with writing (Berkenkotter).

One important and often overlooked set of problems growing out of collaborative writing activities has to do with the nature of personal interaction that takes place in the small groups that often serve as the primary vehicle for collaborative work. Teachers have only begun to realize the complexity of social interaction that characterizes the workings of these groups, especially during the face-to-face oral exchanges that punctuate and bound the processes of writing and collaboration (George, "Working"; Herreman; Whitworth). Teachers have noticed, for example, that students working in small collaborative writing groups may fail to respond frankly to the problems they see in a draft because of their "allegiance to peers" (Trimbur 615) or their antipathy toward peers (Whitworth).

As we begin to understand that collaborative writing groups are micropolitical environments that reflect the unequal distribution of power in our larger culture (Lunsford and Ede; Myers; Trimbur), we also begin to see that not all members of such groups contribute equitably to group collaboration or have the opportunity to participate in the same way within collaborative ventures (Herreman; Lunsford and Ede; Whitworth). Teachers have noticed that group members with high status within the culture at large (e.g., whites, males, people with high socioeconomic status, etc.) can come to control group discussions and collaborative endeavors while those group members who have relatively low status within the larger culture (women, older students, students of different races, handicapped students) are frequently afforded less privilege (Lunsford and Ede; Selfe 1988). Hence, some group members speak more than others and some group members are silenced or marginalized.

This essay explores the use of computer-based conferences as forums for collaborative activities and suggests that these environments may offer alternative patterns of communication and exchange. It begins with an overview of the research on such conferences, proceeds to an explanation of how computer-based forums for collaboration may function to change the nature of collaboration, and ends with a series of suggestions for setting up electronic environments for collaborative projects.

Current Research on Computer-Based Conferences

Although much of the evidence on computer-based collaborative activities as they function within composition classrooms is preliminary and anecdotal, it suggests that such activities may have the potential for encouraging vigorous, egalitarian written exchanges among students working in writing groups. Reports of on-line discussions via networks, for example, indicate that such forums encourage more people to participate in group discussions and efforts than do similarly constructed face-to-face meetings (Fersko-Weiss; Kiesler, Seigel, and McGuire; Pfaffenberger; Pullinger; Spitzer, "Writing Style"). Computer networks, further, have been reported to make collaboration possible for writers and readers in different geographical locations (Holvig; Pfaffenberger; Spitzer, "Computer Conferencing"); for individuals who are handicapped (Batson) or do not find it possible, because of age or economic constraints (Holvig; Ludtke) to get to a traditional classroom where they can participate in collaborative academic exchanges; and for individuals who do not find the traditional classroom a conducive environment for intellectual discussion (Hiltz; Meeks).

Claims about the value of computer-based forums as environments for collaborative activities have not been based solely on the grounds that such settings facilitate group connectedness when participants' schedules do not allow them to meet in person. Claims have also been made about how such environments may change the nature and the dynamics of group discussions and collaboration. Studies of computer-based communication in business environments, for instance, indicate that on-line forums may also encourage fluency in written communication (Czajkowski and Kiesler) and that up to 60% of the messages sent within a computer-based conversation may contain "new information";

that is, "information respondents reported they would have gotten (or sent) no other way if there were no electronic mail" (Sproull and Kiesler 1509). Further, work by Kiesler et al. indicates that computer-based discussions are less inhibited and often include more critical evaluation than face-to-face discussions because situations are depersonalized in certain ways. The anonymity and "weak social feedback" (99) often characteristic of computer-based conversations may contribute to this phenomenon.

This evidence suggests that, when used carefully by teachers in academic settings, computer-based conversations may provide a particular kind of language-based learning that encourages groups of writers to take risks with their interpretation of texts, to explore and challenge ideas with written language, and to question and negotiate the nature of textual authority (Cooper and Selfe; Lanham). It is important to note, however, that many of the claims for computer-based collaboration have not been systematically tested within reading- and writing-intensive classrooms and that many of our hopes for these conferences are based on preliminary evidence.

Collaboration and Power

The characteristics of computer-based forums for group discussion and collaboration are important because they may represent one way of addressing problems of participation, involvement, and the equitable distribution of power in collaborative groups that must otherwise depend primarily on face-to-face discussion.

Frequently, collaborative learning and writing activities, as they are set up in classrooms, are negotiated and shaped in small groups during a series of face-to-face conversations designed to help group members reach agreement on various aspects of the writing task. In these groups, depending on a teacher's pedagogical approach, students explore and negotiate the nature of the writing assignment, the audience for the task, the responsibilities involved in the task, or all of these subjects. Many teachers also have students work in these small groups to write or create text, to critique text produced by group members, and to analyze and evaluate the text produced by the group in its collaborative effort (cf. Bruffee, "Conversation"; Elbow; NCTE Committee on Classroom Practices in Teaching English).

However, the workings of these small groups as they come to a consensus about their representations of writing tasks, a process often completed through a series of face-to-face discussions, may well contribute to some of the problems mentioned earlier, notably the differential exercise of power on the part of various group members and the resultant marginalization or silencing of some individuals. Although scholars who write about collaboration recognize this set of problems, they differ in their interpretation and in the solutions they pose.

To understand the nature of their disagreement and why it is so important to the current discussion, it is necessary to start with a definition of collaborative learning. For the purpose of this paper, I will use one offered by John Trimbur. This definition contains his interpretations of similar definitions offered by Kenneth Bruffee ("Conversation") and Harvey Weiner. Trimbur explains:

> ...collaborative learning may be distinguished from other forms of group work in that it organizes students to work not just together on common projects but more important to engage in a process of intellectual negotiation and collective decision making. The aim of collaborative learning...is to reach consensus through an expanding conversation. (602)

It is around the notion of "consensus" and the processes of reaching consensus that much of the controversy about collaboration turns. Bruffee, especially in his early work ("Practical Models"), ties his notion of collaborative consensus to that of democratic power sharing and those "nonauthoritarian styles of leadership and group life" (Trimbur 605) growing out of educational reforms of the 60s and 70s. Bruffee ("Conversation") maintains that "to learn to think well as individuals, we must learn to think well collectively — that is, we must learn to converse well" (640) within a democratic "community of status equals" or peers (642) that comes to agree on or share conversation and, hence, knowledge.

Bruffee notes that teachers are responsible for designing collaborative assignments that help students move toward consensual understanding by encouraging an expanded conversation that is as similar "as possible to the way in which we would like them eventually to read and write." (642) He adds, "The way they [student learners] talk with each other determines the way they will think and the way...that they will write" (642) and reminds teachers that the community of collaborative groups in which students function "approximates" the communities within which they will function "in everyday life, in business, government, and the professions" (642).

Greg Myers and, in a slightly different way, John Trimbur find Bruffee's notion of consensus and its implications problematic. These two authors see consensus as a theoretical construct that has been naively interpreted as "acculturative" (Trimbur 612). If Bruffee is right in thinking that collaborative groups mirror the normal workings of groups in government, industry, and busines — Trimbur and Myers point out — teaching students to value consensus and the process of reaching it means that we also teach them to accept "the current production and distribution of knowledge and discourse as unproblematical and given" (Trimbur 610). Such an approach is difficult to support, these authors point out, in light of the way that our capitalist system "perpetuates...economic, racial, and sexist injustices" (Myers 156–157) by suppressing or excluding interests that are not accommodative to such a system.

Trimbur and Myers suggest, in other words, that teaching students to value a normative notion of consensus as they work in groups can lead to a silencing or marginalization of students who may hold views contrary to the dominant ideology, who may be members of a minority group, who may be women, who may be disabled, who may simply be reluctant to compete in the verbal marketplace of ideas replicated in most traditional classrooms. As Myers notes, "Any teacher who uses group discussions or projects has seen that they can, on occasion, be fierce enforcers of conformity" (159).

To combat such a vision of consensus within collaborative groups, both authors offer a more critical vision of consensus as "the result of conflicts" (Myers 166) that must be acknowledged. These authors would teach students to value "dissensus" and a "collective investigation of differences" (Trimbur 615) rather than consensus in collaborative projects. Bruffee himself, in later writings ("Conversation"), recognizes the need for groups to value both "abnormal discourse" (648), a term borrowed from Rorty, which "challenges the authority of knowledge" (649), and accommodative discourse in the work of collaborative groups.

Problematically, however, these authors fail to recognize the difficulties in translating their ideas into practice. Most collaborative groups operate within traditional classroom settings and depend primarily on competitive face-to-face discussions as forums for knowledge transfer, negotiation, and creation. Students accustomed to the values of such traditional forums may well find it difficult or impossible to resist or challenge existing cultural power structures replicated or mirrored in small groups.

In fact, the nature of the traditional classroom setting as a forum for such group activities promotes some of these problems. Students who are more verbally articulate in collaborative projects that depend heavily on face-to-face discussions as a vehicle for information exchange are rewarded for verbal assertiveness by both teachers and students with increased attention, and often by competitive grading schemas that identify verbal participation as a valued behavior. Hence, students who are already assertive about their verbal group input, often because they enjoy a confidence born of privilege, get more rewards. In such settings, women, who traditionally speak less than men (Rich; Spender) and are interrupted more often (Zimmerman and West) are at a disadvantage, as are students less articulate in oral than in written discourse. Group members who want to take time to think about their response before they offer it or students who are merely polite are often out of luck. Older student group members, who may be hesitant to add their views; or students with physical handicaps, who cannot verbalize, may also be at a disadvantage in such a collaborative setting.

Linguistic research on oral conversational exchanges supports the contention that power in face-to-face discussions is not exercised in an equitable fashion. In face-to-face conversations, one variable that has been cited frequently in studies of groups engaging in problem-solving discussions (meetings of departmental faculty members and other participants of conversations, Sacks, Schegloff, and Jefferson) involves turn taking. Such research indicates that women are interrupted more frequently in their turns and speak less often than do men in the same situation, a finding that should concern teachers of English who use face-to-face small group discussions as the basis for most of the collaborative work that their students do.

Linguists have also studied topic initiation and maintenance to identify how individuals exert power on a "micropolitical" scale (West and Zimmerman 102) within the conversations of two or more persons. In such conversations, findings indicate that women initiate more topics than do men, but men's topics receive more attention (Fishman, 1983, 1978). Agreement and disagreement have also been noted as markers of power patterns in conversations; dominant individuals, who have power, disagreeing more often than do less powerful individuals and offering fewer supportive "agree" statements than do those same individuals (Brown and Levinson; Edelsky). Finally, linguists have used the number of questions asked and the number of apologies made by individuals to study characteristic power relationships (Brown and Levison). In cross-sex studies, investigators have noted that females ask more questions (Fishman, 1983, 1978), make more apologies (Eubanks; Kalcik), and exert less power than males in certain conversational settings.

Hence, while several scholars note that collaborative groups should be taught to value differences of opinion rather than strive for premature and normative consensus, little work has been done to suggest how this more sophisticated vision of collaboration can be played out successfully in traditional classroom settings where pedagogical, cultural, and linguistic patterns of face-to-face discussions support traditional power differentials among individuals.

A Case Study of Computer-Based
Collaboration: Megabyte U.

To teachers who use small group face-to-face meetings as forums for collaborative projects that go on in a classroom, such realizations are disturbing indeed and threaten to outweigh some of the most valued benefits of collaborative activities. They point, certainly, to the advantages of establishing alternative forums for collaborative endeavors that are not constrained by the same power structures operative within face-to-face discussions in traditional classroom settings.

In this context, computer-based forums have some potential for providing teachers with supplemental environments for collaborative activities, settings that diminish many cues of status, gender, race, and handicap. Perhaps because they have grown out of hackers' bulletin boards and a computer culture only marginally related to traditional academic endeavor, such forums — when shaped by reformist educators — have been reported by some teachers to encourage a focus on ideas rather than on personalities and to provide a reduced-risk setting in which writers can be encouraged to examine the nature and value of dissensus as they learn.

Preliminary research findings on such forums operating in business and industry support this contention. Computer-based exchanges have been observed to minimize some cues of gender, race, and social status in established organizational hierarchies, especially when pseudonyms are used to disguise writers' identity (Kiesler, Seigel, and McGuire; Sproull and Kiesler). The ability to minimize social and hierarchical cues, in turn, contributes to more egalitarian participation by individual group members engaged in a common task and the decreasing potential for group domination by individuals (Kiesler, Seigel, and McGuire; Spitzer, "Writing Style").

These findings and others have been tested recently in a discourse-based study of an on-line forum called Megabyte University, a collection of approximately seventy English teachers who participate in an electronic exchange of written information about using computers to teach writing- and reading-intensive classes. This conversation, held on Bitnet, was created by Fred Kemp of Texas Tech University in March 1989 as an attempt to extend the face-to-face discussions initiated at two academic conferences beyond the temporal and geographic limitations characterizing such short-term professional gatherings.[1] As Kemp noted in an early explanatory note on Megabyte, the network was "intended not as a chat net or a technical exchange, but as a continuing discussion regarding important aspects of an emerging field, Computers and English." Megabyte contributors have collaborated in writing tasks of interest to the group, in solving problems at individual contributors' sites, and in analyzing problems within the profession at large.[2]

Like many electronic conferences, both in and out of classrooms, Megabyte resembles most closely an on-line letter exchange in which participants send "messages" or "texts" to a common location, where they are then collected into a longer document constituting a public conversation or dialogue. These longer documents, consisting of multiple messages from a number of participants, are sent, within a day or two, to each individual on the Megabyte mailing list. Thus, Megabyte can also be described as an asynchronous exchange that depends heavily on electronic wide-area networks (WAN) such as Bitnet and Edunet as vehicles for exchanging messages and conversations.

Given this relatively common setup for asynchronous on-line conferences, participants on Megabyte sign on to their computers, read the collected on-line messages sent by Kemp from Texas Tech, write a reply to one or more of the messages or topics someone has written (using a Bitnet address supplied by Kemp), and send this reply via Bitnet to a computer at Texas Tech University, where it is added to the common conference files to be distributed. Although, given individual participants' personal schedules, individual messages are sent to Kemp daily, collected messages (referred to henceforth as the Megabyte conference exchange) are distributed on a more occasional basis depending on the time Kemp has to attend to the Megabyte traffic and the relative heaviness of that traffic. Collected messages usually arrive every day or so, sometimes skipping a long weekend or a vacation period. For the most part, Megabyte participants sign their own names to the messages they send, much as they would in sending a regular letter by post. However, some participants have used pseudonyms for "signing" messages. Collaborative writing tasks have also been undertaken on Megabyte.

To become involved in this collaborative exchange of written information, participants must have access to a computer linked to one of the WANs that can communicate with the Texas Tech location. In most cases, participants use a personal computer, linked by modem or local-area network (LAN) to a university-based mainframe computer that is tied into one of the national WANs.

There are characteristics of Megabyte that make this conference similar to many on-line conferences used by teachers in composition or literature classrooms: it involves a number of participants, some of whom know each other and some of whom do not; it is *asynchronous*, or incapable of supporting conversations as they happen (as opposed to *synchronous*, or capable of supporting "real-time" conversations); and it focuses discussions or collaborative writing tasks of common interest to participants.[3] In other ways, however, the Megabyte conversation is quite unlike the on-line discussions that students might be involved in. Among these differences, Megabyte participants communicate via a national wide-area network (WAN) rather than on a local-area network (LAN) as used in most academic classrooms and on many campuses. In addition, Megabyte participants are professional educators who choose to participate and collaborate in this on-line setting given their common interest in composition studies, while most students involved in on-line collaboration are required to participate as a function of the course in which they are enrolled.

For the study of Megabyte, a 40-day sample of the conversation was chosen: 20 days of network exchanges in which participants signed their real name to messages and 20 days immediately following a decision to try a pseudonym-optional period of exchange. The sample periods were selected to provide two reasonably large and continuous chunks of Megabyte conversation, as well as a basis for examining claims about involvement, power, and pseudonym use in this on-line conference. During the periods under study, 296 individual messages were sent by 33 different participants (18 males and 15 females from 16 different states), an average of 7.3 messages a day. Excerpts from a typical day's collection of messages are represented in the appendix. Of the total number of sample messages, 107 were sent in the first 20-day period and 189 in the second 20-day period.

In addition, because this was a study of involvement and power structures in written on-line exchanges, two independent variables, sex and professional status (as factors having a relationship to power and status within conversations) were noted for each message and analyzed in relationship to the dependent variables. As noted earlier, sex is considered an important variable in linguistic studies of individual, face-to-face conversations because it is closely associated with power differentials.

Professional "profile" was chosen as the primary marker of social status within the Megabyte group because most members function within a university or college system that places high value on national publication or distribution of the faculty members' work, and because such work results in a wider visibility within the computers and composition studies field. Colleagues who speak frequently at national meetings, publish articles on computers in nationally distributed academic journals, or market and author software are more well known by their colleagues than those who do not. Professional visibility for participants was marked "high" if an individual had published at least one article on computers and composition in a nationally distributed academic journal or if an individual was associated with the marketing, demonstration, or discussion of at least one highly visible commercial software package at national conferences—attaching her name to a product as author or user, appearing in the exhibitors' area of such conferences during demonstration sessions, or speaking at conference sessions about the use of the software package. For the sample, 11 males and 10 females were identified as "high" visibility, 7 males and 5 females identified as "low" visibility.

At least three findings in this study are of particular interest in connection with the preceding discussion about collaboration and dissensus. First, given the very nature of this asynchronous, on-line discussion, no participants were ever interrupted as they contributed to the conversation. In addition, all participants held the floor for as long as they wished during each "turn" that they took in the conversation — that is, participants could make each message as long as they desired. This pattern of exchange differs from face-to-face conversations in which interruptions are often used to dominate conversations and exercise power. In the Megabyte conversation, all four groups of participants had equal access to the on-line exchange and had the opportunity to contribute as much as they wanted to the conversation.

Second, there were additional, albeit more subtle, indications that the patterns of conversation in Megabyte differed from those in face-to-face conversations. Although males and high-profile individuals contributed more messages to the conversation and were more verbally assertive (as measured by the number of disagreements they initiated), for example, women participants in Megabyte often wrote longer messages. In addition, there were no significant differences in the proportion of direct personal references made to participants in any of the four groups. Because direct references, in this study, were used as one index of the attention participants paid to the ideas of individuals within the on-line conversation, this result provides another small indication that the attention given to participants in the Megabyte exchange was not based on sex and profile differences. The Megabyte conversation also showed no significant differences in the number of politeness markers — agreements, questions, apologies — among the four groups. Within face-to-face discussions, in contrast, such politeness markers are typically associated with the conversation of women and low-power individuals.[4]

Finally, the pseudonym-optional period of the Megabyte conversation offers another indication that exchanges held on-line may encourage different patterns of engagement for participants and may support dissensus in ways that face-to-face conversations do not. During the pseudonym period — although men and high-profile individuals continued to write significantly more messages and to be more verbally assertive than were women and low-profile participants — the conversation was also characterized by a prolonged and controversial exchange about the use of pseudonyms, the exercise of power, and the relationship of these two activities to gender and status within the Megabyte community. The controversy focused on whether the Megabyte conversation, when it used real names to identify participants' messages, unintentionally marginalized some participants and whether the option of using pseudonyms alleviated such patterns of exchange if they did, indeed, exist.

During this discussion, the group's dissensus on the issues was extended and thoroughly examined. During a period of approximately twenty days, some vocal participants — often, although not exclusively, male — continued to express doubt about the value of using pseudonyms and noted that such an activity could become counterproductive. In contrast, other participants — generally, although not exclusively, female and low-profile — continued to note that they considered the option of using pseudonyms liberating and explored the reasons why they thought this was so. Certainly, there was a wide range of opinion on this set of issues. Several participants noted that it was the reduced-risk environment afforded by the pseudonym-optional period that allowed this extended discussion of sensitive and volatile issues to take place. There is no way of proving, of course, that a similarly extended and controversial discussion could not take place in an environment where identities were more directly revealed, but in the Megabyte environment, at least, it did not. In fact, as the group collectively and slowly abandoned the pseudonym-optional mode, the discussion of gender, status, and power issues faded correspondingly. Final contributions on the subject, interestingly, were made using pseudonyms even though the conversation, in general, had moved away from this practice.

In applied terms — while these findings must be interpreted cautiously as describing only limited aspects of one particular group of collaborators and their processes — they lend some support to previous research indicating computer-based conferences can provide alternative forums for cooperative, collaborative exchanges of written information. If these collaborative forums are carefully crafted, it may be possible for teachers and students to use them to encourage different kinds of collaborative patterns for group members.

Suggestions for Teaching with On-Line Collaboration

Although these early findings represent a case that is far from complete, they can suggest to classroom teachers who employ collaborative writing assignments several methods for adding computer-based support in their courses and for studying the results. When we get some preliminary experience in using these methods and informally observing their effects on our students and their collaboration, we can begin to test in a systematic fashion the claims for computer environments as productive forums for collaborative activities.

Interpreting and Analyzing Collaborative Tasks

One method of supporting students as they begin to explore and analyze a collaborative writing task is to provide a computer-based conference as a forum for some of their discussions about the assignment. Allowing individual participants the option of using pseudonyms in such a setting might provide those participants who have relatively little power in the face-to-face discussions with a different kind of voice. In such a reduced-risk environment, where, as Michael Spitzer ("Writing Style") notes, "powerful ideas...have more impact than... powerful personalities" (20), group members might be at once more likely to proffer opinions that differ from the majority opinion and to consider marginal interpretations that might otherwise be dismissed in face-to-face conversations.

Such a forum could, in Trimbur's words, provide a place wherein students are encouraged to express their interpretations of a task and then undertake a "collective investigation of differences" (614) in their opinions—without the same kinds of social embarrassment that constrain behavior in face-to-face exchanges. This forum could, in turn, allow collaborative groups to see more clearly the value of dissensus and might even serve to delay premature decisions in one particular problem-solving direction.

Preliminary research evidence supports these suggestions. Kiesler, Seigel, and McGuire note that groups collaborating on decisions via computers took longer to reach a decision, were more "uninhibited" in their discussion (their commentary contained more hostile remarks and swearing than did that of similar face-to-face groups), and demonstrated a higher incidence of changing their original position on a topic than did face-to-face groups. Further, these investigators speculated that the relative lack of social and nonverbal cues in computer-based conferences may have allowed participants to "ignore social pressure to reach consensus" (1129).

Completing Collaborative Tasks

Teachers in writing-intensive courses can also use computer networks and conferences to support groups as they begin writing collaboratively. Individuals have reported success in using computers to support the generation of ideas (Burns and Culp; Spitzer, 1989), the discussion of ideas (Spitzer, "Computer Conferencing"), and the drafting and revision of collaborative papers (Bernhardt and Appleby; Pullinger). During the writing process, computerized prewriting or invention aids, word-processing packages, spelling and style checkers, graphics packages, data bases, and on-line library searches may also support on-line group composition.

Finally, computers can allow groups to "meet" and write without having to coordinate schedules or physical locations—not a small advantage when collaborative groups contain members who live far from each other or members who cannot, for economic or physical reasons, travel frequently to a common meeting location.

Critiquing and Revising Collaborative Projects

One of the greatest challenges reported by teachers who employ collaborative activities is to get students to read each other's work critically and to provide productive feedback to other group members (Bruffee, "Conversation"; George, "Working"; Whitworth). As Weiner points out, groups not given sufficient guidelines or protocols for collaborative writing tasks may "just pat each other on the back, attack each other counterproductively, or fall silent" (56).

Often, students' lack of strategies for effective critiquing is complicated by social constraints. In writing classrooms, without knowing how students interact with each other outside class hours, teachers may unwittingly ask students to provide effective critical, and often sensitive, evaluations of the work of their roommates, their supervisors in organizational or work situations, or their dating partners. Those of us who have found our own face-to-face critique sessions with certain colleagues difficult, alienating, patronizing, or falsely encouraging know just how powerful such social constraints can be.

Using a computer-based forum to support critiquing—in addition to providing careful direction for commenting on written texts—could alleviate some of the pain and embarrassment involved in students' exchange of critical commentary on drafts.

On-Line Collaboration and Exploring the Value of Dissensus

As a profession, we do not yet know enough about how individuals collaborate—within face-to-face groups or on-line. Early findings about on-line conferences, however, indicate that teachers may be able to employ them productively as forums for collaborative writing projects.

Although these forums may require writers to operate within a unique set of constraints (the difficulty of reviewing long documents on line; the constraints that a small screen places on both writers and readers; the problems of struggling with awkward network, hardware, or software), they may also, under the direction of a skillful teacher, provide an alternative forum for the exchange of information within a group. Indeed, many teachers are already reporting that computer-based collaboration is serving such purposes. Preliminary claims for these on-line environments indicate that they limit some of the social and visual cues that inhibit face-to-face conversation and, in doing so, create an environment in which individuals who are less powerful in traditional collaborative exchanges can find a more central role or voice, can feel more able to take risks.

To assess our success in creating such environments, teachers who use computer-based collaboration can contribute by exploring in a systematic fashion the effects computer-based forums have on the collaborative writing activities of their students. Among other projects, they can undertake efforts to examine students' attitudes toward collaborative activities, observe the processes they employ within on-line collaborative writing tasks, identify group members' perceptions of consensus and dissensus, collect data that describe on-line conversations and collaborations, and analyze how group members handle agreement and disagreement.

If on-line collaborative forums do indeed present group members with a reduced-risk environment, then these settings may also help them explore the value of "difference without domination" (Trimbur 615) and examine, in a productive way, the "conflicts inherent in an unequal social order and in the asymmetrical relations of power in everyday life" (609). Teachers, under these circumstances, may be able to work with students to construct a more critical vision of collaborative learning as "not merely...a process of consensus-making but more important...[as] a process of identifying differences and locating these differences in relation to each other" and to understand how "collective agreements" can be based on "collective explanations of how people differ, where their differences come from, and whether they can live and work together with these differences" (610).

Notes

1. These two conferences—the 1989 Conference on College Composition and Communication in Seattle, Washington, and the fifth annual Computers and Writing Conference in Minneapolis, Minnesota—were particularly rich gatherings of scholars interested in the teaching of composition and the use of computers.

2. Megabyte participants, for example, have collaborated by reading and commenting on several drafts of a paper entitled "Computer-Based Forums for Academic Discourse: Testing the Claims for On-Line Conferences" that I wrote late in 1989 and early in 1990. A number of Megabyte participants collaborated with John Slatin (University of Texas at Austin) in writing a formal response to a published article in *Academic Computing*. This on-line response was published in *Computers and Composition* in August 1990. More informal collaboration—in the form of group analysis, problem solving, and evaluation—takes place every day on Megabyte.

3. It is important to interpret all findings in this paper with caution, given the limitations of the Megabyte study and the nature of the conference itself. Findings in the Megabyte study cannot be generalized to conferences for student populations. Megabyte, for example, is a voluntary conversation among colleagues, not a compulsory conversation among students in connection with an academic class.

4. For further explanation of this study—including details on the methodology, statistical analyses, findings, and further cautions for interpreting the

data — see "Computer-Based Forums for Academic Discourse: Testing the Claims for On-Line Conferences," by Cynthia L. Selfe and Paul Meyer.

Appendix: Sample Megabyte Conversation

From TTACS::YKMBU "Megabyte U" 20-SEP-1989 07:11:06.50 To: @national
CC: Subj: Query about Garrison (Larry H.)

Date: Tue, 19 Sep 89 16:38 EST From: Larry Hunt <LSHNCE@ RITVAX> Subject: off the point....

This is completely off the point, and I desperately hope that it's not setting a precedent, but....

did ANYone out there happen to get an audio copy of Garrison Keillor's bit "The Lutheran's Guide to the Orchestra" last week?????

I'd like to use a pseudonym to avoid claiming responsibility for such an abuse of MBU as this, but that would sort of defeat the purpose, right?

Larry H. lshnce@ritvax

From: TTACS::YKMBU "Megabyte U" 20-SEP-1989 07:12:35.04 To: @national
CC: Subj: In on the tweak (Incognito)

From: Incognito

Ted, Your take on the issue of "light names" interests me. You look at it from the writer's point of view, and seem especially sensitive to the "economics" — who gets "credit" and for what. But your account doesn't exactly consider how the community decides what is "dumb" stuff and ought to disappear and what is "good stuff" and therefore deserves to be mentioned to others and cherished. Gypsy, as I recall, seemed to think that some voices carried more weight than others not by virtue of what they said but by virtue of who was saying it. And Trent has already admitted that the gender of an author colors and disturbs his reading, every bit as much as his awareness of gender influences his reactions in face-to-face exchanges. These seem to me to be the real issues. I'm pleased that Terrence now feels free to flap away and that freedom is closely tied to his sense of accountability for what he says. Anonymity gives him room to experiment out loud without fearing that his contributions will come home to haunt him—that future contributions will come with the tag "already-said-some-dumb-stuff-here-and-probably-ought-not-to-be-taken-too-seriously. Everything we include in "reputation" is at stake here, but even more important to me is how those reputations come to be what they are in the first place. And that's why I'm going underground. Not because I fear accountability or want credit to my name, but because we need to have a good look at how the group distributes power and authority within the comfortable domain we have already achieved . . . [ellipses mine]. So count me in on the "tweak."

Incognito

From:TTACS::YKMBU "Megabyte U" 20-SEP-1989 07:14:09.14 To: @national
CC: Subj: Collectives only? (Louie C.)

Date: Tue, 19 Sep 89 18:54 EST From: Louie Crew <LCREW @DRACO> Subject: Collectives only?

> The myth of the writer writing individually and in isolation> is a function of the Platonic/Augustinian/Romantic bias> in pre-post-modern literary criticism, and a holdover from> the 19th century demolition of rhetoric as a discipline> by philologists, grammarians, and literature cultists.> (whew!)

You mean even those women who thought they weren't networking, were? You mean we have no privacy? Or that we should not?

Sorry, I've spent much of my life fighting bullies, and this philosophy sounds like it could empower some others, especially those who favor doublespeak.

I would like to see you relate this to one of the questions I've raised about risk. Does diversity surface much on networks? As much as conformity?

Diversity surfaces all over the library. Or have I completely misunderstood?

From: TTACS::YKMBU "Megabyte U" 20-SEP-1989 07:15:48.44 To: @national
Subj: MBU as text (John S.)

Date: Tuesday, 19 September 1989 6:53pm CST From: John Slatin
EIEB360@UTXVM.BITNET

Neat question, Trent, and I surprise myself by being quite sure that
I *don't* consider that set of messages about evaluation to constitute a
"text"; I think the criterion I'm using is that if it were mine to do with
as I liked, I wouldn't publish it as is. It's perhaps a draft — which of
course means that I don't (I must not) consider a draft as a text. A
draft is what's going to become a text when it's "finished," or at least
when the person working on it has stopped working on it for a while.
And yet I would consider the individual messages comprising that
discussion as texts — since they each underwent some such process (or,
if not, as mine often don't, it isn't because it's impossible to revise and
polish — as Ishmael noted a few messages ago). Whew, what a sentence.
But I hope I make myself relatively clear: the set of messages comprising
the MBU discussion of evaluation does not constitute a text, but the
individual messages do constitute texts. Contradictory? No doubt. But
wait till you hear what just struck me: that if I were to *print* those
messages, so as, e.g., to "pore over them" (Ishmael's phrasing again —
that Melville's a powerful writer!) and analyze them as Cindy's trying
to do, *then* I'd regard the printout as a text. No, not quite: I'd
regard the body of messages as constituting a text. I think it must have
something to do with the perhaps illusory sense of closure that's involved
in, for instance, printing out a set of messages (as if there aren't going
to be any more on that subject), or simply in constituting an object of
study for the purpose of writing about it: does it become a text because
one regards it in a certain way?

Whoever said that about the eloquence and elegance of all these
dashed-off messages must not have been reading mine!

Confused (as ever), John

Works Cited

Batson, Trent. "The ENFI Project: A Networked Classroom Approach to
Writing Instruction." *Academic Computing* Feb.–March 1988: 32–33,
55–56.

Berkenkotter, Carol. "Student Writers and Their Sense of Authority over
Text." *College Composition and Communication* 35 (1984): 312–319.

Bernhardt, Steven, and Bruce Appleby. "Collaboration in Professional Writing
with the Computer." *Computers and Composition* 3.1 (1985): 29–42.

Bowen, Betsy, and Jeffrey Schwartz. "What's Next for Computers: Electronic
Networks in the Writing Classroom." Paper given at the annual meeting of

the National Council of Teachers of English. San Antonio, TX, November 1986.

Brown, Penelope, and Stephen Levinson. "Universal in Language Usage: Politeness Phenomena." *Questions and Politeness: Strategies in Social Interaction.* Ed. Esther Goody, Cambridge, MA: Cambridge UP, 1978. 56–289.

Brownell, Winifred, and Dennis R. Smith. "Communication Patterns, Sex, and Length of Verbalization in Speech of Four-Year-Old Children." *Speech Monographs* 40 (1973): 310–16.

Bruffee, Kenneth A. "Collaborative Learning: Some Practical Models." *College English* 34 (1973): 634–43.

———. "CLTV: Collaborative Learning Televison." *Educational Communication and Technology Journal* 30.1 (1982): 26–46.

———. "Collaborative Learning and the 'Conversation of Mankind.'" *College English* 46 (1984): 635–52.

Bump, Jerome. "Radical Changes in Class Discussion Using Networked Computers." Unpublished Paper, The University of Texas at Austin, 1988.

Burns, Hugh, and George Culp. "Stimulating Invention in English Composition through Computer-Assisted Instruction." *Educational Technology* 20.8 (1980): 5–10.

Butler, Wayne B. "The Construction of Meaning in an Electronic Interpretive Community." Paper presented at the annual convention of the NCTE. Baltimore, MD, November 1989.

Cooper, Marilyn, and Cynthia L. Selfe. "Computer Conferences and Learning: Authority, Resistance, and Internally Persuasive Discourse." *College English* 52 (1990): 847–69.

Czajkowski, Alex, and Sara Kiesler. "Computer-Mediated Communication: Or the Next Best Thing to Being There." *National Forum* 3 (1984): 31–34.

Daiute, Collette. "Issues in Using Computers to Socialize the Writing Process." *Educational Communication and Technology Journal.* 33.1 (1985): 41–50.

Duin, Ann H. "Implementing Cooperative Learning Groups in the Writing Curriculum." *Journal of Teaching Writing* 5 (1986): 315–23.

Eakins, Barbara, and Gene Eakins. *Sex Differences in Human Communication.* Boston: Houghton, 1978.

Edelsky, Carole. "Who's Got the Floor?" *Language in Society* 10 (1981): 383–421.

Elbow, Peter. *Writing Without Teachers.* New York: Oxford UP, 1973.

Eubanks, Sheryl, B. "Sex-based Language Differences: A Cultural Reflection." *Views on Language.* Ed. R. Ordoubadian and W. von Raffler Engel. Murfreesboro, TN: Inter-University, 1975. 109–20.

Faigley, Lester. "Subverting the Electronic Notebook: Teaching Writing Using

Networked Computers." *The Writing Teacher as Researcher: Essays in the Theory and Practice of Class-Based Research*. Ed. Max Morenberg and Donald Daiker. Portsmouth, NH: Boynton/Cook, 1990. 290–311.

Fersko-Weiss, Henry. Electronic Mail: The Emerging Connection. *Personal Computing* (1985): 717–19.

Fishman, Pamela M. "Interaction: The Work Women Do." *Language, Gender, and Society*. Ed. Barrie Thorne, Cheris Kramarae, and Nancy Henley. Rowley, MA: Newbury, 1983. 89–102.

———. "What Do Couples Talk About When They're Alone:" *Women's Language and Style*. Ed. Douglas Butturff and Edmund L. Epstein. Akron: L and S Books, 1978. 11–22.

George, Diana. "Working with Peer Groups in the Composition Classroom." *College Composition and Communication* 35 (1984): 320–26.

———. "The Politics of Social Construction and the Teaching of Writing." *Journal of Teaching Writing* 8.1 (1989): 1–10.

Hawkins, Thom. *Group Inquiry Techniques for Teaching Writing*. Urbana: ERIC Clearinghouse on Reading and Communication Skills and the NCTE, 1976.

Herreman, Dana. "None of Us is as Smart as All of Us." NCTE Committee on Classroom Practices in Teaching English. *Focus on Collaborative Learning: Classroom Practices in Teaching English*. Urbana: NCTE, 1988. 5–12.

Hiltz, Starr Roxanne. "The 'Virtual Classroom': Using Computer-Mediated Communication for University Teaching." *Journal of Communication* 36.2 (1986): 94–105.

Holvig, Kenneth. "Voices Across the Wires through Breadnet and Clarknet." Paper given at the Conference on College Composition and Communication. Los Angeles, CA, March 1987.

Kalcik, Susan. "'...like Ann's Gynecologist or the Time I was almost Raped': Personal Narratives in Women's Rap Groups." *Journal of American Folklore* 88 (1975): 3–11.

Kiesler, Sara, Jane Seigel, and Timothy McGuire. "Social Psychological Aspects of Computer-Mediated Communication." *American Psychologist* 39 (1984): 1123–34.

Kiesler, Sara, et al. "Affect in Computer Mediated Communication." *Human Computer Interaction* 1 (1985): 77–104.

Lanham, Richard. "Convergent Pressures: Social, Technological, Theoretical." Paper presented at the The Future of Doctoral Studies in English conference. Wayzeta, MN, April 1987.

Ludtke, M. "Great Human Power or Magic: An Innovative Program Sparks the Writing of America's Children." *Time*, 14 September 1987: 76.

Lunsford, Andrea, and Lisa Ede. *Singular Texts/Plural Authors: Perspectives on Collaborative Writing*. Carbondale: Southern Illinois UP, 1990.

Meeks, Bryan. "Overview of Conferencing Systems." *BYTE*, Dec. 1985: 169–184.

Myers, Greg. "Reality, Consensus, and Reform in the Rhetoric of Composition Teaching." *College English* 48 (1986): 154–74.

NCTE Committee on Classroom Practices in Teaching English. *Focus on Collaborative Learning*. Urbana: NCTE, 1988.

Pfaffenberger, Bryan. "Research Networks, Scientific Communication, and the Personal Computer." *IEEE Transactions on Professional Communication* PC 29.1 (1986): 30–33.

Pullinger, D. J. "Chit-Chat to Electronic Journals: Computer Conferencing Supports Scientific Communication." *IEEE Transactions on Professional Communication* PC 29.1 (1986): 23–29.

Rich, Adrienne. *On Lies, Secrets, and Silence: Selected Prose 1966–78*. New York: Norton, 1979.

Rodrigues, Dawn. "Computers and Basic Writers." *College Composition and Communication* 36 (1985): 336–39.

Sacks, Harvey, Emanuel Schegloff, and Gail Jefferson. "A Simplest Systematics for the Organization of Turn Taking in Conversation." *Language* 50 (1978): 696–735.

Selfe, Cynthia L. "Technology in the English Classroom: Computers Through the Lens of Feminist Theory." *Computers and Community: Teaching Composition in the Twenty-first Century*. Ed. Carolyn Handa. Portsmouth, NH: Boynton/Cook, 1990. 118–39.

Selfe, Cynthia L., and Johndan Eilola. "The Tie That Binds: Building Group Cohesion through Computer-Based Conferences." *Collegiate Microcomputer* 6 (1988): 339–48.

Selfe, Cynthia L., and Paul Meyers. "Computer-Based Forums for Academic Discourse: Testing the Claims for On-Line Conferences." *Written Communication* 8: 163–92.

Selfe, Cynthia L., and Billie Wahlstrom. "An Emerging Rhetoric of Collaboration: Computers and the Composing Process." *Collegiate Microcomputer*, 4 (1985): 289–95.

Spender, Dale. *Man Made Language*. London: Routledge and Kegan Paul, 1980.

Spitzer, Michael. "Writing Style in Computer Conferences." *IEEE Transactions on Professional Communication* PC 29.1 (1986): 19–22.

———. "Computer Conferencing: An Emerging Technology." *Critical Perspectives on Computers and Composition Instruction*. Ed. Gail Hawisher and Cynthia Selfe. New York: Teachers College Press, 1989. 187–99.

———. "Local and Global Networking: Implications for the Future." *Issues in Computers and Writing*. Ed. Deborah Holdstein and Cynthia Selfe. New York: LA, 1990. 58–70.

Sproull, Lee, and Sara Kiesler. "Reducing Social Context Cues: Electronic

Mail in Organizational Communication." *Management Science* 32 (1986): 1492–1512.

Thorne, Barrie, Cheris Kramarae, and Nancy Henley, eds. *Language, Gender, and Society*. Rowley, MA: Newbury, 1983.

Trimbur, John. "Consensus and Difference in Collaborative Learning." *College English* 5 (1989): 602–616.

Weiner, Harvey S. "Collaborative Learning in the Classroom: A Guide to Evaluation." *College English* 48 (1986): 52–61.

West, Candace, and Don H. Zimmerman. "Small Insults: A Study of Interruptions in Cross-Sex Conversations between Unacquainted Persons." *Language, Gender, and Society*. Ed. Barrie Thorne, Cheris Kramarae, and Nancy Henley. Rowley. MA: Newbury, 1983. 103–18.

Whitworth, Richard. "Collaborative Learning and Other Disasters." NCTE Committee on Classroom Practices in Teaching English. *Focus on Collaborative Learning*: *Classroom Practices in Teaching English*. Urbana: 1988. 13–20.

Zimmerman, Don H., and Candace West. "Sex Roles, Interruptions, and Silences in Conversation." *Language and Sex: Difference and Dominance*. Ed. Deborah Holdstein and Cynthia Selfe. Rowley, MA: Newbury, 1975. 105–129.

9

Responses to the Essays

Readers are themselves collaborators, drawing from texts the meanings that are most significant to themselves. In the spirit of this kind of collaboration, the last two pieces of this book form a unit consisting of readers' responses to the essays. The first piece, a review essay by John Clifford, offers a critical "re-vision" of the essays with an emphasis upon the essays' ethical dimensions. The second piece, a series of letter exchanges between the essayists, highlights issues raised in the essays that influenced the thinking of the respondent(s) or that, in the eyes of the respondent(s), demand further consideration by the essayist(s) in future study of collaborative writing. By implication, this final section invites readers to enter such active collaboration as well, as they reflect on the essayists' varied attempts to formulate new visions of collaborative writing.

Toward an Ethical Community of Writers
John Clifford

Learning, Richard Rorty suggests, is primarily a shift in a person's relations with others. In the midseventies, after having taught English in a working-class high school in Brooklyn for a decade, I joined the composition program at Queens College. I had read Bruffee's 1973 essay on collaborative learning and was impressed with the range and sophistication of the nontraditional relationships between teachers and students. In the early seventies, I had enthusiastically experimented with various alternative learning strategies to the teacher-as-dispenser-of-knowledge pedagogy encouraged in my high school. But there is something about the high school experience, with its sequential classes, its *in loco parentis* atmosphere, its deadening monotony that mitigates against our best intentions to fully engage students.

Consequently, the confluence of Bruffee's suggestions that we need to make changes in ourselves to run an effective collaborative class and my own liberation from the constraints of my traditional high school, inspired me to pursue the efficacy of collaborative learning in earnest. I had not yet finished my Ph.D. and had no strong preference for a dissertation topic. Experimental designs were still typical for classroom research—the ethnography projects on process and revision that would inform writing studies in the early eighties were not common. And since I was under real-world pressure—the funding for the open admissions experiment in the CUNY colleges was about to be drastically slashed—I decided it would be pragmatic to do a research project testing the effect collaborative learning had on the writing ability of freshmen. Reading from Bruffee's bibliography, I especially remember Mason's *Collaborative Learning* and Abercombie's *The Anatomy of Judgement* offering important perspectives on how people could learn and work together. At the time I was planning the study, the overt political activism of the sixties was waning; however, my suspicion of authoritarian education, my commitment to participatory democracy and the active involvement of learners in their own education, was still strong. Collaboration seemed a more humane, natural, and potentially effective way to teach writing, while also displacing the stupifying authority of the hidden curriculum implicit in traditional education.

The study that eventually evolved from my reading of collaborative theory, my belief in a community of learners, and my situation as a writing instructor in the Queens program was weighted in favor of orchestrated peer feedback in small groups, a strategy I felt would provide the context of a real audience. I thought then, rather simply, that collaborative strategies would provide "a supportive interactive environment" to risk the changes and the self-consciousness necessary for growth in writing. With Janis Forman's assistance, the study demonstrated that collaborative learning without direct instruction did help students write better.

Since that study I have continued to use various collaborative strategies in writing as well as in literature classes. Collaborative techniques are especially compatible with reader-response criticism since both encourage learners to bring their own values and ideas to the fore within a social community. The dramatic interest in collaboration in the last several years is, no doubt, due to the obvious connections between collaboration and the social turn composition studies have taken since 1985. In this context, I was pleased to be asked to respond to this exciting collection since I have a keen interest in how collaborations's leading theorists are confronting the problems and promises that have emerged over such concepts as group consensus, the integrity of individual expression, political alignments, and the influence of culture on group dynamics.

Anne Gere and Laura Roop's "For Profit and Pleasure" reminds us that our current advanced theories were often someone else's common practice. Postmodern thinking about discourse often revolves around a Foucauldian consideration of power: who has it and who doesn't. Invariably men have it and exercise it discursively within institutions. Those forbidden access to these conversations are pushed to the margins where their counter-hegemonic voices find solace in small communities. The women's groups Gere and Roop describe made the best of just such an inside/outside polarity. These women collaborated as a survival strategy, as a way for literate females to maintain a life of the mind and a sense of identity, while also finding respite from a patriarchal culture that diminished and isolated their contributions. Gere and Roop are careful to note that these were less revolutionary cells than social communities privileging friendships, intertextual dialogues, and supportive spaces to strengthen performances of gender not allowable elsewhere. Without a coherent theory, these women intuitively collaborated, creating an empowering transitional site that would later serve as a basis for more explicit interventions into an exclusionary male culture. As a harbinger for the growth of feminist criticism, women's clubs are prescient; as a resistance model for the multiple discourses still marginalized in our institutions/culture/discipline,they are inspirational.

John Trimbur and Lundy Braun's "Laboratory Life and the Determination of Authorship" gives us a rare and much needed look behind the scenes at collaboration as real-world praxis as well as the difference between a contextual theory and messy reality. It also raises difficult ethical problems for instructors of advanced and technical writing courses in college. Fifteen years ago the connection between preparing writing students for meaningful work and the political responsibility of intellectuals was tangential. It has since moved in from the periphery to occupy a perplexing place for the reflective practitioner of collaboration. Collaboration in university writing classrooms has been clearly associated with a progressive agenda. In Lunsford and Ede's terms it has been a dialogic, not a hierarchical, movement. We have privileged peer feedback, multiple responses, and democratic arrangements because we believed in these ideas professionally and politically. It was the democratic thing to do, the ethically right thing to do. But Trimbur and Braun convincingly demonstrate that the sites students occupy beyond the university will not be so committed to equality. Merit, status, and seniority, for example, can quickly unbalance the carefully designed arrangements found in collaborative classrooms. Although the modern workplace is often collaborative, the distribution of influence and rewards is often asymmetrical. People are often exploited. In Jürgen Habermas's terms, workplaces are almost always success-oriented; they exist to turn out a competitive product, a pragmatic solution. Unlike our collaborative classrooms, they do not exist to increase self-esteem, to engage all regardless of merit. Perhaps the dialogic collaborative classroom is utopian, or perhaps it is simply unworldly and as such fails to adequately prepare students for the actual demands of work. Regardless, I feel strongly that these and other ethical questions need to be made explicit in the classroom. Students will probably not have the opportunity to confront these issues with anything like the freedom that a university can provide. As with biomedical ethics, the need for writers to understand the multiple and contradictory ethical contingencies of the workplace is crucial if we have any sense of a wider societal responsibility. By clearly encouraging students to foreground their differences rather than sublimate them for a consensual greater good, we can help them learn firsthand how domination and resistance work. The challenge is how to tolerate our multiple differences while still struggling communally to produce literate and responsible discourse. That is just the challenging enterprise members of a reflective university are confronting every day. And although we have hardly succeeded, it would be illuminating if students realized that it is possible to work toward democratic principles even in a hierarchical institution. If the collaborative classroom would confront the inequities rampant even in an enlightened university, our student writers might be able to meld their ethical and professional selves more harmoniously.

Kitty Locker's essay, "What Makes a Collaborative Writing Team Successful?" is a clear reminder that collaborative strategies are not beyond failure. In my experience, in fact, the possibilities for going astray are greater in a collaborative environment than in the teacher-controlled conventional classroom. The rewards are qualitatively greater when collaboration works, but first a conducive context must be created, trust must be established, responsibilities must be clearly agreed upon, the distribution of authority must be settled. But most of all everyone must be committed to the project's goals and method. In composition classrooms, such a desideratum is hard won, over time and with a high tolerance for frustration. In a work site with desultory leadership, an effective collaborative writing project seems unlikely indeed. Jim was simply unwilling or psychologically unable to join this specific collaborative community. As in traditional classrooms and workplaces, dissent from the general values of the group must be confronted in a democratic dialogue. Unless that responsibility is admitted and measures taken, the center will not hold and good work will not happen.

Charlotte Thralls's "Bakhtin, Collaborative Partners, and Published Discourse" usefully expands the notion of collaboration beyond the rather limited vision I had in 1975. Working within a postmodern idiom, Thralls holds that all writing is inherently collaborative. This interesting notion echoes Barthes's and Foucault's ideas about texts that are authored not by single individuals but by the language and ideas current in discourse communities, by the structures of language, by past and future meanings of words. Using Bakhtin, Thralls develops this idea to clarify the multiple ways writing involves authors inter-textually as they seek on the one hand to build on or struggle against previous discourses and on the other to anticipate the responses of intended and imaginary audiences. Rhetoric becomes fully dialogic in this view. Thralls's extended illustration of the interlinked chain of authors involved in the publication of a journal article argues yet again for a rethinking of our traditional privileging of the lone expressive voice.

Some of the recent backlash against collaboration centers on just this point. Traditionalists remember conceiving of themselves as rugged individualists, forging a unique writing style and a distinctive cast of mind. But their obliviousness to the social forces shaping just such an illusory view of their role as institutional mavericks also enables them to hold on to the false polarity individual/society. Academics have never existed as autonomous agents outside disciplinary or institutional discourse. Opposition from these traditional liberals is often dramatic and emotional, as they conjure up visions of *1984* and *Brave New World*. It seems to be difficult indeed to reorient one's academic socialization, one's belief in the sanctity of literary ownership, one's struggle to transcend the mediocrity of the crowd. Thralls's use of Bakhtin, however, should help to demonstrate that our language can never be wholly ours to shape at will, that all our writing can only be a partially successful intertextual struggle with countless other voices. But the traditional humanist objection to collaborative work is not, I think, primarily intellectual. It emanates instead from a sense of dis-placement, a sense of loss and betrayal of the writer's expressive/individualist values that cogency probably cannot transform. The case for collaboration as an intertextual reality is, after Thralls's essay, difficult to dispute.

Gender studies have grown in importance in the last few years. It is, then, no surprise that collaborative group work, with its emphasis on personal interaction between men and women, would be fertile ground for inquiry. Mary Lay's "The Androgynous Collaborator" is a strong intervention into our current spirited discussions about masculine and feminine characteristics. The author obviously has an agenda, one that would privilege the kind of traditional female behavior discussed by Carol Gilligan, such as the ability to maintain group harmony while deflecting disruptive and aggressive talk. For Lay, groups work best when differences in ideology as well as conversational style are self-consciously accepted, when competitive impulses are sublimated for group coherence. Although I support her general goals, I would have preferred that she speak of masculine and feminine subject positions to reinforce the idea that she is not suggesting that men are by their very nature more confrontational or women more contextual. The risk of essentializing is always great when theorists discuss actual behavior. Lay does seem to attribute behavior to socialization and not essence, but she might have improved her argument by noting that both men and women can occupy masculine subject positions both within discourses and within groups. Many men are, in fact, uncomfortable with the conventional subject positions of authority and dominance that they are expected to assume in institutions. Similarly we should also not assume that the positions women have been forced to adhere to are somehow authentic. Group work does indeed take cooperation, trust, respect for difference, and a temporary transcendence of independence and individual achievement, but many of the men I have worked with over the years seem to understand that the contingencies of a particular collaborative context require that they highlight some attributes of their multiple selves while diminishing those that are less situationally pragmatic. An effective collaborative group requires both men and women to, as it were, create themselves anew. The key move here is akin to Kenneth Burke's call for identification, for an attempt on the part of rhetors to locate themselves within the culture, to interrogate whose interest they serve with their work, to situate their work space within a fully contextualized sociopolitical landscape. Lay's essay reminds us how important gender is within any rhetorical situation and how crucial it is that we are conscious of its complex effects.

John Schilb's essay on "The Sociological Imagination and the Ethics of Collaboration" extends the need for careful scrutiny of both one's purposes within a collaborative framework and the larger social and political implications of the work being carried on by the group. Schilb is rightly concerned that writers not block out the societal context within which we all must work. In this sense his interesting notion that we look at the other meaning of collaboration — collusion with the enemy — is provocative. Again Kenneth Burke is a useful intertext, especially his fear that we may be carefully but unwittingly raising sheep for the marketplace. Some writing theorists are concerned that the classroom not become merely a site for the replication of dominant values, that we do more than merely provide business and industry with literate apolitical workers. The connection with the Trimbur/Braun essay is obvious: both pieces hope to raise our consciousness about the ethical implications of our work, collaboration or otherwise. Schilb usefully provides a heuristic to do just that, one suggested by C. Wright Mills's inquiry into sociology/ethics/politics. His questions probe the effect our work would have on the structures governing our culture: how human nature would be affected, how change would be accounted for, and so forth. Such an exploration could easily be blended into collaborative work. We may eventually choose to reproduce the existing culture within our classrooms, or we may struggle to transform inequalities, but we have little choice about the professional imperative to allow those and other ethical issues to be discussed explicitly and dialectically. I would hope that students, indeed all writers, would want to be sure others, especially those close at hand, were not exploited or marginalized; however, an equally pressing goal is to prevent dichotomous thinking about self/society and feelings of impotence about changing cultural values. Collaborative work needs to allow for difference, for alterity, for multiple voices. Consensus might be necessary at work sites, but within our classrooms, unless we encourage and expect dissent, collaboration runs the risk of being little more than conformity. To collaborate without hegemony — that is the more intellectually and ethically challenging agenda.

Cynthia Selfe in "Computer-Based Conversations and the Changing Nature of Collaboration..." is well aware of these problems, as indicated in her characterization of collaborative groups as micropolitical environments that reflect the struggles of domination/individuality that Mary Lay, Trimbur/Braun, John Schilb, and others in this collection are so concerned about. We cannot see ourselves nor our students as somehow outside difficult political problems. Students in the classroom bring the world with them; they are in the world while they are in our collaborative groups, and they go back to the world after: there is really no polarity between inside/outside, private/public, individual/society. As with many of the issues facing collaborative work, instructors need to problematize what seems commonsensical. Men and women often bring to groups conventionally constructed selves unfamiliar with alternatives; students are often unaware that there is more than one acceptable discourse within a discipline; collaborators often assume that the goals of the group and of the institution are given and beyond debate. It is our responsibility to convince students that we do not privilege groupthink or mindless harmony, and that they need to and are rewarded for working out their socialized values and expectations within the group.

From this perspective, I had some reservation about Selfe's suggestion that computers might allow for dissensus and a more open negotiation of differences. Students' efforts at writing individually on a computer as a kind of electronic bulletin board are theoretically intriguing, but certainly have some drawbacks. I have seen electronic bulletin boards in action and the results are mixed. Students were, indeed, more open and less inhibited about a range of issues, including some rather crude racial and gender biases. Nevertheless, the experiment is worth pursuing, but only in conjunction with other socially interactive arrangements. Perhaps a balance of face-to-face and computer-based collaboration will more realistically achieve the kind of acceptance of difference without domination that is at the heart of Selfe's project.

Interestingly, Rogers and Horton's essay on exploring face-to-face collaboration takes the opposite position from Selfe, seeing more promise within groups than in isolation. Selfe certainly has a compelling point, but the felt experience of actually sitting down with others to work should remain the linchpin in collaborative practice. For it is in actual groups that we must clarify who we are and how we can work together. Foucault would certainly agree that the site at which the collaborative discourse takes place influences our thinking in hundreds of subtle ways. Corporations, universities, and institutions of all sorts have their own ideologies. Indeed, Louis Althusser would contend that all these groups exist under the umbrella of a larger societal ideology and that universities, for example, mask their values under various guises. This may be a cogent insight, but regardless of its validity, as institutional workers we can only continue our contradictory tasks: we must help our students learn alternatively: the complexity of effective collaborative work while still maintaining an ethical space from which they can critique the very enterprise we challenge them to master.

Correspondence Between the Authors

Dear Anne Gere and Laura Roop:

Your essay "For Profit and Pleasure: Collaboration in Nineteenth Century Women's Clubs" made me realize, once again, how inventive individuals and groups are in devising strategies and forms of social organization to make literacy popular. As writing teachers, we are too often locked into the frames of reference that formal education takes for granted, and we may thereby cut ourselves off from the rich sources of self-sponsored reading and writing that are located outside of educational institutions. Your work is helpful in this respect, in pushing us to expand our sense of what literacy means and to think about how people incorporate reading and writing into their everyday lives — and how they do this collaboratively.

I'm particularly interested in how ordinary people use literacy, as you describe it, to create a space outside the academic world. Indeed, these kinds of cultural spaces offer settings "where learning could be safe and joyful." I would just add — as I think you imply — that part of what makes such learning joyful is the fact, at least in the case of the women's clubs you describe, that these women have evaded the patriarchal world to create for their own purposes spheres of cultural activity.

In the study and teaching of writing, we like to talk about the empowering potentialities of literacy, but too often we think that what makes reading and writing empowering is the way they can help students negotiate the transition from private to public life — public meaning jobs, careers, professional credentials, expertise, citizenship, and so on. What I particularly like about your essay is the way it offers another way to think about what the term "empowering" might mean. It gives us a way to see "empowering" as a collaborative activity by which individuals invest power in each other. Your subjects, of course, are middle-class women, tied apparently to their husbands, their homes, and the round of domestic obligation. I don't get the sense that many of them are radicals out to change the world, though it is interesting that Julia Ward Howe was a prominent advocate of women's suffrage. But what I find "empowering" is not the explicit politics but the micropolitics of the women's clubs you have studied — in particular, how people in subordinate positions, cut off from full participation in public life, make do by turning to forms of collaborative activity to overcome their atomization and social isolation — in the case you have studied, the powerful constraints on women of the regime of domesticity. In this sense, the phenomenon of women's clubs seems to me to represent something more than an adaptation to the patriarchal order or what Blair and Martin see as a "way-station between private and public life." It's also a creative way of resisting the logic of cultural power and of carving out new and alternative cultural spaces where women can come together to exercise their powers as readers and writers.

What I would like to know more about is how people collaboratively employ these strategies of resistance, evasion, and making-do in a variety of settings and how self-sponsored reading and writing help them to accomplish their ends. You're right, I think, to emphasize the pleasure of participating in collaborative forms of social life — the pleasure, I'd add, not only of common activity and the company of one's peers but also of getting away with it in a social order that isolates women in the home.

Who gets to speak, to read, to write? These are questions that have been answered in advance by a meritocratic social order that relies on experts and professional credentials. The question your essay raises for me is, How do people excluded from the dominant discourse — whether women or members of other subordinate groups — invent collaborative strategies to make their voices heard?

John Trimbur

Dear John Trimbur and Lundy Braun:

I was especially delighted to be given the opportunity to respond to your essay, "Laboratory Life and the Determination of Authorship," not only because so much of John's work and thinking is included in my own essay for this collection, but also because your combined thinking has helped me understand something important about using collaboration in my own classroom.

I have always told teachers, and myself, that we can learn quite a bit by simply listening to students. If we listen carefully enough, I have said, we usually can hear what is important to students, as writers and as fellow humans struggling to make meaning. But sometimes, as your essay taught me, listening is not enough; sometimes, we can hear students say things and *still* fail to understand the import of their comments. Such has been the case with students' comments about the collaborative activities I have had them do in my classes for the last six or seven years. Your essay helped me to understand why students I work with have been saying the things that they have about their collaborative work.

In most of my writing classes, I include one or more writing assignments that allow students to work collaboratively on a composition task of their choice. Often, because I teach at a technological university and in a program of technical communication, such assignments will involve using written and graphic communication to solve some sort of technical communication problem: writing an improved manual for beginning students who want to use a video camera, revising a poorly designed brochure targeted at a particular readership, rewriting technical guidelines to address the needs of a dissatisfied or frustrated user.

In the past, I have been fairly satisfied with these assignments. Most students have given them high reviews in end-of-the-semester course evaluations and have expressed delight in being able to combine forces with their colleagues in approaching a truly difficult and multi-faceted communication problem. Such assignments, the students have told me, allow each team member to contribute according to his or her own abilities and talents. But, while students have always focused on the benefits of these assignments (probably in an attempt to reward me for a learning experience they find useful), they have also consistently sent me subtle messages about the difficulties attendant on such collaborative projects. And it is these subtle, yet persistent messages that I have failed to understand until I read your piece.

Almost always in these more critical comments, there is some kind of statement from one or more students who felt they carried more of the load than the other team members. Frequently, there are also comments from students who feel that they did the major work on *the* most important part of the communication project — writing the first draft, analyzing the audience, testing the document on users, proofing and editing later drafts, performing layout and design services — and, were, therefore, deserving of more recognition. Almost always, students provide comments that speculate about the difficulties of giving each team member appropriate credit for his or her contributions. To address the problems behind these comments, I have allowed individual team members to identify their own and others' contributions, to keep complicated writers' logs that document their contributions to the project, even to give themselves grades for their involvement. But, with all these approaches, I still missed the main point of what my students were saying and have, thus, missed a valuable opportunity for teaching about the political nature of language and language use.

What my students were trying to tell me, in these comments that I have consistently misunderstood and undervalued, was what your essay also revealed in great detail: collaborative writing projects are typically the sites for complex social and political struggles, for the difficult negotiation of credit, for the building of power bases and public profiles. All of my attempts to evaluate individual contributions to collaborative projects missed this important point because they did not allow class members to discuss the dilemmas that are *part and parcel* of collaborative processes. As a teacher, I was attempting to resolve the struggles that characterize collaboration, when I might have been focusing students' attention on the implications and characteristics of such struggles as they occur naturally among human beings engaged in creative work. Your essay made me realize that I could build into my classes the time for foregrounding these struggles in discussions of collaborative writing and that I could encourage individual groups to focus part of their effort on thinking about these issues as well. At least part of our discussions in every class might address how different academic disciplines and professional groups perceive collaboration. Another part might identify the different strategies these groups have for dealing with the struggles that are part of collaborative authorship. All of this discussion probably should be aimed at identifying alternative ways of dealing with multiple authorship and collaborative creativity.

All of this thinking convinces me that our discipline needs to encourage more research projects on collaboration and multiple authorship. First, I suspect that we need to continue the kinds of descriptive studies that you have undertaken. As scholars of writing, we need to look at a variety of collaborative situations and to chart the patterns of interaction evident therein. This kind of work will allow us not only to tease out common operational concerns in connection with multiple authorship, but also to identify both positive and negative strategies for dealing with these concerns. You rightly point out in your conclusion that, as teachers of writing, we need to examine — critically and carefully — the data such studies produce. We need to look closely at the practices of industry, government, and business, and the ideological premises on which these practices are based, before deciding whether or not to bring them into our classrooms. But we should also note that a discussion of these practices, based on descriptive research projects such as yours, may provide teachers and students with a starting point for rethinking and experimenting with collaborative authorship in creative and realistic ways.

In connection with such descriptive projects, I would encourage investigators to ask the following kinds of questions: What percentage of multiple authorship projects in particular workplaces show evidence of asymmetrical power relationships? Do they all? Do the projects that do show such evidence share any common characteristics: Are they the most important projects? The least? The most public? Those tied most closely with the reward structure? Are there any multiple authorship strategies used in these settings that seem equitable? If so, on what ideological premises are these strategies based, and why? What characteristics tend to be associated with those individuals who receive little or no credit as an author: Are such authors generally male? Female? Young? Old? How does one move from receiving little or no credit as an author to receiving appropriate credit for multi-authored contributions?

While we are answering such questions about writing in the workplace, I think we can also concentrate on further studies of collaboration in our own writing classrooms. Among the questions we have to answer in these academic settings are the following: What patterns of power and power relationships are evident in the collaborative activities of student writing groups with which we work? Do student projects in various writing-classroom settings indicate the presence of asymmetrical power relationships? If so, on what characteristics are such relationships based: Gender? Age? Race or ethnicity? Language proficiency? Writing experience or ability? Academic major? Knowledge in a topic area? Access to, or experience with, electronic writing technologies such as computers and computer networks? Further, we can ask questions such as these: What collaborative strategies do our students bring with them to writing classes? On what ideological premises are these strategies based? Why? Which of these strategies seem to be effective and which dysfunctional for our purposes? On what bases can, or should, composition teachers make such evaluations of collaborative strategies? How and when can we best teach those collaboration strategies we consider most productive?

Well, these are just a few of the many questions your fine work has prompted me to think about. As you know from your own efforts and from my incomplete list, there seems to be plenty of work to do. I suspect that this particular area of inquiry will provide fertile ground for explorations by many scholars. I want to thank you for providing me the opportunity to respond to this essay and to explore more carefully my own thinking about collaboration.

Cynthia L. Selfe

Dear Kitty Locker:

I very much enjoyed your story about collaboration at The Ohio Legal Rights Service. I was especially interested in your approach, which I would characterize as cultural analysis based on fieldwork, the aim of which is to produce social knowledge about an "other," the other in your study being the two collaborative teams.

This approach places your work in the forefront of writing research, where we find increasing interest in writing (for example, collaborative writing) as a cultural phenomenon. Cultural analysis based on qualitative methods, we assume, can allow us to describe writing behaviors and then use these descriptions to build general theories about writing processes. In the case of cultural analyses of collaboration, such as yours, the aim is to identify factors characteristic of successful collaborative teams in order to build toward a theory of effective collaborative strategies.

What's troubling, however, about our efforts at cultural analysis — and what your essay helps us see — is how difficult it is for us to come to terms with the status and objectives of the descriptions we produce. We seem uncertain, for example, about the nature of knowledge we hope to generate from our research, and we seem uneasy about the kinds of claims we legitimately can make on the basis of our observations and interviews. Do we wish to claim that the representations of cultural life we produce are in some sense objective, designed to reveal the realities of a world external to us, from which we can generalize about collaborative strategies? Or, do we wish to claim that our representations are *only* subjective stories, more reflective of our interpretive moves than a culture "out there?"

One of the most significant problems for those of us attempting cultural descriptions is reconciling these oppositional claims, as they are defined within an objectivity/subjectivity framework. Most of us try to balance both claims, implying that our descriptions of cultural life — of collaborative behaviors — are both objective and subjective. We take the position that our descriptions can be *subjective accounts of an objective world*; that cultural descriptions — a phenomenologically based inquiry — can somehow be made to match an empirical world — a positivist goal. This position, unfortunately, creates contradictions in our research because our subjective accounts are at odds with our objectivist aims. For example, when we hold that our stories are subjective and provisional, and therefore dependent on our beliefs and language, we contradict ourselves when we then try to use our stories to get in touch with an external world somehow beyond our language and stories. Conversely, when we maintain that our cultural descriptions should be able to match an objective reality and reveal some larger truth about collaboration or other writing processes, then we find our indeterminate stories an insurmountable barrier to this task.

Your description of the collaborative teams suggests that you are thoroughly familiar with the difficulties involved in working within a subjectivity/objectivity framework, juggling these oppositional claims. For example, as you begin your article, you are careful to establish a hermeneutic context for your story, announcing the sense in which your text is the subjective and open-ended translation of a dialogue between you — the interpreter — and the collaborative teams — the interpreted. In detailing your methodology, you allude explicitly to this interpretive activity, establishing your narrative presence through the confessional "I," and acknowledging that "other stories," "other truths" could coexist with your version of collaborative behaviors at the agency.

As you move into the actual story about the collaborators, however, there is a discernible shift away from these claims of subjectivity toward implicit claims of objectivity, namely that your story is a closed, authoritative, and empirically verifiable account of events that took place at the Ohio agency. These claims are communicated through various objectification strategies that dominate the style of your text construction. For example, as the actual story begins, the personal and fallible first-person presence established in the methodology section of your article disappears and is replaced by an omniscient and authoritative third-person narrator. This shift in narrative presence tends to marginalize the subjective conditions of your fieldwork, relegating the confessional and overtly subjective aspects of your study to introductory, subordinate status in the article. At the same time, this third-person rhetorical stance produces an objectifying distance between you and your subjects. Finally, the progression of the article — from methodology to findings and conclusions — gives the article the aura of an empirical research report, suggesting perhaps that an inductive process can facilitate the move from subjective facts to larger empirical truths about collaboration.

In seeing you work through these opposing claims, I was struck by parallels in your work and my own efforts to come to grips with the challenges and difficulties we face in representing cultural behavior. More specifically, your article forced me to grapple with problems that are implicit in a subjectivity/objectivity framework, and to speculate on ways of resolving the contradictions that arise when we think about our culture-based research within such a framework.

As contemporary theorists are now pointing out, the greatest problem in thinking about our qualitative research within a Cartesian objectivity/subjectivity split is that this framework forces us to posit a world in which there exists a necessary and inevitable split between our subjective language or selves and an objective reality external to us. Such a binary split, Thomas Kent maintains, assumes that "knowledge lies beyond language" and that "language forms a barrier or a medium between us and the world, and to get to the world, we must move through the medium of language that in some way corresponds or represents" events in the world. (Thomas Kent, "Ethnography and Objectivity," *Social Perspectives on Professional Communication*, ed. Nancy Blyer and Charlotte Thralls [Newbury Park: Sage, forthcoming].) What we need, Kent argues, is a new metalanguage, a new way of talking about our knowledge as something, not "*beyond* language," but "*in* language," for "knowledge cannot be separated from the languages we employ in our discourses" (emphasis mine).

This new metalanguage for conceptualizing cultural descriptions is beginning to emerge in the work of theorists, such as Thomas Kuhn, Mikhail Bakhtin, and Richard Rorty, who posit that language and knowledge are essentially human and social creations. For Kuhn, reality and knowledge are constructed and provisional, while for Bakhtin, this social construction of knowledge is collaborative and public: an interplay of voices, of rhetorically positioned utterances produced through our dialogues with others. According to Kent, these theorists help us realize that our knowledge about a culture "derives only from our linguistic descriptions of the world and does not hook on to a world out there." When knowledge is thus construed as a product of language, Kent explains, we no longer have to juggle objectivity/subjectivity claims; "we no longer have to worry about something 'in here' and something else 'out there' at which language aims." Instead, we have an alternate vocabulary, which allows us to "tell a different story about the stories we tell." In this different meta-story, reality is understood as something we construct, and thus our cultural accounts are always inventions rather than representations of culture. In other words, because there is no larger story or truth beyond what we construct in our cultural accounts, our cultural descriptions — case studies, ethnographies, and so forth — are all.

An alternate metalanguage that allows us to talk about our cultural descriptions as human and collaborative constructs, rather than as representations of culture, seems terribly liberating to me because it eliminates the fundamental contradiction I have suggested exists when we claim that our subjective stories can somehow represent an objective reality or culture. In even more concrete terms, a metalanguage for cultural analysis that rejects the idea of a split world frees us from the responsibility of connecting our stories to some larger generalization — some totalizing theory — that would permit accurate prediction of effective collaborative behaviors. Many of us, when we attempt cultural descriptions, seem to assume that our stories must be contextualized within such generalizations. It is as if we feel our stories lack significance in and of themselves, and thus they must be justified by some larger truth, which our stories can help reveal. In your article, for example, you seem to say that the real significance of your story lies somewhere beyond your story; that your story is important because it confirms the findings of other researchers — Ede and Lunsford, Forman and Katsky, and others — and that, collectively, these stories can allow us to "draw inferences about the factors that lead to successful collaborative writing"; these stories, you imply, can move us toward some ultimate representation of the important "processes and organizational structures collaborative groups use."

When we think of our cultural descriptions as inventions instead of representations and when we question the efficacy of viewing our stories within a split world (with a subjective in here and an objective out there), we begin to see, I think, that we need not require of our stories that they lead us toward overarching generalizations about collaboration — generalizations aimed at a truth somewhere beyond the stories themselves. To do so is to privilege an objective reality that, in a split world, is forever barred to us.

When we question this split-world framework for talking about our cultural stories, we also need no longer defend our stories, arguing that, *even though* they are inherently subjective, our stories are valuable because subjectivity is the best we can claim. To label our stories subjective is to imply the existence of an opposing term — objectivity — and thus to define our stories negatively in terms of an irredeemable lack.

These problems are alleviated when we adopt an alternate way of talking about our cultural descriptions. When, for example, we view our stories as collaborative constructions, and we accept that knowledge is something in language rather than beyond it, then we are able to clarify what is of considerable value in cultural descriptions like yours. The value is not, I think, in whether your story, with all its rich detail, can put us in touch with the "reality" of events that took place at The Ohio Legal Rights Service, nor whether your story can move us toward a theory of effective collaborative strategies. What is of value in your story is the story itself, because in Rorty's words, "The world does not speak; only we do" (Richard Rorty, *Contingency, Irony, and Solidarity* [New York: Cambridge UP, 1989] 6).

Charlotte Thralls

Dear Charlotte Thralls:

As we reflected about writing to you, we were reminded of Ellen Goodman's observations in a column she wrote for *The Boston Globe* in the summer of 1985:

> Sometimes I think that the telephone call is as earthbound as daily dialogue, while a letter is an exchange of gifts.... There is

> leisure and emotional luxury in letter writing. There are no obvious
> silences to anxiously fill. There are no interruptions to brook. There
> are no *nuances and tones of voice* to distract. (emphasis ours)

Goodman's words came to mind for two reasons. First, because we are writing you a letter, and second, because you, like Goodman, acknowledge the "voices" inherent in communication. On the surface, it appears that, for Goodman, "voice" is the pitch, pace, and timbre we hear when talking on the phone or interacting face-to-face. But, the more enduring "voices" of written messages, which you point out, are also apparent to Goodman. "It's letters that let us take turns, let us sit and mull and say exactly what we mean," she writes.

Mulling over your description of the collaborative nature of all writing provided us with another theoretical perspective for understanding our current research on face-to-face collaborative writing. It has also solidified some personal reflections about current notions of authorship among researchers, and raised some questions you may wish to address in the future.

It occurred to us that your application of Bakhtin's theory might be extended and applied to group contexts. Bakhtin discusses utterances in relationship to intrapersonal and interpersonal communication—he speaks of cognition and the interaction between individuals. Bakhtin does not address group communication per se. However, we find it useful to apply Bakhtin's notion of utterance to the way we think about group communication.

In his essay on speech genres, Bakhtin defines an utterance as a basic unit of speech communication with two major characteristics: 1) boundaries, and 2) finalization (*Speech Genres and Other Late Essays*, trans. Vern W. McGee, U of Texas P, 1986). When Bakhtin says that an utterance has boundaries, he means an utterance has an absolute beginning and an absolute end. These boundaries are clearly demarcated by a change of speakers; that is, individual utterances are determined by the interaction of the communicators rather than by grammatical or semantic units, such as sentences. An utterance is finalized, Bakhtin suggests, when a "speaker has said (or written) *everything* he wishes to say at a particular moment or under particular circumstances" (76). In other words, finalization occurs when the utterance can be evaluated as a whole. For example, when a drill sergeant says "Halt!" or when a scholar publishes an article in a scientific journal, intention is completed or, as Bakhtin would say, each utterance is finalized. Neither utterance exhausts the communication topic—the sergeant will continue to teach her subordinates about commands and the scholar hopes his article will prompt peer response—yet, each utterance is finalized because it is placed before a hearer or reader who senses an end or completeness that makes response possible.

Your essay builds upon Bakhtin's notion that these utterances are also inherently *responsive*. As you explain, Bakhtin is not suggesting that responses are always immediate. Rather, he is proposing that eventually what is heard or read will find a response in subsequent speech or behavior. However, while each utterance is linked to past and future utterances, it is also independent, possessing its own uniqueness and boundaries. In this way, an utterance is not a mere reflection or repetition of what already existed, but it "always creates something that never existed before" (119–120).

We believe Bakhtin's notion of utterance provides a theoretical framework for considering collaborative writing sessions in which authors plan, draft, and revise group documents face-to-face. Consider, for example, a face-to-face collaborative writing session as a bounded, finalized, and inherently responsive "group utterance." This group utterance is bounded in the beginning, by the group's first words and in the end, by the emergence of the group with their completed document. While the group's utterance is unique — through their collaboration they create written and spoken texts that never existed before — it is also colored by their need to account for the past and to anticipate the future. This accounting and anticipating raises certain questions and concerns that the group must address. These questions include: What have we done? What do we know? What should we do? What should we say or not say? By addressing these questions the group completes a document, which marks a decision to say no more and anticipates a response. With the completed document their utterance is bounded and finalized. We believe this theoretical description can be expanded to build a case for collaborative writing sessions in which groups originate and complete written messages.

Now we leave the theoretical and share more personal reflections about collaborative partnership in relation to the research community. In our experience, individualistic views of authorship too frequently dominate academe, inhibiting collegiality, personal growth, and the free exchange of ideas. The individualistic approach to authorship one finds in academe may also contribute to *institutional* competitiveness for research stars; that is, individual researchers whose reputations will increase the status of the organization. The dark side of this kind of competition, observes Henry Rosovsky, former dean of the Faculty of Arts and Sciences at Harvard University, is "too much movement by professorial stars from one university to another in relentless pursuit of personal gain; a consequently lower level of institutional loyalty; invidious comparisons between fields giving excessive advantages to those subjects where 'market power' is strong (as in computer sciences vs. English); and not least, the deleterious effects of a Wall Street mentality that focuses too much on short-term highly visible achievements at the expense of the long run and the unfashionable" (*The University: An Owner's Manual*, Norton, 1990, 31–32).

Moreover, references to collaborative partners are often needlessly negative in tone. For example, typically researchers establish the significance of their work by positing the insufficiency of previous research. As Swales and Najjar explain, research article introductions often employ negative language to describe past research efforts ("The Writing of Research Introductions," *Written Communication*, April 1987). They write: "Sometimes negation will . . . be expressed through quantification (*little, no, none of, few*), and sometimes it will be realized through the choice of verbs like *fail, neglect, lack, been restricted to*, and the like" (179). Such language neither acknowledges nor encourages the "collaborative partnership" you observe.

More than language, the circumstances in which writers collaborate may cause them to overlook their collaborative partnerships. Your description of the collaboration between authors, editors, and reviewers provides an example. Here, as you explain, a text results from a series of responsive reactions among collaborators. However, the ultimate acceptability of that text rests in the hands of the reviewers and especially the editors rather than the author. This fact raises a number of questions: How does a hierarchical relationship impact collaboration? How is inequitable decision-making power reflected in the responsive utterances of collaborators? Do collaborative relationships of this sort alienate collaborators and invite individualistic views of authorship? These are questions you may wish to address.

Collaborative partnerships may even prove difficult among peers, particularly peers from other disciplines. This fact strikes close to home. One of us is an experimental psychologist; the other is trained in communication and composition. Consequently, we have very different ideas about what constitutes "evidence"—one finds statistics incomplete; the other finds textual analysis imprecise. We believe the quality of our work is improved by our collaboration; although, along the way our differing perspectives and methodologies sometimes impede our progress and accent our individuality rather than our partnership.

There are signs that researchers are moving away from an individualistic to a collaborative view of the academic endeavor, however. For example, Lunsford and Ede challenge the notion of first author and dramatize the seamless weaving of their ideas by alternating their names all over the cover of their new book, titled *Singular Texts/Plural Authors* (Southern Illinois U P, 1990), and the Association of Business Communication Research Committee recently revised the criteria for administering the Outstanding Researcher Award to acknowledge publications authored collaboratively.

Perhaps even more importantly, we are beginning to acknowledge the value systems that underlie our methodologies. In a comparative analysis of four discourse studies from four different disciplines, Karen Tracy observed: "Different assumptions and argument styles may reflect different intellectual commitments, perhaps even incompatible versions of what is significant knowledge" ("A Discourse Analysis of Four Discourse Studies," *Discourse Processes* 11, 1988, 244). As we acknowledge the values that our methodologies reveal, we may more readily collaborate to create more multilayered studies.

Your essay is encouraging. Your application of Bakhtin and the notion of collaborative partnership provide us with a richer perspective and vocabulary for discussing, and perhaps even promoting, a less individualistic and more collaborative academic environment.

Priscilla Rogers and Marjorie Horton

Dear Mary Lay:

We read your article "The Androgynous Collaborator: The Impact of Gender Studies on Collaboration" with great interest for at least two reasons. First, our work on collaboration in nineteenth-century women's clubs touches on many of the same issues. Second, the effects of gender on collaboration is a practical concern; we both work in male-dominated institutions that are in the process of experiencing dramatic changes as women assume more powerful roles within the university and within the hierarchy of public schooling. We discuss gender's effect on collaboration informally and incessantly — as we negotiate with colleagues at the workplace and even as we write this response together. We've noticed the obvious: Women seem to choose collaboration more often than men and facilitate collaborative relationships by listening carefully, speaking tactfully, and pushing for consensus.

Perhaps because we so admire what our female colleagues bring to collaboration, we are troubled by your argument concerning androgyny's desirability. You discuss the problematic nature of the term "androgyny," the implied binary opposition, the negative effect the term has had on women historically, but you do not reject it outright. Why not? The essence of your argument is that the male-defined workplace should recognize the value of female-typed strategies for its collaborative work. We agree. However, male-typed strategies hardly need affirming in institutions that have been designed by men.

While we concur that it is useful to think about the ways women can change the nature of collaboration within organizations, we urge that you also consider the nature of the institutions within which collaboration occurs. Perhaps an analogy will help. In the early days of women's studies, most curriculum reformers adopted the "add women and stir" model. Rather than examine the existing academic structures of courses, departments, and disciplines, scholars assumed that adding content about women would introduce sufficient change. As time passed, feminists began to recognize that more comprehensive change was required. They saw the need to question the very nature of academic structures — courses, programs, and departments — to insure the health of women's studies on campus. Similarly, we think the nature of the workplace in which collaboration occurs merits further analysis. How can the patriarchal reward structure be altered? What features within the organization reinforce masculine-typed collaboration? How can the self-reflective qualities that you urge for collaborators be extended to the organization surrounding the collaborative community?

Finally, we suggest that you extend your investigation of journals written during collaboration to include more gender analysis. Participants in such research might be encouraged to reflect upon gender specifically. When asking group members to reflect on how they perceive the collaborative process, for example, you could include gender as a category of analysis. In reporting responses of individual group members, you could identify their gender, thereby providing the basis for broadening your own gender analysis. You might consider answering questions such as these: How can the concept of gender, which in your description seems rooted in and defined by family/domestic/private, be connected with public social systems such as the workplace? How can we describe the relationship(s) of gender and power within collaboration? We believe it would be extremely useful for you and other researchers to discuss the role gender plays in particularized classrooms and businesses. "Thick description," with an eye toward gender's effect on collaborative work, would enrich and temper any generalizations we're all tempted to make in professional and personal conversations.

As we said at the outset, we enjoyed reading your article, and find your work interesting. We look forward to the next installment.

Anne Ruggles Gere
Laura Jane Roop

Dear John Schilb:

As always when I read your work, I'm struck by the intelligence, the learning, and the insight you bring to your topic. Your article suggests two implications for my own work; it also raises issues that you might want to explore more fully at some point.

First, your article reminds me to be more sensitive to the downside of collaboration. In my own article in this volume, I present "Jim" as an obstructive individual. That may not be fair to him. Collaborative writing certainly places a premium on consensus and group problem solving at the expense of the individual. Perhaps I and other scholars ought to try to identify and calculate those costs. I assume that "Jim" was wrong and his superiors were right in their definitions of what constituted good writing for his agency. But the superior may not always be right. Betty Evans White tells the story of a supervisor who introduced mechanical errors into the writing of a subordinate during the cycling process; supervisors whose native language is not English or who are addicted to purple prose or bureaucratese may not improve a document. In my consulting workshops with middle-level managers and professionals, the most burning question is always, "How can we implement the advice we've learned here?" In almost every organization I've worked with, subordinates are convinced that their superiors want passives, nominalizations, clichés, and obfuscations. It occurs to me that we have few detailed studies of collaboration in groups or organizations where only a small number of people possess a good writing style or are sensitive to demands of audience and purpose. Can collaboration succeed, either in terms of process or product, in those conditions?

Mills's questions about the structure of society and your thoughtful analysis of the ways we might apply these in the writing classroom raise a second point for me. Most of us in business and technical writing, I think, privilege the writing done by high-level white-collar managers in prestigious firms at the expense of blue-collar and low-level white-collar workers in those firms and at the expense of small businesses and nonprofit organizations. Certainly MBA students at Harvard, Dartmouth, and Stanford need to learn how to communicate effectively; certainly they should be encouraged to explore the ramifications of the power structures they will join and hope to perpetuate. Certainly we can learn much from studying the communication patterns of executives in Fortune 500 firms. But perhaps all of us in this field need to give equal time to people in less prestigious organizations and to blue-collar workers. These people communicate too. In fact, research assistants Elizabeth Bonfield and Jane Greer have recently helped me document the extensive—and partially underground—writing done by factory workers in a company that makes components for automobile manufacturers.

To build on what you've done here, you might want to investigate why academicians in the humanities so devalue collaborative work. Is it simply that the humanists have traditionally worked independently in the library while scientists work collaboratively in the laboratory? Or is it also that collaboration involves compromise, and compromise seems to threaten academic freedom? If you have access to them, cases where collaboration has the potential to affect academic freedom and individual integrity would be fascinating.

You argue convincingly that collaboration is ethically suspect·if it merely reinforces a suspect organizational structure. Do cases exist that show a marginalized person using collaboration to transcend the prejudices of other members or to transform the values of the organization? What techniques can best help someone from a devalued group who must work with others who are given more status and prestige by the organization or the society? Right now, we still have comparatively few detailed case studies of collaborative groups, and even detailed studies rarely give "equal time" to all members of the group. If further research shows that suppression of the contributions of some members is the norm, should we in academia lobby business to use less collaborative writing? And how might we do that, given the practical and philosophical benefits of collaboration, in spite of the possibility for misuse that you so cogently address?

Finally, I'd like to see you rethink your analysis of LeFevre and your advice to students in the situations she describes. LeFevre, after all, is writing about invention — thinking of ideas and strategies — not about selection. Good papers, like good ads, often come after brainstorming many ideas and approaches and discarding most of them. In the passage you quote, it seems to me that LeFevre is simply saying that traditional invention techniques do little to help students or professionals whose problem is not that they cannot think of anything to say, but rather that they can think of only two things to say: one approach that is proscribed by the political and situational constraints, one approach that they find repugnant. Studying who is empowered and who is marginalized by those constraints and how those systems came to exist is interesting, challenging, and worthwhile. But redefining the rhetorical situation in this way does little to help the worker faced with an ethical as well as a rhetorical problem. Can we offer any invention techniques for such situations? You also suggest that the students "ought to consider just what circumstances would compel them to leave." When I assign problems with ethical dimensions, I am distressed that my students initially polarize the situation, assuming that they must either resign or go along with the status quo. Faced with the specter of large student loans to repay, few of them are willing to resign. It seems to me more productive to try to help them realize that a range of alternatives are possible and to examine in particular the uses of language in expressing and shaping those alternatives. You yourself suggest a promising alternative in what is almost a throwaway line: "Also, they ought to see if they can collaborate with anyone else at work in expressing their concerns to their supervisor." This approach suggests looking for other alternatives; it also suggests using collaboration to change the system in precisely the ways you call for.

Kitty O. Locker

Dear Priscilla Rogers and Marjorie Horton:

I believe that you have opened up an essential area for investigation: the benefits of face-to-face collaboration. If professional writers must at times collaborate to achieve a "uniform and consistent message" for internal and external audiences, particularly on sensitive and controversial issues, then we must prepare future writers for this type of interaction. You have done an excellent job of pointing out the importance of face-to-face collaboration and increasing our understanding of it. In particular, you have given instructors guidelines for designing and choosing cases that allow students to experience face-to-face collaboration. The case criteria that you provide in Appendix D are valid, thoughtful, and immediately useful. I intend to use your list to select the cases I assign students in my courses.

After reading your study, I would suggest a few directions for your future research. For example, if the benefits of face-to-face collaboration — as you put them, understanding the rhetorical situation, examining language choice, considering ethical dimensions, and reappraising decisions — are clear, how often do professional writers choose to draft and revise together? If the answer is, as you suspect, "infrequently," have we discovered all the individual and organizational obstacles that block more frequent face-to-face collaboration? Do writers encounter frustration primarily because of interpersonal conflict or conflict over ideas when planning, drafting, and revising collaboratively? Do managers as well as writers assume that collaborative writing is simply too time-consuming? If upon reading your essay, writers and managers are convinced that the benefits of face-to-face collaboration outweigh the problems, could you help writers who do not work in the same building or on the same job site somehow simulate face-to-face collaboration? Finally, as you suggest, should we study more to what extent individual voices are repressed and the least controversial language selected during this collaborative process? In particular, how can instructors train students engaging in face-to-face collaboration to avoid "groupthink"? These questions seem to be natural extensions of the research you report in your essay. Moreover, your topic lends itself well to the current interest in the interdisciplinary nature of professional writing, as scholars in small group communication and conflict resolution could help us prepare students for collaborative assignments.

You state, "The extent to which face-to-face collaborative writing is employed in these professional contexts is unknown." However, as you discovered, interviews with and surveys of business and technical writers reveal that writers frequently consider that drafting and editing are best done individually. I would be interested in finding out whether those who supervise and manage writers share this attitude and therefore encourage their writers to collaborate only after they have produced individual drafts. Or, do managers consider collaboration so time-consuming that they might discourage collaboration during the drafting stage despite the benefits you point out? You have convinced me that during "corporate crisis situations requiring managers to present a unified message, and business situations involving the education of new employees" face-to-face collaboration is required. I wonder if in-depth interviews with writers and those who supervise them might also reveal even more situations in which face-to-face collaborative drafting and revising could outweigh the increased time and frustration, the inevitable conflict and negotiation.

When recommending that instructors prepare students for "argumentation, negotiation, and consensus reaching," you recognize that conflict can either evoke ideas or damage interpersonal relationships. The cases that we develop for the classroom should, as you suggest in Appendix D, deliberately include areas of conflict. Cases in which each student "owns" unique information sharpen information gathering as well as negotiating skills. I wonder, however, if collaborators might experience more conflict in the drafting stage than in the planning or revising stages or if collaborators experience more interpersonal conflict during early stages of collaboration and more conflict over ideas during later stages or vice versa? If you conduct future case studies of face-to-face collaboration, you might consider analyzing if different degrees and types of conflict are inherent in the early and late stages of face-to-face collaboration. Or, if it is impossible to separate types and degrees of conflict, could you suggest how instructors can better help student collaborators handle conflict in general?

In the new discourse communities that we must prepare our students to enter, face-to-face communication may be impossible. While collaborators might be located within the same building, they might as likely be separated. Can writers in this situation simulate face-to-face collaboration, perhaps through electronic mail? Although electronic mail eliminates the nonverbal cues that enhance communicators' ability to understand messages, because it involves drafting and recording words, could electronic mail to any extent simulate face-to-face collaboration? Could collaborators experience any of the benefits you suggest if they must draft and revise at a distance?

Finally, I think that you have reminded us of a potentially dangerous consequence of face-to-face collaboration because collaboration is essentially group decision making. As you illustrate, the students in your case study did have to evaluate the "truth of their words" but may have "evaded" an issue to "preserve group cohesiveness." We might hope that within collaborative groups "the benefits to be gained from face-to-face collaborative writing are used for good"; but again, do other disciplines provide us with the means to help students confront, not avoid, ethical choices? And, how can we better ensure that as the group reaches consensus on any ethical questions within its message, individual voices are not lost?

The questions I offer may be as much a reflection of my interest in your essay as directions for future research. Your own suggestions for continued research are solid and include long- and short-term benefits of face-to-face collaboration. In particular, your questions about the types of relationships developed during collaboration and the tools that support collaboration are well worth exploring. I think that readers from academe and industry have much to gain from a careful study of your essay.

Mary M. Lay

Dear Cynthia Selfe:

Thanks for your essay on "Computer-Based Conversations and the Changing Nature of Collaboration." I learned much from it. In general, it usefully pushes teachers of writing to explore how computers might facilitate their work. More specifically, I was interested by your idea that anonymous on-line exchanges might promote equality—that perhaps they can "limit some of the social and visual cues that inhibit face-to-face conversation and, in doing so, create an environment in which individuals who are less powerful in traditional collaborative exchanges can find a more central role or voice, can feel more able to take risks." At the same time, I appreciate your acknowledging that these are "preliminary claims," which still need verifying. The research agenda you go on to propose for writing teachers strikes me as quite sensible: "they can undertake efforts to examine students' attitudes toward collaborative activities, observe the processes they employ within on-line collaborative writing tasks, identify group members' perceptions of consensus and dissensus, collect data that describe on-line conversations and collaborations, and analyze how group members handle agreement and disagreement."

Let me note here four issues that I especially hope researchers will explore. First, I would like to know how a student's attitude toward computer-based conversation might reflect his or her particular learning style, and how writing classrooms might accommodate various kinds. I suspect there will always be some students who find anonymity congenial and others who prefer face-to-face interaction. Second, I would like to know how students' collaborative behavior can be affected by the assignment they have to fulfill. The Megabyte case perhaps sheds light on students' computer interactions, but given that Megabyte emphasizes "continuous discussion" while writing courses emphasize task-oriented, time-bound assignments, we need to acquire data about the possible effects of the latter. Presumably this inquiry would entail distinguishing the various kinds of activities that now fall under the general rubric of "collaboration."

Third, I would like to know how variables such as gender, race, and class might continue to affect on-line exchanges even when they preserve anonymity and result in equitable turn taking. More specifically, I wonder how such variables might influence the *nature* and *quality* of conversational moves, whatever their distribution. Obviously I assume that students will not, cannot, just slough off the effects of their gender, race, and class by adopting pseudonyms and/or communicating from a distance. Consider Linda Brodkey's February 1989 *College English* article "On the Subjects of Class and Gender in 'The Literacy Letters.'" It showed how a group of teachers operated with a middle-class ideology when they consistently ignored concerns of the working-class people with whom they corresponded. Consider, too, how researchers like Carol Gilligan, Deborah Tannen, and the authors of *Women's Ways of Knowing* have found women more concerned than men with maintaining relationships in their ethical stances and communications. Might not this distinction have played some part in the hacker culture's being primarily male? One study of computer conversations you cite found that the participants engaged in "more hostile remarks and swearing than did similar face-to-face groups." Can we assume many women would welcome such "uninhibited" behavior? They might even think it signifies deeper inhibitions at work! They might think, too, that it bears some connection to the hostility displayed in the acts of sexual harassment that have occurred on several campus computer networks. It would be useful to know what "ground rules" computer networks can set up so that "risk taking" is not equated with "hostile remarks."

Finally, any research into computer use should keep in mind who gets access to computers and who does not. You sensitively and justifiably point out that computers enable people to converse when they otherwise might not be able to meet. Undoubtedly, you share my additional hope that computer resources are equitably distributed so that we do not wind up with yet another system of "have" and "have nots." In fact, it would be interesting to learn what differences of style as well as content there are between the computer conversations of the politically powerful and those of marginalized groups now using computers on behalf of concerted social movements.

Of course, the issues I raise comprise too large an agenda for any single researcher. They call for—guess what!—"collaboration." Meanwhile, I am grateful for the research you yourself have undertaken thus far.

John Schilb

Contributors

Lundy A. Braun is Assistant Professor of Medical Sciences at Brown University. Her research is on human papilloma viruses and cervical cancer, and she is interested in the social context of scientific research and laboratory life.

John Clifford is a professor of English at the University of North Carolina at Wilmington, where he teaches courses in literature, writing, and theory. He has coauthored several textbooks and his essays and reviews have appeared in *College English, College Composition and Communication, Reader*, and *Rhetoric Review*, as well as in several anthologies, most recently an essay on Eiseley in *Literary Nonfiction*, on Althusser in *Contending with Words*, and a piece on literacy in *A Right to Literacy*. He also edited *The Experience of Reading: Louise Rosenblatt and Reader-Response Theory*.

Janis Forman established and now directs the management communication program for the Anderson Graduate School of Management at UCLA. She has published extensively on collaborative writing, most recently in the *Journal of Business Communication*, the *Journal of Business and Technical Communication*, and *Evolving Perspectives on Computers and Composition Studies: Questions for the 1990s*. She is also the author of *The Random House Guide to Business Writing*. Her current research interests include a study of hypertext and collaborative writing.

Anne Ruggles Gere is Professor of English and Professor of Education at the University of Michigan, where she codirects the Ph.D. Program in English and Education. She is currently working on a book about the literacy activities of women's clubs.

Marjorie S. Horton is Senior Research Engineer at the Electronic Data Systems Center for Machine Intelligence in Ann Arbor, Michigan. She has designed and evaluated computer-supported meeting rooms as well as software. Her research interests include human-computer interaction and computer support for collaborative work groups. Recent publications of her research appear in *The Bulletin of the Association of Business Communication* and *Proceedings of the 1990 Conference on Human Factors in Computing Systems*.

Mary M. Lay is Associate Professor in the Department of Rhetoric at the University of Minnesota — Twin Cities. She is Immediate Past President of the Association of Teachers of Technical Writing and is author of *Strategies for Technical Writing* (Holt, Rinehart and Winston 1982) and coeditor of *Collaborative Writing in Industry* (Baywood 1991). She attended an NEH seminar on the "Woman Question" at Stanford University in 1986 and has since been studying gender issues in professional communication.

Kitty O. Locker is an Associate Professor of English at The Ohio State University. She is the author of *Business and Administrative Communication*

(Irwin, 1989) and coeditor of *Conducting Research in Business Communication* (Association for Business Communication, 1988). She received the Alpha Kappa Psi Award for Distinguished Publication in Business Communication in 1986, and again in 1988, for articles on the history of dunning letters and the history of business jargon, respectively. Her current research includes work on negative messages, on the way corporate culture is revealed in written documents, and on collaborative writing in the workplace and the classroom.

Priscilla S. Rogers is Assistant Professor of Management Communication and Director of the MBA Writing Program at the University of Michigan School of Business Administration. She has also implemented corporate communication programs for automotive and medical managers. Her research interests include managerial writing assessment and collaborative writing in managerial contexts. Recent publications of her research appear in *The Journal of Business Communication*, *The Journal of Business and Technical Communication*, and *Management Communication Quarterly*.

Laura Jane Roop is Language Arts Consultant for the Oakland (MI) Schools and a published poet.

John Schilb is Assistant Professor of English and Director of the Freshman Writing Program at the University of Maryland, College Park. His main interest is the relation between composition theory and literary theory. He has coedited two anthologies on this subject, *Contending With Words: Composition and Rhetoric in a Postmodern Age* and *Writing Theory and Critical Theory*.

Cynthia L. Selfe teaches at Michigan Technological University and is the author of *Computer-Assisted Instruction in Composition: Create Your Own* (NCTE) and *Creating a Computer-Supported Writing Facility* (Computers and Composition). She has coedited *Computers in English and Language Arts: The Challenge of Teacher Education* (with Dawn Rodrigues and William Oates, NCTE), *Critical Perspectives on Computers and Composition Instruction* (with Gail Hawisher, Teachers College Press), and *Computers and Writing: Theory, Research, and Practice* (with Deborah Holdstein, Modern Language Association). Selfe is the coeditor (with Gail Hawisher) of *Computers and Composition*, a journal for teachers of English.

Charlotte Thralls teaches in both the graduate and undergraduate rhetoric and professional-communication programs at Iowa State University. She was also cofounder and coeditor of the *Journal of Business and Technical Communication* (JBTC). In her forthcoming anthology (*The Social Perspective in Professional Communication*, Sage Publications, coedited with Nancy Blyler), Professor Thralls explores social-based rhetorical theory in relation to organizational culture and visual media.

John Trimbur is Associate Professor of English in the Department of Humanities at Worcester Polytechnic Institute. He has published a number of articles and chapters on collaborative learning, literacy theory, and cultural studies and is coeditor of *The Politics of Writing Instruction* (Boynton/Cook, 1990).